SCHOLASTIC LATIN

AN INTERMEDIATE COURSE

Page intentionally left blank

SCHOLASTIC LATIN

AN INTERMEDIATE COURSE

RANDALL J. MEISSEN, LC

Pontifical Athenaeum Regina Apostolorum
Via degli Aldobrandeschi, 190
00163 Rome, Italy

Scholastic Latin : an intermediate course / Randall J. Meissen
Rome: Pontifical Athenaeum Regina Apostolorum, 2012

ISBN: 9780615708805

8 7 6 5 4 3 2 1

FIRST EDITION

Cover Image: *Abbaye Fontevraud, Cloître du Grand-Moûtier*,
Wikimedia Creative Commons 3.0/J.-C. Benoist

Page intentionally left blank

INTRODUCTION

This book was prepared for the purpose of teaching a refresher course to first year philosophy students studying at the Pontifical Athenaeum Regina Apostolorum in Rome. Hence, rather than providing a presentation of Latin grammar from the beginning, it seemed more appropriate to compile a series of guided readings. Marginal notes throughout the text direct students toward relevant passages in Nunn's grammar, which is included in the appendix.[1] Except where otherwise noted, the reading passages have been taken from Signoriello's *Lexicon peripateticum philosophico-theologicum.*[2]

Students are frequently frustrated to find that a large portion of Thomistic vocabulary is absent from the standard Classical Latin dictionaries (Oxford, Collins, Langenscheidt, etc.). The following dictionaries are better suited for reading Scholastic authors:

BLAISE, A., *Dictionnaire latin-français des auteurs du Moyen-age*, Brepols, Turnhout (Belgium) 1994.

DEFERRARI, R. J., *A Latin-English Dictionary of St. Thomas Aquinas : based on the Summa theologica and selected passages of his other works*, St. Paul Editions, Boston, MA 1986.

DEFERRARI, R. J. - BARRY, M. I. - MCGUINESS, I., *A Lexicon of Saint Thomas Aquinas : based on the Summa theologica and selected passages of his other works*, Loreto Publications, Fitzwilliam, NH 2004.

LEWIS, C. T. - SHORT, C., *A Latin Dictionary*, Oxford University Press, Oxford 1984.

STELTEN, L. F., *Dictionary of Ecclesiastical Latin*, Hendrickson, Peabody, MA 2003.

---

1 H. P. V. NUNN. *An Introduction to Ecclesiastical Latin.* University Press, 1922.
2 NUNZIO SIGNORIELLO. *Lexicon peripateticum philosophico-theologicum in quo scholasticorum distinctiones et effata praecipua explicantur.* Pignatelli, 1872.

Another indispensable resource is the on-line version of the *Index Thomisticus*, (http://www.corpusthomisticum.org/) produced by Father Roberto Busa, S.J. (November 13, 1913 – August 9, 2011). The *Index* was a pioneer work in the digital humanities. The work commenced in 1949 after Fr. Busa convinced IBM founder Thomas J. Watson to support the project. Initially, the work was recorded on computer punch cards, and it grew to encompass the entire corpus of St. Thomas' writing: approximately 11 million words, each of which was morphologically tagged and lemmatized by hand. Nearly three decades of meticulous labor were required before the publication of the 56 printed volumes of the *Index Thomisticus* in 1976. [3]

---

3 «Roberto Busa», in *Wikipedia, the free encyclopedia*, Page Version ID: 517341193, in http://en.wikipedia.org/w/index.php?title=Roberto_Busa&oldid=517341193 [1-11-2012].

Page intentionally left blank

Contents

Page intentionally left blank

Page intentionally left blank

LESSONS AND READING PASSAGES

Page intentionally left blank

Chapter 1

Vocabulary

orior, -iri, ortus, *arise*
conor, -ari, *attempt; try*
progredior, progredi, progressus, *go, proceed*
paulatim, *gradually*
ultra, *beyond*
pertingo, pertingere, *to reach, to get as far as*
quatenus, *as far as, in so far as*
ius, iuris, neut., *law*
praeter, *beyond, before*
prout, *as; just as*
praecipuus, -a, -um, *particular, especial*

Grammar

◊ **Impersonal verbs** are used frequently in scholastic texts. Many impersonal verbs appear only in the third person singular and in the infinitive and gerund forms. They are usually translated in English with "it" as an impersonal subject. Verbs like *videtur* and *relinquitur* are used impersonally in the passive voice.

constat, *it is plain, evident*
accidit, *it happens*
placet, *it pleases*
patet, *it is clear, evident, well known*
decet, *it is becoming, proper*
necesse est, *it is necessary*
refert, *it concerns*
relinquitur, *it remains*
licet, *it is allowed*
libet, *it pleases*
videtur, *it seems*
oportet, *it is fitting, one ought*
interest, *it concerns*

BEWARE:
licet, verb = it is allowed
licet, adv. = although

◊ **The relative pronoun, qui, quae, quod** occurs in virtually every paragraph of scholastic philosophical writting. The relative pronoun agrees in gender and number with its antecedent; however, its case is determined by the function it serves within its clause.

It is worth quickly refreshing one's memory of the way the relative pronoun is declined.

BEWARE:
quod has many functions
1. relative pronoun = which
2. conjunction = because
3. conjunction = that

3

	singular			plural		
	m	**f**	**n**	**m**	**f**	**n**
n	qui	quae	quod	qui	quae	quae
ac	quem	quam	quod	quos	quas	quae
g	cuius			quorum	quarum	quorum
d	cui			quibus		
ab	quo	qua	quo	quibus		

	sing	pl
n	res	res
ac	r.em	res
g	r.ei	r.erum
d	r.ei	r.ebus
ab	r.e	r.ebus

orta est => orior, -iri
progrédiens => pro-
gredior
conatur => conor, -ari

remotus
remot.ior
remot.issimus

veritátis inveniéndae
vitae...instituéndae
gerundive phrases,
see Nunn §190

	sing (fem.)
n	domus
ac	dom.um
g	dom.us
d	dom.ui
ab	dom.o

Readings

1.   Metaphysica.[1] Quaestiónes de <u>rerum</u> intérna natúra, de mundi hominísque orígine ac fine, de Deo ipso ab antiquíssimis tempóribus hóminum ánimos movérunt. Hinc paulátim metaphýsica sciéntia <u>orta est</u>, quae ultra phýsicam rerum natúram sénsibus apparéntem <u>progrédiens</u> ad altióra pertíngere <u>conátur</u>. Metaphýsica enim illa philosóphiae pars est, quae rerum, quátenus in se spectántur, ratiónes <u>remotió-</u><u>res</u> invéstigat. Lógica et éthica (cum philosóphia iúris), quae sunt praeter metaphýsicam áliae partes philosóphiae praecípuae, de rebus tractant, non prout in se considerántur, sed quátenus ad intelléctum et voluntátem referúntur, ítaque leges <u>veritátis inveniéndae</u> et <u>vitae recte instituéndae</u> docent.

2.   Finis operántis—Finis óperis. *Finis óperis* est illud ipsum, quod per operatiónem effícitur. *Finis operántis*, qui dícitur étiam *finis intentiónis*, est illud, quod sibi propónit agens in sua operatióne. E. g., « **forma <u>domus</u> est finis términans**

---

1 from J. DONAT, S. J., *Ontologia*. Oeniponte: Felicianus Rauch, 1914.

operatiónem aedificatóris; non tamen ibi terminátur inténtio eíus, sed ad ulteriórem finem quae est habitátio; ut sic dicátur, quod finis operatiónis est forma domus, intentiónis _vero_ habitátio [2]». Item, « bonum córporis potest esse finis virtútis, quasi quidam términus, vel efféctus virtuósae operatiónis; non autem sicut _in quo stet_ virtútis inténtio; quia, _cum_ virtus _sit_ perféctio ánimae, quae est córpore nobílior, et _cum_ nihil _agat_ _propter vílius se_, non potest esse _quod_ in bono córporis inténtio virtútis _quiéscat_[3]».

Dícitur quoque _finis óperis_ id, ad quod opus natúra sua spectat; _finis_ autem _operántis_, illud, quod agens ad líbitum sibi propónit, e. g., respéctu eleemósynae, subsídium páuperi ferre est finis _óperis_; _cháritas_, aut inánis glória est _finis operántis_; item, respéctu aedificatiónis domus, cómmoda habitátio est finis _óperis_; _lucrum_, vel áliud est finis _operántis_. Aliquándo finis _óperis cum fine operántis_ conspírat, uti cum architéctus própriam sibi aedíficat domum.

3. **Finis Cuiúslibet Rei Est Bonum.** Nam finis cuiuslíbet rei est id, in quod terminátur eíus appetítus: appetítus autem cuiuslíbet rei terminátur ad bonum: _cuiuslíbet_ ígitur rei finis est áliquod bonum [4].

---

2 *Qq. dispp., De Pot., q. III, a. 16 c*
3 *In lib. IV Sent., Dist. XLIX, q. I, a. 1, sol. 1 ad 4*
4 *Contr, Gent., lib. III, c. 16. Vid. Signoriello, Omne agens agit propter bonum* litt. O

Marginal notes:

vero = autem

in quo stet (subj.)
cf. Nunn §150

cum...sit; cum...agat
cf. Nunn §156a

propter vílius se
(*prep. + acc. neut.*
comp. adj. + abl. of
comparison)

quod...quiescat
(=quiescit)
cf. Nunn §116

charitas = caritas

lucrum ≈ pecunia

cuiuslibet => qui.libet

Page intentionally left blank

Chapter 2

Vocabulary

finio, -ire, -ivi, -itum, *to limit, bound*
intellego, intellegere, intellexi, intellectum, *understand; realize*
actus, -us, masc., *act*
equidem, *truly; indeed*
huiusmodi, *of this sort; such*
possideo, possidere, *to possess*
ideo, *therefore*
exinde, *thence, from that*
exurgo, exurgere, exurrexi, exurrectus, *to arise, to come to being*
infero, inferre, intuli, illatus, *to infer*
nempe, *namely*

huiusmodi
also used as a pronoun, in imitation of Greek (οἱ οὕτως = οἱ τοιοῦτοι): huiuscemodi autem Christo Domino nostro non serviunt, Rom. 16, 18 (cf. Nunn §71)

Grammar

◊   **quod, quia, quoniam** are used in post-Classical Latin to introduce indirect statements (instead of the Classical accusative+infinitive construction). Following verbs of speaking, thinking, feeling, believing, etc., the conjunction **quod, quia,** or **quoniam** often introduce a clause with it's verb in the indicative mood.

◊   **Substantive use of participles**: when a participle is used substantively, it is often necessary to translate in English with a phrase. E.g. **finitus** = something limited; a finite thing.

◊   Most **adverbs** are derived from adjectives by modifying their termination. This is similar to English, where we can make adverbs by adding the suffix "-ly" to an adjective (eg. quick =>quickly). In Latin, adjectives from the 1st/2nd declension are transformed into adverbs by changing their ending to "-e", while adjectives from the 3rd declension become adverbs by adding "-iter" to the stem (stems ending in "-nt" add only "-er").

clar.us => clar.e
fortis => fort.iter
prudens => prudenter

◊   Other **adverbs** come from the following sources:

1. The ablative neuter or feminine singular of adjectives, pronouns, and nouns can produce adverbs (e.g. **falso,** *falsely;* **recta,** *straightaway;* **vulgo,** *commonly;* **vero,** *in fact, truly*)

BEWARE:
vero, adv. = in fact
vero, conj. = but

2. Idiomatic phrases which have merged into single words (e.g. **scilicet,** *that is to say, namely;* **nihilominus,** *nevertheless;* **videlicet,** *it is easy to see, clearly, to wit;* **postmodo,** *presently*)

3.   Adverbs ending in "-tim" (e.g. **separatim,** *separately;* **passim,** *everywhere, in many cases, indiscriminately;* **interim,** *meanwhile;* **generatim,** *generally;* **paulatim,** *gradually*)

Readings

finitis => finio, -ire

actu
ablative, "in act"

*si...exurgeret, iam...
possideret, ideoque
non esset...*
see Nunn §169
regarding use of the
imperfect subjunctive in conditional
statements

inferri => inferre

dicemus => dicimus

1.   **Infinítum Impossíbile Est Esse Ex Finítis.** Intellígitur de illo, quod est *actu* infinítum. Équidem, si huiúsmodi infinítum ex finítis exúrgeret, iam *actu* ómnia non possidéret, ideóque non esset actu infinítum. Exínde abnórmitas pantheísmi inférri potest, secúndum enim hoc systéma, Infinítum, nempe Deus, ex rerum finitárum collectióne exúrgeret.

2.   **Actus—Poténtia.** Actus signíficat 1° operatiónem; e. g., actus intelléctus, et eiúsdem operátio idem sunt. *Actus* hoc sensu accéptus *actus secúndus,* ut mox dicémus, appellári consuévit, eíque oppónitur poténtia, seu facúltas, quae est próximum princípium, ex cuius virtúte operátio prodúcitur. 2° Signíficat vel id, quod rem detérminat, seu pérficit; unde *actuáre* est determináre, seu perfícere; e. g., ánima est actus córporis; rationálitas est actus animalitátis: vel quod ex áliqua re edúcitur, cuiúsmodi est ignis, qui ex ligno evólvitur, aut figúra Cáesaris in marmóre inscúlpta. *Actus,* cui haec significátio adnéctitur, vocátur actus *formális,* eíque e contrário respóndet poténtia *passíva,* seu *subiectíva,* quae est capácitas subiécti ad recipiéndum actum formálem sive substantiálem,

adnectere
to join, add

sive accidentálem, v. g., disposítio córporis ad recipiéndam ánimam, perlucíditas aeris ad lumen suscipiéndum, capácitas marmóris inelaboráti ad recipiéndam figúram etc. 3° Quandóque usurpátur pro ipsa entitáte, seu existéntia rei, qua ratióne quidquid est extra níhilum, sive exístit, dícitur *actus entitatívus*, vel *habére actum entitatívum*; eíque oppónitur *poténtia obiectíva*, quae est mera rei possibílitas, seu non repugnántia ad existéndum, in qua poténtia modo est Antichrístus, qui <u>licet</u> non exístat, potest tamen exístere.

licet = quamquam = quamvis

Page intentionally left blank

Chapter 3

Vocabulary

scilicet, *that is to say, namely*
sumo, sumere, *to take, grasp, understand*
ratio, rationis, f., *reason; the act of reasoning; the product of reasoning, concept, notion, idea; plan, pattern; argumentation, proof*
albus, -a -um, adj., *white*
albitudo, albitudinis, f., *whiteness*
visio, visionis, f., *vision*
aliquid, *something, anything*
patet, *it is clear, evident, well known*
pendeo, pendere, pependi, -, *hang, hang down; depend*
quemadmodum, *as, just as; to the extent that*
adnoto, adnotare, adnotavi, adnotatus, *to note, jot down; to notice*
e.g. (exempli gratia), *for example*
denomino, denominare, denominavi, denominatus, *to designate, to give a name to*
siquidem, conj., *accordingly; if indeed*

Grammar

◊ **ratio**: the original meaning of ratio pertained to business transactions (e.g. rationem ducere, to compute; rationes subducere, to settle accounts). Subsequently, more figurative meanings developed (e.g. rationem habere, to make a calculation of any kind). From this arose the meanings most commonly employed in scholastic language: plan (e.g. ratio studiorum), method of procedure, nature, kind, notion. By analogy, ratio came to be applied in philosophy to the faculty of mind responsible for planning, reason itself, and thus also to the products of reason: concept, idea, theory, doctrine, philosophical system, and the act of adducing a proof or of reasoning.

Consider this passage from Vatican II, *Gaudium et spes* §57:

Sane hodiernus progressus scientiarum artiumque technicarum,	Clearly today's progress of the sciences and technology,
quae vi methodi suae <u>usque ad intimas rerum rationes</u> penetrare nequeunt,	which by virtue of their methods are unable to penetrate <u>to the most profound explanations</u> of things,

cuidam phaenomenismo et agnosticismo favere potest,	can foster a certain phenomenalism and agnosticism
quando methodus investigandi, qua disciplinae istae utuntur,	when the methods of investigation which these sciences use
immerito pro suprema totius veritatis inveniendae regula habetur.	are wrongly considered as the supreme rule of seeking the whole truth.

◊ **3rd person verbs**: Philosophical texts, like modern academic writing, tend to employ verbs in the third person. This gives a tone of objectivity; there is no place for "I," "you," and "we" when speaking of carefully reasoned truths. This also makes reading philosophical texts much easier! Be sure to recognize the active verbs ending in -t (he, she, it), -nt (they). The passive 3rd person endings require more care. When you see verbs ending in -tur and -ntur, ask two questions: 1) is the verb ordinary or deponent, 2) is the subject of the verb expressed (e.g. res dicitur alba= a thing is called white), or unexpressed/impersonal (dicitur quod...=it is said that...).

Readings

1. **Abstractum Est Forma Concréti.** Scílicet, abstráctum est id, a quo concrétum denominátur; e. g., ab albitúdine res dícitur alba, et a visióne res dícitur visa. Ex quibus exémplis patet *formam* hic sumi pro ratióne, per quam áliquid denominátur, quae necésse non est ut sit in ipsa re, cum possit étiam esse áliquid princípium extra rem, et a quo ista pendet, síquidem *vísio*, ex qua res denominátur *visa*, est extra rem *visam*. Hac ratióne, quemádmodum s. Bonaventúra adnotávit, áliqui hómines ex Divinitáte denominántur divíni, ut *diviníssimus Paulus*, vel *diviníssimus Ioánnes*[5].

hic = in hoc loco

sumi => sumere
pres. passive infin.

necesse est + ut +subjunctive
cf. Nunn §123

cum possit...
cf. Nunn §156a

---

5 *In lib, III Sent.*, Dist. XI, dub. 3.

2.   Áccidens Est Entis Ens. Et Accidentis Esse Est Ines-

se. Nimírum: Áccidens, si secúndum própriam et intrínse-

cam ratiónem spectétur, est quidem áliquod ens; sed quó-

niam ens simplíciter et principáliter signíficat *esse per se,* ac

proínde substántiam; *esse* autem accidéntis éxigit inhaerén-

tiam substántiae, ídeo áccidens dícitur *entis ens*, quia refértur

ad substántiam, ac proínde non habet *esse simplíciter*, nempe

ita perféctum, sicut substántia. « **Esséntia, subdit s. Thomas,**

próprie et vere est in substántiis, sed in accidéntibus est

quodámmodo, et secúndum quid [6]».

Quocírca vi huius effáti senténtia Lóckii refutátur as-

seréntis substántiam in qualitátum complexióne consístere.

Qualitátes enim sunt accidéntia. Atqui accidéntia, cum sint

entis éntia, principáliter et perfécte non sunt ens. Ergo sub-

stántia, si ex ipsis qualitátibus constituerétur, non esset pró-

prie et perfécte ens; id quod eíus notiónem déstruit.

3.   Ex hoc theorémáte illud álterum séquitur: Accidéntis

esse est inésse. Non quidem ita ut inésse signíficet *esse* ac-

cidéntis absolúte, sed modum esséndi, qui sibi convénit ex

órdine ad subiéctum, cui inháeret. Ínsuper accidéntis *esse*

est *inésse*, non quátenus ad esséntiam accidéntis requíritur,

ut actu inháereat subiécto, sed quátenus áccidens necessário

órdinem habet ad hoc, ut álteri insit, et recipiátur in subiécto

sibi accommodáto[7]. Hinc accidéntia absolúta, de quibus su-

---

6 *De ente et essentia, c*
7 Vid. s. Thom., *In lib. IV Sent.*, Dist. XII, q. I, a. 1, *sol.* 1 ad 1

---

nimirum
without doubt

exigit => exigere
to require, demand

inhaerentia, -ae
an inherence or existence in something

nempe =
that is to say

subdit = ait

quodammodo
in a certain measure

sententia Lockii...asserentis
the opinion of John Locke asserting...

atqui = sed
si...constitueretur, non esset
cf. Nunn §169

pra [8], non sunt huiúsmodi, ut subsístant per se, quemádmodum substántia, sed sustinéntur a Deo sine subiécto, et *actu*
quidem non sunt in substántia, *potestáte* vero et *exigéntia* in
substántia sunt, quia étiam dum actu exístunt sine substántia, póstulant esse in substántia.

8 Signoriello, Pag. 8

Chapter 4

Vocabulary

mendacium, mendacii, neut., *lying, falsehood, untruth*
idest, *that is*
abstraho, abstrahere, abstraxi, abstractus, *to abstract, to remove from*
induco, inducere, induxi, inductus, *induce, influence; introduce*
abstractio, abstractionis, f., *abstraction*
supra, adv., *above, previously (ut supra dictum = as said previously)*
alterum...alterum, *one thing...the other*
nego, negare, *to deny, refuse, negate*
adeo, adv., *to such an extent*
dummodo, conj., *provided [that...]*
affingo, affingere, affinxi, affictus, *add to, attach*
quamvis, conj. or adv., *although*
siquidem, conj., *accordingly; if indeed*
item, adv., *likewise, besides*
mentior, mentiri, mentitus sum, (deponent), *to lie, deceive*

Grammar

◊ **Guessing vocabulary**: thousands of Latin words have come directly into English, so it is often possible to correctly guess the meaning of a Latin word when it is encountered in context. However, pay close attention to the context; the meaning of the English words derived from Latin are often similar but not 100% the same as their cognates. For verbs, a good rule of thumb is to work from the present infinitive.

1) sometimes Latin verbs ending in -are have the ending -ate in English. E.g. **separare**=>*separate*, **elevare**=>*elevate*, **resuscitare, supplicare, illuminare, immolare, liberare, communicare, celebrare, cooperare, creare, donare, expiare, cogitare, congregare, cremare.**

2) sometimes verbs ending in -are or -ere change to an -e ending in English. E.g. **observare**=>*observe*, **praeparare**=>*prepare*, **inclinare, implorare, evadere, intercedere, praecedere, praesumere, absolvere, adorare, salutare, residere.**

3) sometimes verbs simply drop the Latin infinitive ending. E.g. **errare**=>*err*, **abstrahere**=>*abstra[ct]*, **considerare**=>*consider*, **manifestare, visitare, convertere, descendere, discernere, ascendere, respondere,**

formare, reformare.

4) verbs ending in -ficare in Latin have the ending -fy in English. E.g. **sanctificare**=>*sanctify*, **vivificare**=>*vivify*, **justificare, pacificare, glorificare**.

Readings

1.   **Abstrahéntium Non Est Mendácium.** Idest, qui ábstrahit, non ídeo in errórem indúcitur, quia ábstrahit. Intelligéndum autem hoc est non quidem de abstractióne *negatíva*, sed de *praecisíva*, de quibus supra. Qui enim álterum cognóscit, omitténdo álterum, nihil negat, adeóque non errat; síquidem error non est rem áliquam ex parte cognóscere et intellígere, dúmmodo nihil ei repúgnans, aut extráneum affingátur. Hinc qui consíderat hóminem, quin in eo consíderet ratiónem, non mentítur. Item, « **intelléctus mathematicórum non est falsus, quamvis nulla línea sit abstrácta a matéria in re [9]**»

2.   **Intellectus Ábstrahit A Matéria.** Tum quia ultra singulária, seu materiália se exténdit; tum quia, ut ait s. Thomas, res singuláres *facit intelligíbiles in actu per abstractiónem speciérum a conditiónibus* materiálibus [10]. Quod ut magis perspícuum fiat, in memóriam revocándum est quamlíbet cognitrícem poténtiam nihil sine quadam abstractióne apprehéndere posse; síquidem poténtia cógnitrix áliquid apprehéndit, quá-

intelligendum = it must be understood

omittendo, gerund by omitting

hinc = hence
quin = without, while not

quamvis = quamquam

---

9   S. Thom., *In lib. I Sent.*, Dist. XXX, q. I, a. 3 sol
10   I, q. LXXIX, a. 3 c

tenus *áccipit formam apprehénsi, non secúndum esse, quod habet in eo, quod apprehénditur,* sed *secúndum esse repraesentatívum.* Iam vero huius abstractiónis gradus divérsi sunt, <u>prout</u> divérsae sunt poténtiae [11]. Étenim sensus exterióres ábstrahunt quidem formam a matéria, quátenus rerum spécies in eis recipiúntur sine matéria, eádem ratióne, qua cera ánnuli figúram sine ferro, vel auro récipit; sed non ábstrahit a preséntia matériae, nec ab eíus *appendícibus.* Quas matériae *appéndices* éxplicans <u>Albértus M.</u> ait esse « **conditiónes et proprietátes, quas habet subiéctum formae quod est in tali, vel tali matéria; v. g., talis membrórum situs, vel talis color faciéi, vel talis aetas, vel talis figúra cápitis, vel talis locus generatiónis; haec enim sunt quaedam individuántia formam, quae sic sunt in uno indivíduo uníus speciéi, quod non sunt in álio [12]»**.

Poténtia autem imaginatíva ábstrahit a matéria, et a praeséntia matériae, sed non ab eíus appendícibus; e. g., Sortem non praeséntem imaginámur, sed tamen crispum, et album, senem, vel iuvénem etc. At intelléctus, cum sit facúltas inorgánica, in rebus neque matériam, neque áliquid, quod ex matéria fluit, sed tantum quidditátem, sive esséntiam eíus cognóscit, ac proínde ábstrahit non solum a matéria, et eíus praeséntia, sed étiam ab eíus *appendíciis.* Hanc ob ratiónem spécies, per quam intelléctus rem cognóscit, *simplíciter ab-*

prout ≈ sicut

Albertus Magnus
St. Albert the Great, teacher of St. Thomas Aquinas

---

11   Vid. Alb. De *Anim.* lib, II, tract. 3, c. 4
12   Vid. Alb. De *Anim.* lib, II, tract. 3, c. 4

strácta étiam vocári solet. Divérsos autem gradus, quibus haec abstráctio intellectíva fíeri potest, explicábimus, ubi distinctiónem tradémus inter matériam *sensíbilem* et *intelligíbilem*.

Chapter 5

Vocabulary

notus, -a, -um, adj., *known*
quam, conj., *than*
virtus, virtutis, f., *strength, power, virtue*
lateo, latere, latui, -, +accusative = *lie hidden [from some-one], escape notice [of someone]*
vel, conj., *or*
secundum quod, *in as far as, as*
occulto, occultare, occultavi, occultatus, *to hide, conceal*
dum, *while, as long as*
immo [or imo], adv., introduces a sentence correcting a mistake, implied doubt, or understatement, *nay, nay but, nay rather; on the contrary; more correctly*
secus, adv., *otherwise*
talis, talis, tale, adj., *such*
nisi, *unless*
effatum, effati, neut., *axiom, proposition, a saying*
repraesento, repraesentare, repraesentavi, repraesenta-tus, *to represent, show*

Grammar

◊ guessing vocabulary: many Latin adjectives ending in -ius and nouns ending in -ium have cognates in English that end in -y. E.g. **voluntarius**=>*voluntary,* **necessarius**=>*necessary,* **contrarius**=>*contrary,* **mysterium**=>*mystery,* **studium**=>*study,* **anniversarius, legionarius, remedium, colloquium, subsidium, matrimonium, seminarium.**

◊ **Conditional phrases** employ the following conjunctions:

si, si non   (if, if... not)
nisi   (unless)
quod si   (and if)
si minus, sin autem   (but if)

Types of conditions:

REAL:	
Pres, or Fut Indicative or Imperative (is...is)	Si vis amari,ama.

Perf, Indicative	Si eum occidi, recte feci.
POTENTIAL:	
Present Subjunctive (were...would be x-ing),	Hanc viam si asperam esse negem, mentiar.
Perfect Subjunctive (were...would)	Si a corona relictus sim, non queam dicere.
IRREAL:	
Imperfect Subjunctive (should ...was)	Si amici adessent, consilii non indigerem.
Pluperfect Subjunctive (had been...would have)	Si ibi te esse scissem, ad te ipse venissem.
INCOMPLETE ACTION:	
dum, modo, dummodo (provided that)	Nil obstat tibi dum Deum credas.

Readings

notior...quam
cf. Nunn §204

1. **Operátio Nótior Est, Quam Substántia.** Hoc effátum ita explicátur a s. Bonaventúra: « **Dicéndum, quod verum est de operatióne extrínseca; de intrínseca autem non habet veritátem; multae enim res sunt nobis notae, qua-**

nos latent
cf. Chap. 5 Vocab.

rum virtútes et operatiónes nos latent. Vel dicéndum, **quod**

quod hoc locum habet = quod hoc [effatum] est verum

hoc locum habet in operatióne naturáli, non in operatióne voluntátis. Operátio enim naturális, secúndum quod naturális est, ita se naturáliter nata est repraesentáre, nec se oc-

nec substantia = nec substantia se occultáre potest

cultáre potest, sicut nec substántia; immo per ipsam manifestátur substántia, dum plus habet de ratióne actualitátis, ac per hoc manifestatiónis et lucis. In operatióne autem

cum...repraesentet
cf. Nunn §156a

voluntária secus est; nam, cum substántia se naturáliter

repraeséntet, sicut naturáliter est, sic se occultáre non potest; operátio voluntária sicut **voluntárie** exit in esse, ita et voluntárie manifestátur, et ita occultári potest; immo non manifestátur, nisi homo **velit**; tália autem sunt, quae latent in secréto consciéntiae nostrae [13]».

vountari.e =>
voluntari.us

velit => vult

2.   **Substántia — Áccidens.** *Substántia*, prout constítuit primum *praedicaméntum*, est ens, cui convénit exístere *per se*. « Rátio substántiae intellígitur hoc modo, quod substántia sit res, cui convéniat esse non in subiécto [14]». Dícitur, *prout constítuit primum praedicaméntum*, quia aliquándo *substántia* súmitur pro *esséntia*: Substántia duplíciter dícitur. Uno enim modo dícitur substántia, prout signíficat ratiónem primi praedicaménti... Álio modo dícitur substántia illud, quod signíficat quid in ómnibus rebus, sicut dícimus quod definítio signíficat rei substántiam; et hoc modo quidquid positíve dícitur, in quocúmque génere sit, substántia est, vel substántiam habet; sic enim substántia pro esséntia súmitur [15]». Iam vero, cum pro *esséntia* súmitur, vagátur per ómnia *praedicaménta*; quodlíbet enim praedicaméntum est áliqua esséntia. *Áccidens* contra, prout oppónitur categóriae substántiae, est ens, cui convénit exístere in álio, seu illud, cuius natúra éxigit, ut álio fulciátur, ipsíque inháereat. Iam patet substántiae

---

13   *In lib. II Sent., Dist. VIII, p. 2, a. I, q. 6 ad arg. Exinde infert sanctus Doctor nullam creaturam nec angelicam, nec humanam posse conscientiae humanae secreta cognoscere, nisi per signa vel conjecturas, vel nisi ea noverit Dei revelatione, aut hominis denunciatione*
14   *Contr. Gent., lib. I, c. 25*
15   *In lib. II Sent., Dist XXXVII, q. I, a. 1 sol*

notiónem non consístere in eo quod accidéntibus substat; síquidem ab hoc substántia denominátur, velut a notióri proprietáte, eódem modo quo lapis dícitur a laedéndo pedem, sed non essentiáliter in hoc sustentáculo constitúitur. Qua enim ratióne substántia posset accidéntia sustentáre; nisi esset in seípsa? Quómodo autem nótio entis *per se* distinguátur a notióne entis *a se*, alíbi explicátum est. Ínsuper *accidéntia absolúta* a Peripatéticis admíssa, uti sunt quántitas, quálitas etc., licet *actu* non exístant in álio, tamen non exístere *per se*, ideóque non esse substántias, étiam explicátum est. Dénique pro sacrae Theológiae tyrónibus illud étiam adnotándum censémus: ratiónem substántiae exclúdere quidem subiéctum, a quo ipsa fulciátur, non vero suppósitum, cuius sit, seu persónam, a qua terminétur.

3.   Hinc natúra humána Christi, licet subsístat in Verbo, a quo assúmpta est per incarnatiónem; tamen est substántia, quia non exístit in Verbo tamquam subiécto, cui inháereat, sed quátenus terminátur a Persóna Verbi. Neque ex hoc, quod non subsístit per própriam personalitátem, séquitur ipsam non exístere *per se*. Ut enim substántia dicátur compléte *per se* exístens, súfficit ut hábeat personalitátem vel sibi *própriam* vel *appropriátam*. Natúra autem humána Christi habet *personalitátem* Divínam sibi *appropriátam*, ut haec in ómnibus gerat vices *personalitátis* ipsíus natúrae humánae.

Chapter 6

Vocabulary

vetus, veteris (gen.), adj., *old, ancient*
indífferens -éntis, adj., *indifferent;* **indifferénter:** *adv.*
non modo...sed etiam, *not only...but also*
siquidem, conj., *accordingly; if indeed*
seu, conj., *or*
quodlibet, *whichever, whatsoever,*
per se, *for itself; taken in itself; through oneself; according to one's own nature and essence*
tamquam, conj., *as, just as, just as if; as it were*
potissimus, -a, -um, *chief, primary, principal, most prominent*
tot, *so many, such a number of*
lignum, ligni, neut., *wood*
fio, feri, factus sum, semideponent verb, *happen, come about; result (from); be made/created*
fere, adv., *almost, nearly*
quot, adj., *how many, as many*
penes, prep., *in the power of, belonging to*

Grammar

◊ **Connective relative pronouns:** A relative pronoun often stands at the beginning of a sentence and must then be translated into English by *and* followed by a personal pronoun. Connective relatives are used in the Vulgate to translate the Greek ὁ δέ. EXAMPLES:

Qui cum recedissent, ecce angelus Domini apparuit in somnis Joseph...qui consurgens accepit puerum.
And when they had departed, behold an angel of the Lord appeared to Joseph in a dream...and he arose and took the child. Matt. 2:13.

Quorum fidem ut videt, dixit...
And when he saw their faith, he said... Lk. 5:20.

◊ Some **compounds of *quis* and *qui*** decline the *"qui"* portion of the word.

1. The addition of the suffix "-que" gives a sense of universality: **quisque,** *everyone,* **quique,** *every*

2. The addition of "ali-" gives the pronoun **aliquis,** *someone,* and the adjective **aliqui,** *some (***aliqua** as the feminine nominative singular*)*

Nunn § 66

23

3. Compounding with "-libet" produces **quílibet, quaélibet, quódlibet, pronoun,** *any, anyone, anything whatsoever;* **adjective,** *any, any at all, any you wish*

4. The suffix "-dam" produces **quidam, quaedam,** and **quoddam, pronoun,** *a certain person or thing,* **adjective,** *a certain, a kind of*

Readings

1.   **Forma—Matéria** Sunt duo princípia, ex quibus non modo secúndum Scholásticos, sed étiam secúndum plerósque véteres, recentésque Doctóres quodvis phýsicum compósitum exúrgit; <u>síquidem</u> docent compósitum naturále generári ex <u>praesuppósito</u> subiécto, quod introductiónem formae cum privatióne ipsíus praecédit. Iam *matéria,* seu *matéria prima* est princípium substantiále indífferens <u>ad quodlíbet constituéndum</u>. *Forma* seu *forma substantiális* est princípium substantiále per se ad id ordinátum, ut cum *matéria prima* compósitum naturále, tamquam potíssima huius differéntia, constítuat. Scílicet, <u>cum matéria vaga sit</u>, atque indífferens ad quodlíbet compósitum, a *forma,* quam récipit, determinátur, <u>ut sit haec</u>, et non <u>ália compósiti naturális spécies</u>.

Exémplum áccipe ab artefáctis. In his lignum, e. g., est matéria commúnis, ex qua quaelíbet státua fíeri potest, figúra <u>vero</u> ab artífice indúcta lignum ad determinátam státuam constítuit, ita ut idem lignum, <u>dum</u> habet figúram Cáesaris, fiat státua Cáesaris, et <u>dum</u> habet figúram equi, fiat státua equi. Eódem fere modo *matéria* naturálium compositórum

siquidem = since, inasmuch as

praesuppositum = something presupposed

ad quodlíbet constituéndum = to making up anything; cf. Nunn §190

cum materia vaga sit: here *cum* = *quamvis* or *licet;* cf. Nunn §166

ut sit haec = to be this [thing]

vero, adverb

dum = during the time in which, as long as

eádem et commúnis ómnibus intellígitur, sed dum várias formas súscipit, in várias substántiae spécies tráhitur; dum enim habet *formam* hóminis, fit homo; dum *formam* equi, fit equus; dum *formam* árboris, fit arbor. Hinc tot sunt <u>penes Peripatéticos</u> *formae substantiáles*, quot sunt divérsae physicárum substantiárum spécies.

penes Peripateticos
= apud discipulos
Aristotelis

2.   Ut autem ista Scholasticórum plácita clárius innotéscant, haec adnotámus: 1° *Matéria* ab Aristótele esse dícitur quod *non est quid, nec quale, nec quantum, nec áliquid eórum, per quae ens determinátur, sed est commúne horum subiéctum*; nempe *matéria* neque ulla determináta spécies entis est, neque áliquid eórum, quibus esséntia compléta rei determinátur, sed est velut áliquid, quod potest in se recípere esséntiam rei, et ea, quibus esséntia determinátur. E. g., *matéria*, ex qua fit ignis, non est ipse ignis, nec eíus quántitas, color, figúra, motus, aut quodvis símile, nec primum eíus princípium actívum, sed est *commúne eórum subiéctum*, nempe intellígitur tamquam illud quod subiícitur iis ómnibus, quae in se recípere potest [16].

2° *Matéria*, ut consequítur ex dictis, non habet per seípsam existéntiam talem, e. g., existéntiam ligni, ferri etc., sed per formam ligni, ferri, etc., quia matéria *per se* neque

---

16   « Hylen namque Graeci, cura de natura disserunt, materiem quamdam rerum definiunt, nulla prorsus modo formatam, sed omnium corporalium formarum capacem; quae quidem in corporum mutabilitate utcumquc cognoscitur; nam per seipsam nec sentiri, nec intelligi potest »; s. Aug., *Contra Faustum*, lib. XX, c. 14

lignum est, neque ferrum etc. Quinímmo Thomístae, aliíque plures addunt matériam nullum habére actum entitatívum, seu omníno existéntia sui próprie destítui, atque tantum exístere per existéntiam tótius compósiti. Id maniféste docet s. Thomas. « **Dícere, ipse inquit, matériam praecédere sine forma est dícere ens actu sine actu** [17]». Atque ínsuper: « **Matéria prima non exístit in rerum natúra per seípsam, cum non sit ens in actu, sed poténtia tantum** [18]». Hinc *matéria* neque est ens simplíciter, neque non ens simplíciter, seu nihil, sed áliquid médium inter utrúmque; exístit enim, ut s. Bonaventúra inquit, *secúndum, realitátem poténtiae*, sive *per modum inchoatiónis entis*[19].

3.   3° *Forma*, cum constítuat et detérminet matériam, ut sit aer, aqua, ignis etc., dici solet *actus*, sicut e contrário matéria dícitur *poténtia*, eo quod est indífferens ad quamlíbet spéciem entis. A Graecis *forma* vocátur étiam ἐντελέχεια, idest perféctio, eo quod omnis perféctio, qua res gaudet, fit per *formam*, sicut capácitas perfectiónis est per *matériam*.

4° *Forma* est quidem *actus* respéctu constitutiónis alicuíus rei, at in se est *poténtia* respéctu existéntiae, quia in se haud invólvit últimum actum, qui est existéntia; in éntibus enim finítis esséntia ab existéntia distínguitur [20]. Hinc *forma*

---

17 I, q. LXVI, a. 1 c
18 I, q. VII, a. 2 ad 3
19 *In lib. II Sent., Dist. XII, a. I, q. 1 ad arg*
20 Vid. s. Thom., I, q. LXXV, a. 5 ad 4

non est *purus actus*, id quod solíus Dei est, in quo existéntia idem est ac esséntia.

Page intentionally left blank

Chapter 7

Vocabulary

dupliciter, adv., *in two ways, doubly*
se habere, *to be (in a certain circumstance or condition)*
subintelligo, -ere, subintellectus, to *understand implicitly,
    to imply*
omnino, *entirely, altogether*
ita, *so; thus; in such a way*
talis -is -e, adj., *such, such kind*
secundum quid, *literally "according to something"; to some
    extent, in some respect, only in the sense noted*
suppositio, suppositionis, f., *a supposition; a meaning*
positio, positionis, f., *a formulation, thesis, proposition*

quomodo te habes?
How are you?"

quid = aliquid
after the words *si,
nisi, num,* or *ne,*
and also in certain
static phrases like
secundum quid, the
word *quid* is short for
aliquid

Grammar

◊   **Verbs taking the Dative:** The Dative case is used following many verbs which are intransitive in Latin. In English,
we "forgive someone," "believe someone," or "obey someone."
In Latin, however, the equivalent ideas would be to "give for-
giveness to someone," "give credence to someone," or "pay
heed to someone." The following verbs usually take the Dative
in Latin: **credere,** *to believe*; **evangelizare,** *to preach the gospel*; **ignoscere/remittere,** *to pardon*; **imperare,** *to command*;
nocere, *to injure*; **obedire,** *to obey*; **parcere,** *to spare*; **placere,**
to please; **resistere,** *to resist*; **servire,** *to serve*; **suadere,** *to persuade*

◊   **Compound verbs + Dative:** Verbs compounded with
a preposition are usually followed by a Dative, especially compounds of **esse.** (cf. Nunn §37)

Readings

1.   **Simplíciter— Secúndum quid.** « Simplíciter potest

áccipi duplíciter. Uno modo dícitur, quod nullo álio áddito

dícitur. Álio modo simplíciter idem est, quod omníno, vel

totáliter [21]». Hinc 1° *simplíciter* áliquid tale esse dícitur, cum

---

21 3, q. L, a. 3 c

nullo alio subintellecto
Ablative absolute, cf. Nunn §51

ita se habet, nullo álio subintellécto; *secúndum quid* vero, cum, ut ita se habére dici possit, sub áliqua positióne accipiéndum est. E. g., Deus *simpliciter* exístit, seu nulla facta suppositióne; creatúra autem, *secúndum quid*, nempe suppósita Dei Voluntáte. 2° *Simpliciter* sub omni respéctu; *secúndum quid* sub quodam tantum respéctu rem talem esse signíficat. E. g.; « id, quod est último perféctum, dícitur bonum simplíciter; quod autem non habet áliquam perfectiónem, quam debet habére, quamvis hábeat áliquam perfectiónem, in quantum est actu, non dícitur perféctum simplíciter, nec bonum simplíciter, sed secúndum quid [22].

2. Hinc étiam « **nihil próhibet áliquid esse secúndum quid simplex, in quantum caret áliqua compositióne, quod tamen non est omníno simplex; unde ignis, et aqua dicúntur simplícia córpora, in quantum carent compositióne, quae est ex contráriis, atque invenítur in mixtis; quorum tamen unum quodque est compósitum tum ex pártibus quantitátis, tum étiam ex forma et matéria** [23]». 3° *Simpliciter*, aut *secúndum quid*, seu in *sensu accómmodo* de quodam subiécto praedicátum enunciátur, absque ulla, vel cum áliqua contractióne. E. g., substántia cógitans est *simpliciter* spirituális; homo *secúndum quid*, seu *in sensu accómmodo*, scílicet quoad corpus, est mortális. 4° « **Considerátur áliquid tale simpliciter, prout est secúndum seípsum tale. Secúndum**

caret + abl.
to lack (something); to not have (something)

---

22 I, q. V, a. 1 c
23 *In lib. Boet. De Hebd. lect. I*

quid autem, prout dícitur tale secúndum respéctum ad álterum [24]». Quo sensu idem signíficant ac *Absolúte — Comparatíve*; vel *Secúndum quod ipsum—In órdine ad álterum.* 5° *Simplíciter* idem signíficat, ac secúndum sui própriam ratiónem: *secúndum quid* idem est, ac secúndum áliam ratiónem. E. g., dícitur áliquid *ens simplíciter* quoad *esse substantiále*; síquidem ens *dicit próprie esse in actu,* ac proínde *secúndum quod primo discérnitur ab eo quod est in poténtia tantum,* nempe *secúndum esse substantiále. Per actus autem superáddites dícitur áliquid esse secúndum quid;* sicut esse album signíficat esse *secúndum* quid [25]. Inde íterum patet illud, quod est *última mo perféctum,* esse bonum *simplíciter;* quia « **bonum dicit ratiónem perfécti, quod est appetíbile, et per cónsequens dicit ratiónem últimi** [26]». 6° *Simplíciter* convénit alícui illud, quod ei convénit *secúndum totum;* sin *secúndum partem,* dícitur ei conveníre *secúndum quid.* Hac autem in re illud monet s. Thomas, quod « **si áliquid natum sit conveníre alícui, secúndum totum et partem, si convéniat ei solum secúndum partem, dícitur conveníre ei secúndum quid, et non simpliciter;sicut dícitur Áethiops albus secúndum dentes: secus autem est de eo, quod non est natum inésse, nisi secúndum partem, sicut áliquis dícitur simplíciter crispus, si hábeat capíllos crispos** [27]».

---

24 I, q. LXXXII, a. 3 c.
25 I, q. V, a. 1 c
26 I, q. V, a. 1 c
27 *Qq. dispp.*, q. *De Unione Verbi Incarnati*, a. 3 c.

Page intentionally left blank

Chapter 8

Vocabulary

porro, *then, afterwards, next, furthermore*
eo quod, *to the extent that*

Grammar

◊   The word **cum** has several, completely unrelated meanings.

    1. As a preposition, **cum** is translated as *with* or *together*. It is compounded with some pronouns, especially **tecum, mecum, vobiscum, nobiscum**, and **quibuscum**

    2. As a conjunction, **cum** can introduce three distinct types of subordinate clauses:

        a. Temporal clauses: **cum** = *when*

        b. Causal clauses: **cum** = *since, because*

        c. Concessive clauses: **cum** = *although*

See Nunn §§ 153, 154, 156, 166, 210

Readings

1.   **Locus Est Immutábilis Términus Continentis.** Scílicet, locus non dícitur movéri, quando áliquid secúndum locum movétur. Étenim, ut paulo ante díximus, « **motus locális non váriat rem secúndum áliquid ei inháerens, sed solum secúndum áliquid extrínsecum** [28]». Atqui « **quando illud, secúndum quod áliquid mutári dícitur, est extrínsecum, tunc in illa mutatióne non mutátur, sed immóbile persevérat** [29]». Ergo locus est immutábilis términus continéntis. Quod quidem perspícuum est « **eo quod per locálem motum**

ut paulo ante diximus in the original context, this paragraph was preceded by a discussion about motion. **Paulo** *is the ablative of* **paulum, -i, neut.,** *which becomes an adverb = a little bit (cf. Chap. 2, grammar)*

---

28 *Cont. Gent.*, lib. III, c. 82, n. 6
29 *Qq. dispp., De Ver.*, q. I, a. 6 c

non dícitur esse succéssio locórum in uno locáto, sed magis succéssio locatórum in uno loco [30]».

2. **Abstráctio formális — Abstráctio totális.** *Abstráhere* signíficat álterum ab áltero separáre; unde res, quae súmitur *separátim* ab iis, quibúscum coniúngitur, dícitur *abstrácte* sumta. Porro abstráctio, quae in sciéntiis occúrrit, non est abstráctio *reális*, seu *materiális*, quae pósita est in vera separatióne eórum, quae naturáliter coniúncta sunt, puta cum ab ave pennae avellúntur; sed abstráctio *intentionális* sive *lógica*.

pennae avelluntur
feathers are plucked
off

Iam haec fit per intelléctum, qui in áliqua re ad unum atténdit, relíctis áliis, quae cum hac iúncta reperiúntur: uti si alicuíus aedifícii sola latitúdo considerátur. Haec autem abstráctio duplex est, scílicet *totális*, seu *universális* et *formális*. Abstráctio *totális* fit, cum natúra supérior, sive universálior sine notis, quibus ad spéciem, vel indivíduum determináta est, spectátur; uti cum de áliquo hómine cógito ipsum esse ánimal rationále, quin cógitem ipsum esse hunc hóminem; vel, cum ánimal consídero, quin ipsum, uti hóminem, inspíciam. Dícitur *totális*, quia natúra commúnior, e. g., *ánimal*, se habet ut totum respéctu natúrae inferióris, e. g., *homo*. Abstráctio autem *formális* fit cum in sui esséntia tantum áliqua natúra accípitur extra subiéctum, in quo subsístit, vel cui inháeret, e. g., *humánitas*, *albitúdo*. « **Duplex, ait s. Thomas, fit abstráctio per intelléctum: una quidem, secúndum quod universá-**

_____

30 *Qq. dispp., De Ver.*, q. I, a. 6 c

le abstráhitur a particulári, ut ánimal ab hómine; ália vero, secúndum quod forma abstráhitur a matéria, sicut forma círculi abstráhitur per intelléctum ab omni matéria sensíbili [31]». Hinc abstráctio, qua corpus naturále considerátur, utpóte constítuens obiéctum sciéntiae phýsicae, non est quidem *formális*, sed *totális*. Circa huiúsmodi dúplicem abstractiónis spéciem haec étiam adnotáre praestat. Abstrácta prióri ratióne, secus ac illa, in quibus abstráctio est *formális*, 1° significári possunt *in concréto*, e. g., « homo significátur ut qui habet humanitátem », 2° « Non prohibéntur habére áliquid áliud, quod non pértinet ad ratiónem (némpe *esséntiam*) horum, nisi solum quod est oppósitum his. Et ídeo homo... potest áliquid áliud habére, quam humanitátem [32]». E contrário, *humánitas* non nisi *in abstrácto* significátur, et quóniam solam rei esséntiam índicat, nihil áliud praeter ipsam exhibére potest [33].

---

31 I, q. XL, a. 3 c
32 Vid. s. Thom., *Super Boet., de Hebdomadibus*, lect. I
33 De abstractione totali et formali vid. Caiet. In Prol. *De Ente et Essentia*

Page intentionally left blank

Chapter 9

Vocabulary

abutor, abuti, abusus sum, deponent, *to misuse, abuse*
ferramentum -i: n., *iron tool;* **medicinalia ferramenta,**
  medical instruments, **tremenda ferramenta,** *instruments*
  of torture
pernícies -éi: f., *disaster, destruction*
miles, militis, m., *soldier*
pater, patris, m., *father,* **patres, pl.,** *fathers, patriarchs*
gens, gentis, f., *nation, clan, people; Gentiles*
pervérsitas -átis: f.; *perversity, error*
verso, versare, versavi, versatus, *to spin, to revolve (around*
  something), to turn
specto, spectare, spectavi, spectatus, *to observe, watch,*
  look at
respício -ere -spéxi -spéctum: *look at, behold, consider, look*
  back, respect, observe
visus, -us, m., *vision, the faculty of sight*
sanctimonialis, sanctimonialis (gen. plural = sanctimo-
  nialium), f., *a nun, a religious*
ódi, odísse, (defective verb which is perfect in form with
  present meaning), *hate, detest*
plerúmque (plúrimum), adv., *mostly, commonly*

abbatissa est modera-
trix et rectrix societa-
tis sanctimonialium

Grammar

◊ **Verbs not taking the accusative:** In Chapter 7, verbs
taking the Dative cases were discussed. However, there are
also two other smaller groups of verbs that take cases other
than the accusitive.

  1. Verbs taking their object in the genitive:

    a. Verbs related to memory take the genitive,
and even worse, several of them are deponent verbs, **meminisse**, *to remember,* **recordari**, *to recall,* **reminisci**, *to
remember,* **oblivisci**, *to forget*

See Nunn §29 for
further explanation
and exceptions

    b. Verbs of pity can take the genitive, e.g. **mi-
serere mei, Domine,** *have pity on me, O Lord*

  2. Verbs taking the ablative case:

    a. Verbs dealing with need or lack typically
require the ablative. E. g. **carere**, *to lack,* **egere**, *to feel the
need of,* **opus esse**, *to need,* **usus esse**, *to be necessary*

    b. The "fantastic five," a group of five depo-
nent verbs denoting use or enjoyment and that take the
ablative: **frui**, *to enjoy,* **fungi**, *to perform (a function or*

See Nunn §57

action), **potiri**, *to be in power of, to take possession of,* **uti**, *to use* **vesci**, *to eat*

Readings

1.   **Ábusus Non Tollit Usum.** Váriis exémplis s. Augustínus hoc effátum explicávit: « **Non ídeo, inquit, contemnénda, vel detestánda virgínitas Sanctimoniálium, quia et Vestáles vírgines** fuérunt; sic non ídeo reprehendénda sacrifícia patrum, quia sunt et sacrifícia géntium [34]». Item: « **Neque enim pro pátria non est armándus miles, quia contra pátriam nonnúlli arma sumsérunt; aut ídeo uti non debent boni doctíque médici ferraméntis medicinálibus ad salútem, quia his ad perníciem étiam indócti pessimíque** abutúntur [35]». Rátio est, quia, aiénte eódem sancto Doctóre, « **non facúltas culpábilis est, sed ea male uténtium pervérsitas [36]»;** quocírca, « **non ídeo debent oves odísse vestiméntum suum, quia plerúmque illo se occúltant lupi [37]».**

a Vestal virgin

nonnulli = aliqui (pl.)
sum(p)serunt

aiente => ait

utentium => utor, uti

odisse
cf. Chap. 9 Vocab.

2.   **Obiéctum materiále—Obiéctum formále.** *Obiéctum materiále* est ea res, circa quam áliqua poténtia, vel disciplína versátur. *Obiéctum formále* est illud, secúndum quod spectántur, et cui ordinántur ómnia, quae ab áliqua poténtia, vel disciplína respiciúntur, seu, ut ait s. Thomas, est illud, « **sub cuius ratióne ómnia referúntur**

---

34   *Contr. Faustum, lib. XX, c. 2*
35   *Contra Crescon, , lib, I, c. 1*
36   *De Doctr. Christ., lib. II, c. 3*
37   *Serm. Dom. in monte, lib. II, c. 2*

ad poténtiam, vel hábitum [38]». E. g., corpus humánum est obiéctum materiále medicínae; ipsum corpus, quátenus sanándum, est eiúsdem artis obiéctum *formále*. Ita quoque homo, lapis etc. sunt obiéctum *materiále* visus, colorátum vero est eíus obiéctum *formále*, quia « **homo et lapis referúntur ad visum, in quantum sunt colorá-ta** [39]». Vel étiam obiéctum *formále* est id, per quod res attíngitur. E. g., conclusiónes in sciéntia sunt eíus obiéctum *materiále*; média demonstratiónis, per quae conclusiónes cognoscúntur, sunt obiéctum *formále*: « **Formális rátio sciéntiae est médium demonstratiónis** [40]». Vel dénique obiéctum *formále* est rátio, propter quam res attíngitur; e. g., últimus finis est obiéctum formále ceterárum nostrárum volitiónum; Bónitas Dei est obiéctum *formále* amóris erga Ipsum. Quo sensu *motívum* étiam appellári solet.

3.   **Finis Est Ménsura Medíorum.** Scílicet 1° cum inter id, quod ad finem órdinem habet, et ipsum finem, uti mox dicémus, propórtio sit opórteat, séquitur, ut rátio eórum, quae ordinántur ad finem, sumátur ex fine, « **sicut rátio dispositiónis serrae súmitur ex sectióne, quae est finis eíus** [41]». 2° Eo média sunt praestantióra, quo fini assequéndo magis convéniunt. Ita, remédia sunt eo praestantióra, quo sanitátem

---

38   I, q. I, a. 7 c
39   I, q. I, a. 7 c
40   *Qq. dispp. De Virtu, q. II, a. 13 ad 6*
41   1ae 2ae, q. CII, a. 1 c

mélius consérvant, aut restítuunt. Hinc s. Thomas: « **Quanto áliquid efficácius ordinátur ad finem, tanto mélius est** [42]».

Atque: « **Dígnitas eórum, quae sunt ad finem, praecípue considerátur ex fine** [43]».

Hanc ob ratiónem grátia *gratum fáciens* est multo excelléntior, quam grátia *gratis data*; nam « **grátia gratum fáciens órdinat hóminem immediáte ad coniunctiónem últimi finis; grátiae autem gratis datae órdinant hóminem ad quaedam praeparatória finis últimi; sicut per prophetíam, et mirácula et ália huiúsmodi hómines inducúntur ad hoc, quod último fini coniungántur** [44]»

---

42 2a 2ae, q. CXLII, a. 5 c
43 2a 2ae, q. CLXXIV, a. 2 c
44 1a 2ae, q. CXI, a. 5 c

Chapter 10

Vocabulary

ratiócinor -ári, deponent : *reckon, compute, calculate*

intelléctus -us, m., *intelligence, sense, meaning, insight, understanding, intellect, the capacity of intuitive knowledge*

sciéntia -ae: f.; *knowledge, science, skill*

intellegíbilis (gen. intelligibilis) -is -e, adj., *intelligible, intellectual*

mediáte, adv., *indirectly, by steps*

immediáte, adv., *directly, immediately*

decúrsus -us, m., *downward path, descent*

quocírca, conj., *on that account, therefore*

intercédo -ere -céssi -céssum: (3), *to go between, to be between; to intercede, intervene*

sórtior, -íri, -ítus, deponent (4), *cast lots, decide by lot, choose, distribute, select, obtain, get*

hábitus -us: m.; *habit, condition, disposition; clothing, religious garb*

Grammar

◊   **ad + gerundive** is a common way of expressing purpose. A gerundive is a verbal adjective and thus agrees in case and gender with the noun it modifies. English cannot replicate this idiom with any word-for-word translation. In English, we typically use the infinitive to express purpose. Examples:

> <u>ad missionem exercendam</u> vocantur (CIC 204 §1)
>
> *they are called to exercise their mission...*

> Omnes christifideles...<u>ad sanctam vitam ducendam</u> atque <u>ad Ecclesiae incrementum eiusque iugem sanctificationem promovendam</u> vires suas conferre debent (CIC 210)
>
> *All faithful Christians ought to use their energies...in order <u>to lead a holy life</u> and <u>to promote the growth of the Church and its continual sanctification</u>.*

◊   **The "Q" words :** we have already seen many of these words, however, they are gathered below in a convenient list. Be sure to take note of the words with which you are less familiar.

qua, *by what road? how? where?*
quacumque adv. *wherever; howsoever*

cf. Nunn §160

CIC = Codex iuris canonici (1983)

Note: in this example, the gerundive *promovendam* modifies two nouns of distinct genders (*incrementum*, neut., and *sanctificationem*, fem.). Thus, it agrees in gender with the closest of the two nouns.

qualis, -e adj. *of such a kind*
qualiscumque, qualecumque adj. *of whatever kind*
quam adv. *how, how much; than (with comparative); as (with superlative)*
quamdiu interrog. *how long?; conj. as long as*
quam ob rem (quamobrem) adv. *for what reason, why*
quamquam conj. *although*
quamvis adv. *however, no matter how; conj. although*
quando adv. *when?; conj. when, because, since*
quandocumque conj. *whenever; as often as*
quantus, -a, -um, *how great, how much*
quantuscumque, -acumque, -umcumque, *however great, however much*
quare (qua re) adv. *by what means; how; why; therefore*
quasi adv. *as it were, so to speak, as if; nearly, almost*
quatenus, *how far, to what point; as far as; insofar as*
quemadmodum (quem ad modum), *in what way, how; just as*
qui, quae, quod, *who, which*
quia, *because; that* (introducing noun clauses and indirect statements)
quicumque, quaecumque, quodcumque, *whosoever*
quid, *how?, why?*
quidam, quaedam, quiddam pron. *a certain*
quidam, quaedam, quoddam adj. *a certain*
quidem adv. *indeed, in fact*
quin adv. *why not?; conj. so that not*
quippe adv. *of course, naturally; conj. since, for*
quisque, quaeque, quidque pron. *each, all*
quisque, quaeque, quodque adj. *each, all*
quo adv. *to what place? where?*
quoad adv. *how far, to what extent; conj. as long as; until*
quocírca: conj.; *on that account, therefore*
quocumque adv. *wherever*
quod conj. *because; as for the fact that; that* (introducing noun clauses and indirect statements)
quodsi conj. *but if*
quomodo adv. how? *in what way?*
quondam adv. *once, formerly*
quoniam conj. *because; that* (introducing noun clauses and indirect statements)
quoque adv. *also*
quot, *how many?*
quotannis adv. *every year*
quotidie adv. *daily*

Readings

1.   Intellígere—Ratiocinári. *Intellígere* est veritátem intelligíbilem *immediáte* apprehéndere. *Ratiocinári* est eam *mediáte* cognóscere, seu procédere de uno <u>intellécto</u> ad áliud, ad veritátem intelligíbilem cognoscéndam[45]: « **Ratiocinátio est decúrsus principiórum ad conclusiónes** [46]». Quocírca inter hos duos actus ratiónis humánae differéntia intercédit, quae inter quiétem, et motum exístit; síquidem intellígere *immediáte* est quaedam quies ratiónis humánae, intellígere autem *mediáte* est quidam motus eíus. Hinc étiam exístit distínctio inter *intellígere*, et *scire*: « **Ipsa cognítio, ait s. Thomas, secúndum quod stat in princípiis, áccipit nomen intelléctus; secúndum autem quod derivátur ad conclusiónes, quae ex princípiis cognoscúntur, áccipit nomen sciéntiae** [47]». Quocírca « **hábitus principiórum dícitur intelléctus, et hábitus conclusiónis sciéntia. Quóniam plúrimum intelléctus lucis et formae habent princípia, propter quod a forma intelléctus nominántur. Sed mínimum et quasi per áliud médium de lúmine intelléctus habet sciéntia; propter quod áliud sortítur vocábulum** [48]»

intellecto => intéllego (intélligo) -ere -léxi -léctum

---

45 Vid. s. Thom., I, q. LXXIX, a. 8 c. « Dixerimus autem eam esse rationem, quae iis, de quibus dubitatur, ex iis, quae sunt certa, et extra controversiam, fidem facit »; Glem. Alex., *Strom.*, lib. II, n. 11
46 B. Alb. M., *De Intellectu et Intelligibili*, lib. I, tract. III, c. 2
47 *In lib. III Sent.*, Dist. XXVIII, q. I, a. 6 sol
48 B. Alb. M., *De Intellectu et Intelligibili*, lib. I, tract. III, c. 2

2. Senténtia Cartésii de instínctu animálium reiíci-

tur. [49] Aestimatívam adésse in animálibus negavérunt car-
tesiáni, qui omnes motus animálium habuérunt tanquam
motus mechánicos. At falso. Nam, ut alíbi iam dictum est no
833), animália distínguunt utília a nocívis, multa ópera, quandóque mirabília, exequúntur finémque suae speciéi próprium
multis médiis óbtinent. Sane ex instínctu naturáli agunt; sed
hic instínctus non est caecus nisi quátenus libertáte et electióne destitúitur; dúcitur autem cognitióne sensíbili et quodam iudício, seu quadam collatióne particulárium sensatió-
num. Quae cognítio experiéntia pérfici potest.

3. Actus hóminis — Actus humáni.

Actus humáni sunt ii, in quos homo virtútem eligéndi, ac
proínde domínium exercére potest, et quóniam volúntas est,
quae per ratiónis consultatiónem, seu deliberatiónem áliquid
prae álio éligit, ídeo actus humáni sunt qui a voluntáte deli-
beráta procédunt. Dicúntur autem *humáni*, quia sunt próprii
hóminis, prout est homo, et a creatúris ratióne caréntibus distínguitur.

Actus hóminis appellántur, qui non sunt próprii hóminis, prout est homo, idest fiunt sine deliberatióne ratiónis, ac
proínde sine electióne voluntátis [50]. Ex his collígitur *humános*
próprie esse illos actus, qui *quoad modum operándi* actiónes
excédunt rerum ratióne caréntium, non item qui tantum

---

49   ELIA BLANC, *Manuale philosophiae scholasticae*, Lugdun, 1901. §851
50   1a 2ae, q. I, a. 1 c

quoad substántiam próprii sunt hóminis, puta intellectiónes, et volitiónes necessáriae; síquidem hae operatiónes, cum penes líberam potestátem hóminis non sint, operatiónibus rerum naturálium quodámmodo assimiléntur.

Page intentionally left blank

Chapter 11

Vocabulary

recipio, recipere, recepi, receptus, *to receive* **(quidquid recipitur**: *whatever is received*)

quidquid, relative pronoun from **quisquis,** *whatever*

propórtio -ónis, f., *proportion, relation between parts*

tamquam, conj., *as, just as*

requiro, requirere, requisivi, requisitus, *to require, seek*

tantúmdem, *as much, just as much*

angustus, angusta -um, (comparative: angustior -or -us) *narrow, steep*

laxus, laxa -um, (comparative: laxior -or -us), *wide, spacious*

imbuo, imbuere, imbui, imbutus, *wet, soak, dip; give initial instruction (in)*

quisque, quaeque, quodque, indef. pron. & adj., *whoever, whatever, each, every*

passim, adv., *here and there; everywhere*

modulus, moduli, m., *a measure (e.g.* like a measuring cup*)*

Grammar

◊ **Comparative adjectives** end in -ior (masc. & fem.) or -ius (neut.) and are declined according to the pattern of the 3rd declension:

	singular		plural	
	m & f	**n**	**m & f**	**n**
n	longior	longiores	longius	longiora
ac	longiorem	longiores	longius	longiora
g	longioris	longiorum	longioris	longiorum
d	longiori	longioribus	longiori	longioribus
ab	longiore	longioribus	longiore	longioribus

◊ The word **quam,** *than,* is used to compare two words. If quam is used, the words compared are in the same case. Examples:

Joannes minor est quam Petrus. *John is younger than Peter.*

◊ **Ablative of Comparison**: If the word to be compared is in the nominative or accusative, *quam* can be omitted and the second word put in the ablative. Examples:

Joannes minor est Petro. *John is younger than Peter.*

Amor melle dulcior. *Love is sweeter than honey.*

Nihil est virtute amabilius. *Nothing is more lovable than virtue.* (Cicero, L*ael*., 8, 28)

Readings

1.   Quidquid Recípitur Ad Modum Recipientis Recípitur. Hoc effátum duo significáre potest: 1° Áliqua debet esse propórtio inter recípiens, et recéptum, tamquam inter actum, et poténtiam; síquidem <u>in subiécto áliquid recipiénte</u> capácitas et disposítio ad illud recipiéndum requíritur, ita ut, prout maíor, vel minor est huiúsmodi <u>propórtio, et capácitas,</u> maíor, vel minor sit recéptio. E. g., fons eádem hora tantúmdem aquae effúndit; ex plúribus tamen vasis, quae ad aquam recipiéndam apponúntur, non ómnia tantúmdem cápiunt; nam quae sunt ore angustióri, <u>minus</u> cápiunt, <u>quam quae laxióri</u>. Item, qui docet, omnes eádem ópera docet, sed non omnes aeque doctrína imbuúntur, sed quisque <u>pro</u> ingénii sui módulo. 2° Quidquid recípitur non recípitur <u>necessário</u> secúndum modum próprium, sed secúndum modum eíus quod dícitur recípere. Hinc materiália recipiúntur in intelléctu, non *reáliter*, et *materiáliter*; sed *spirituáliter*, et *intentionáliter*. Unde *cógnita*, ut passim docet Angélicus, *sunt in cognoscénte secúndum modum cognoscéntis.*

**2.   ** Neque mirum, si áliqua virtus spirituális recipiátur in re corpórea; puta in aqua est áliqua virtus producéndi grá-

---

in subiecto...recipiente
the direct object of *recipiente* is *aliquid*
proportio et capacitas
compound subject

ad aquam recipiendam
cf. Nunn 160

minus...quam quae laxiori
clause of comparison

pro = in proportion to

necessario, adv.

tiam. Nam « **virtus spirituális non potest esse in re corpórea per modum virtútis permanéntis, et complétae. Nihil tamen próhibet, in córpore esse virtútem spirituálem instrumentáliter; in quantum scílicet corpus potest movéri ab áliqua substántia spirituáli ad áliquem efféctum spirituálem inducéndum: sicut et in ipsa voce sensíbili est quaedam vis spirituális ad excitándum intelléctum hóminis, in quantum procédit a conceptióne mentis. Et hoc modo vis spirituális est in Sacraméntis, in quantum ordinántur a Deo ad efféctum spirituálem** [51]». Ad cuius maiórem perspicuitátem adnotánda est dispáritas inter áccidens corpóreum et spirituále. Áccidens enim corpóreum expóstulat subiéctum exténsum, nec recípitur in subiécto, nisi per quantitátem, et idcírco in subiécto spirituáli récipi nequit. Áccidens autem spirituále incomplétum et tránsiens, cum magis sit propter términum, quam propter subiéctum, non debet talem proportiónem cum subiécto serváre, unde potest supernaturáliter récipi in subiécto corpóreo.

Numquam autem illud effátum intelligéndum est hoc modo: Quidquid recípitur, affícitur natúra et conditiónibus recipiéntis, atque rédditur tale, quale est ipsum recípiens. Sic enim ánima rationális, dum infórmat corpus, fíeret corpórea, et indúeret omnes córporis qualitátes.

---

51   3a, q. LXII, a. 4 ad 1. Quomodo virtus spiritualis sit in Sacramentis non quasi ens fixum, explicatur *in lib. IV Sent., Dist, I, q. 1, a. 4, sol. 2*

3.   Intelléctus agens—Intelléctus pátiens. Quóniam esséntiae rerum materiálium, quae sunt obiéctum proportionátum intelléctui humáno, prout sunt extra ánimam, et a phantasmátis repraesentántur, non sunt intelligíbiles actu, duplex intelléctus ad explicándum actum intellectiónis est distinguéndus, *agens* et *pátiens*. Intelléctus *agens* est ea virtus ánimae, quae ex phantasmátis spécies intelligíbiles, rei esséntiam repraesentántes, éfficit, quátenus phantasmáta illústrat, atque ex eis conditiónes materiáles ábstrahit; eódem fere modo, quo fulgor erúmpens ex óculis felis obiécta illústrat, eáque visibília reddit. *Intelléctus pátiens* est ea virtus ánimae, quae spécies intelligíbiles, ab intelléctu agénte elaborátas, in se, tamquam in quoddam spéculum, excípii, et per eas obiéctum ab eísdem repraesentátum apprehéndit. Dícitur étiam *possíbilis*, non quidem quia non sit áliquid reále, sed quia est in poténtia ad spécies rerum recipiéndas, et ídeo a poténtia ad actum intelligéndi progréditur [52].

Hac in re illud adnotándum est, quod cum Aristóteles intelléctum agéntem *hábitum*, aut *artem* nóminat[53], ad modum comparatiónis lóquitur. Nam, sicut ars formam artificiósam indúcit in matériam rudem, quae in poténtia ad illam est, ita intelléctus agens per spécies impréssas tamquam per formas pérficit, et ad actum redúcit intelléctum possíbilem.

---

52 Vid. *Species impressa—expressa*, litt. *S*. Quae ad duplicem hanc intelligendi virtutem spectant, fuse explicata invenies apud Sanseverino, *Phil. Christ., Dynam.*, vol. II, c. VII, aa. 6 sqq, p. 599 sqq, Neapoli 1862
53 *De An., lib. III*

Rursus, intelléctus agens dícitur *hábitus* ad significándum ipsum non esse *privatiónem*, per quam res est in poténtia ad áliquid recipiéndum; síquidem intelléctus agens non est in poténtia ad recipiéndum, sed in actu ad agéndum [54].

---

54 Vid. s. Thom., *In lib. III De An.*, lect. X

Page intentionally left blank

Chapter 12

Vocabulary

adaequatio, adaequationis, fem., *a making equal, equalization, equation*
sicuti, adv., *just as*
refero, referre, rettuli, relatus, *to refer, recall, relate*
unusquisque & unumquodque, *each one, every*
confórmo -áre, *to form, shape, conform, educate*
assecútio -ónis: f., *perception, comprehension, knowledge*
dénique, *at length, lastly, finally*
dícto -áre, *say repeatedly, order, dictate*

Grammar

◊   **Translating Participles:** When translating a participle, its tense must be taken as relative to that of the main verb. **Present participles** refer to actions **contemporaneous** with the action of the main verb. **Perfect participles** refer to actions **prior to** that of the main verb. A future participle refers to action subsequent to that of the main verb. A proper translation of Latin participles must always bear in mind their tense and voice.

    Present active participle: contemporaneous action, active voice.

    Puer vigilans lupum vidit:

The boy keeping watch saw a wolf.

Keeping watch, the boy saw a wolf.

While keeping watch, the boy saw a wolf.

    Perfect passive participle: prior action, passive voice.
    Puer territus clamavit.

The having-been-frightened boy shouted.

The boy, having been frightened, shouted.

The frightened boy shouted.

When he had been frightened, the boy shouted.

◊   Latin participles should frequently be translated in English with subordinate clauses (i.e., temporal [when], causal [since, because], concessive [although]). The context must decide.

◊   Beware of deponent verbs! Their perfect participles

are passive in form but active in meaning. They are frequently used to fill in the gap left by Latin's lack of a true perfect active participle. Examples: **dux locutus**, *the leader having spoken*, **imperator hortatus**, *the general having encouraged*, **miles secutus**, *the soldier having followed*. This is in contrast to **verbum dictum**, *the word having been spoken*, **lupus visus**, *the wolf having been seen*, etc.

Readings

1.   Bonum Et Malum Sunt In Rebus, Verum Et Falsum Sunt In Mente. Scílicet, verum in adaequatióne rei ad intelléctum consístit, ita ut, quando res refértur intelléctui, sícuti est, ratiónem veritátis hábeat. Quocírca verum, etsi fundétur in re, tamen ex eo, quod ab intelléctu cognóscitur, complétam hábeat ratiónem veritátis: « **Verum est in mente..., et unumquódque in tantum dícitur verum, in quantum conformátum est, vel conformábile intelléctui** ». E contrário bonum non ex eo quod ab ánima cognóscitur, sed quátenus est áliquid extra ánimam, bonitátis ratiónem habet: « **Secúndum esse, quod habet in rerum natúra..., est perfectívum bonum, bonum enim in rebus est** [55] ». Quocírca cognítio veri fit per progréssum obiécti ad subiéctum, assecútio autem boni per progréssum subiécti ab obiéctum: « **Intellectíva apprehénsio est secúndum motum a rebus in ánimam... operátio autem appetítus est secúndum motum ab ánima in res** [56] ».

---

55 *Qq. dispp.*, *De Ver.*, q. XXI, a. I c. Vid. etiam, I, q. LXXXII, a. 3 c
56 In *lib. III Sent.*, Dist. XXVI, q. I, a. 5 ad 4

2. Consciéntia—Synderésis. *Synderésis* est hábitus generáliter dictans bonum esse prosequéndum, malum autem declinándum. *Consciéntia* vero est iudícium, quo intelléctus prácticus ápplicat princípia generália synderésis ad particuláres actiónes, seu est actus, quo práctice quis iúdicat hoc esse prosequéndum, quia bonum, áliud declinándum, quia malum . Hic actus, si circa praetéritas actiónes versétur, dícitur *consciéntia cónsequens*; si respíciat actus futúros, dícitur *consciéntia antécedens*; ac dénique *concómitans*, quando actum comitátur. Hinc intelligúntur illi loquéndi modi, scílicet *consciéntiam ligáre, testificári, accusáre*.

3. Bonum Tótius Est Bonum Pártium. Nempe totum non potest bene exístere, nisi ex pártibus sibi consentáneis, seu quae toti cóngruant. Ita, ut exémplo s. Thomae utámur, « **impossíbile est quod bonum commúne civitátis bene se hábeat, nisi cives sint virtuósi, ad minus illi, quibus convénit principári** [57]». Rursus: Quod totum absolúte pérficit, vel in débita perfectióne consérvat, pérficit, et in perfectióne consérvat étiam partes. Hinc fit, ut, cum quidvis suam perfectiónem appétat, pars appétat perfectiónem et bonum tótius. Quod laudátus Doctor éxplicat exémplo manus, *quae expónitur íctui, absque deliberatióne, ad conservatiónem tótius córporis* [58]. Exínde infértur « **quod ille, qui quaerit bonum commúne multitúdinis, consequénter étiam próprium bonum**

[57] la 2ae, q. XCII, a. 1 ad 3
[58] I, q. LX, a. 5 c

quaerit: primo, quia bonum próprium non potest esse sine bono commúni vel famíliae, vel civitátis, aut regni... secúndo, quia, cum homo sit pars domus, vel civitátis, opórtet quod homo consíderet quid sit sibi bonum ex hoc, quod est prudens circa bonum multitúdinis. Bona enim disposítio pártium accípitur secúndum habitúdinem ad totum, quia, ut Augustínus dicit in lib. III *Confess.* c. 8, Turpis est omnis pars suo toti non convéniens, vel non cóngruens [59]».

---

59 2a 2ae, q. XLVII, a. 10 ad 2

Chapter 13

Vocabulary

orior, -iri, ortus, *arise*
vulgo, adv., *generally, usually*
inhaéreo -ére -haési -haésum, *to adhere to, inhere*
indígeo -ére -ui, *to want, need, lack*
quíppe, conj., *for, certainly, indeed, to be sure;* **quíppe** + *qui (quae, quod): inasmuch as he/she/it*
idcirco, adv., *therefore, on that account*

Grammar

◊   **Alius and alter:** the word **alius** means *one* or *another* of an indefinite number while **alter** refers to *the other of two.* Both **alius...alius** and **alter...alter** are used in pairs to contrast two distinct groups or things, or to express reciprocal action.

> *Aliud est sententias exprimere, aliud probare eas.*

> It is one thing to express opinions, another to prove them.

> *Alter frater mortuus est, alter adhuc vivit.*

> One brother is dead, the other still lives.

> *Alius alium spectamus.*

> We look at each other.

Readings

1.   **Suppósitum—Persóna—Subsisténtia.** *Subsisténtia* aliquándo idem signíficat, ac *Perséitas.* Consístit nempe in eo, quod ens non pendet ab álio, tamquam a subiécto, cui inháereat, seu in eo, quo substántia constitúitur in *esse* substántiae. « Substántia est subiéctum, quod non índiget extrínseco fundaménto, in quo sustentétur, sed sustentátur in seípso; et ídeo dícitur subsístere, quasi per se, et non in álio exí-

Perseitas = "per se" + -itas

stens [60]». At vero, quóniam in substántia *incompléta*, quippe quae ad totum substantiále componéndum ordinátur, *esse in se* non perfícitur, nisi in ipso substantiáli compósito, idcírco *subsisténtia* intellígitur, quátenus convénit tantum substántiae *complétae*; haec enim, cum neque in áliquo, tamquam in subiécto, neque in áliquo, tamquam in toto, sit, absolúta ratióne habet *esse per se*; et ídeo dícitur esse *sui ipsíus*. Ítaque *subsisténtia* defínitur: *Actuálitas*, seu perféctio, per quam natúra fit sui ipsíus et non altérius, seu per quam natúra último complétur et terminátur, ita ut sit sui iúris, atque non égeat communicári álteri ad hoc, ut sit, et operétur. Substántia, quae per *subsisténtiam* hoc sensu accéptam iam último compléta et termináta est, nempe substántia singuláris, último compléta, et sui iúris effécta, dícitur *suppósitum*, si intelléctu cáreat; *persóna*, vel *hypostásis*, si sit intélligens.

ultimo, adv.

egeat
cf. Nunn §57

Exínde explicátur definítio *persónae*, quae post Bóetium vulgo in scholis tráditur: *Natúrae rationális indivídua substántia* [61].

2. Dícitur 1° *substántia*; nam accidéntia non subsístunt. 2° *Indivídua*, nempe tum *lógice*, tum *phýsice*. Dícitur áliquid indivíduum *lógice*, quátenus de áliis mínime praedicátur, ut Cícero, Plato, etc. *Phýsice* autem, quátenus totum quoddam est; qua ratióne gutta aquae, quátenus cum Oceáno iúncta est, non appellátur indivídua; separáta vero ab Oceáno indi-

---

60 *Qq. dispp., De Pot., q. IX, a. 1 c*
61 « Persona non dicitur, nisi de individua rationali natura »; s. Ans., *Monol.*, c. 78

vídua dícitur. Iam vero, *persóna*. est natúra indivídua utróque modo: *Lógice* quidem, nam universália, tum quia in intelléctu tantum exístunt, tum quia plúribus commúnia esse possunt, non sunt *persónae*. Ita hóminis *in commúni* nulla persóna est, sed Cicerónis, vel Platónis, vel singulórum individuórum síngulae persónae nuncupántur [62]. *Phýsice* autem, quia substántiae, quae sunt tótius compósiti partes, puta ánima et corpus hóminis, non habent própriam *hypostásim*, sed subsístunt in *hypostási* tótius compósiti. « **Substántia indivídua, quae pónitur in definitióne persónae, impórtat substántiam complétam per se subsisténtem separátim ab áliis, alióquin manus hóminis posset dici persóna, cum sit substántia quaedam indivídua; quia tamen est substántia indivídua, sicut in álio exístens, non potest dici persóna [63]** ».

3. Quod si duae natúrae ita secum uniántur, ut una eárum nullam ex unióne novam perfectiónem adipísci possit, tunc ista rétinet *hypostásim* própriam; áltera autem amíttit in unióne própriam *hypostásim*, atque in *hypostási* perfectióris natúrae subsístit. Ita evénit in mystério Incarnatiónis. Christi enim natúra humána caret própria hypostási, et subsístit in Persóna Verbi. Ex qua explicatióne vocis *indivíduae*, quae in definitióne *persónae* adhibétur, séquitur, ut ipsa sit *incommunicábilis*, scílicet, ut sit substántia singuláris; ínsuper ut sit in

hypostasim
some words taken from Greek have an accusative ending in *-im*

caret
cf. Nunn §57

---

[62] « Essentiae significatio ad aliquid commune videtur pertinere; nomon autem de singularibus hypostasis, quae subsunt huic univorsali, praedicatur ac dicitur »; s. Cyrill. Alex., *De Sanct. Trinit., Dial.*
[63] S. Thom., 3, q. XVI, a, 12 ad 2

se *tota*, sive sui iúris, sibíque ipsi própria, et íntegrum suárum operatiónum princípium; dénique ut non possit ita assúmi, ut trahátur *in personalitátem* altérius [64]. Quae quidem, ut inquit s. Bonaventúra, ipsi ethymológiae nóminis *persónae* respóndent; síquidem, « **persóna dícitur quasi per se unum, per se autem unum próprie dícitur unum, quod est omníno distínctum ab áliis, et in se indistínctum** [65]». At vero, « **non est contra ratiónem persónae communicabílitas assuméntis** [66]»; scílicet nulla repugnántia in eo est, quod Persóna Divína humánam natúram assúmpsit; nam « **persóna dícitur incommunicábilis, in quantum non potest de plúribus suppósitis praedicári; nihil tamen próhibet plura de persóna praedicári. Unde non est contra ratiónem persónae sic communicári, ut subsístat in plúribus natúris** [67]». 3° Dícitur *rationális*, ut distinguátur *persóna* a *suppósito*; non enim próprie dícimus *persónam* equi, aut lápidis, sed persónam vel Divínam, vel Angélicam, vel humánam. Unde *persóna* nihil addit supra *suppósitum*, nisi áliquam dignitátem et excelléntiam pétitam ex natúra intellectuáli.

---

64 S. Thom., *In lib. III Sent.*, Dist. V, q. II, a. I ad 2
65 *In lib. I Sent.*, Dist. XXIII, a. I, q. 1 resol.
66 S. Thom., loc. cit
67 3, q. III, a. 1 ad 2

Chapter 14

Vocabulary

assígno -áre, *to assign, designate, indicate*
áccido -ere -cidi, *to happen, take place, occur*
impedio, impedire, impedivi, impeditus, *to hinder, obstruct*
conficio, conficere, confeci, confectus, *to make, construct, prepare*
deficio, deficere, defeci, defectus, *to fail*

Grammar

◊   **Ut** when it introduces a clause with the verb in the <u>Indicative</u> mood means either *as, when,* or *where* according to the context. The clause that it introduces is either a clause of comparison, a clause of time, or a clause of place. See Nunn §§153–155, 175.

Nunn §105

◊   When **ut** introduces a clause with the verb in the <u>Subjunctive</u> mood the clause may be:

(1) A clause of purpose. See Nunn §§157, 158.
(2) A clause of consequence/result. See Nunn §163.
(3) A noun clause. See Nunn §§116–127, 142, 145.

In all these cases **ut** can be translated by *that* in Eng.

Readings

In Naturálibus Et Morálibus Non Quaeritur Quid Semper Fiat, Sed Quid In Plúribus Áccidat. Cuius rátio assignátur a s. Thoma: « **In rebus naturálibus non quáeritur quid semper fiat, sed quid in plúribus áccidat, eo quod natúra corruptibílium rerum impedíri potest, ut non semper eódem modo operetúr...In morálibus considerátur quod ut in plúribus est, non autem quod semper est, eo quod volún-**

tas non ex necessitáte operátur [68]». Unde cónficit idem Doctor, « in rebus contingéntibus, sicut sunt naturália, et res humánae, suffícere talem certitúdinem, ut áliquid sit verum ut in plúribus, <u>licet</u> defíciat in paucióribus [69]».

licet = quamquam

4.   **Contraríorum Uno Pósito, Négatur Álterum.** Quod intelligéndum est de contráriis immediátis, quae nempe médium inter se exclúdunt; atque respéctu eiúsdem *número* subiécti. Sic Petrus sanus negátur esse aeger. Vel étiam de contráriis *mediátis*, sed ita ut, non pósito, álterum negétur, at, uno subláto, non nisi contingénter ponátur álterum, ut, si páries est albus, uno potest idem esse niger, saltem qua parte albus est, sin albus non est, non séquitur necessário, ut sit niger, quia potest esse ruber [70].

5.   **Causa finális—effíciens—exempláris.** Sunt váriae spécies causae extérnae. *Causa effíciens* est, quae própria actióne prodúcit effÉctum; e. g., sculptor est causa effíciens státuae. *Causa finális* est id, cuius grátia áliquid fit, v. g., cómmoda habitátio respéctu domus, ac proínde ad effÉctus productiónem concúrrit, quia causam efficiéntem ad agéndum movet. *Causa exempláris* est rei faciéndae ídea, quam causa effíciens cogitatióne sua cóncipit, et ad cuius similitúdinem illam prodúcit, e. g., forma domus construéndae in mente architÉcti; quocírca huius causae inflúxus consístit tum in eo,

---

68   la 2ae q. LXXXIV, a. 1 ad 3
69   la 2ae q. XCVI, a. 1 ad 3
70   Vid. Signoriello, p. 70-71

quod dírigit causam efficiéntem ad perficiéndum opus, tum in eo quod detérminat ipsum opus non quidem per intrínsecam constitutiónem, sed per sui imitatiónem, tum quia est velúti finis agéntis, quátenus agens operátur, ut *assequátur similitúdinem, sui* exempláris [71].

---

71 *Contr, Gent.* lib. III, c, 19

Page intentionally left blank

Chapter 15

Vocabulary

exémplar -áris, *n., example, model, copy*
ópera -ae, f., *work, labor, care, attention, aid*
cómputo -áre, *reckon, count, compute*
respéctus -us, m., *respect, care, regard, concern, consideration*
úllus -a -um, *any,* as a pron., *anyone, anything*
infírmo -áre, *weaken, annul, refute, disapprove*
cálor -óris, m., *heat*
supérior -ior -ius, *upper, higher, former,* **supérius, adv.**

Grammar

◊   The **Ablative Absolute.** A noun or pronoun in the Ablative case with a predicative participle, or adjective, or even another noun agreeing with it, is used to denote an incident that accompanies or explains the action of the verb on which it depends like an adverbial clause. This construction is very common in Latin, and is called the Ablative absolute, because it is independent of, or loosed from (*absolutus*), the main structure of the sentence. The noun or pronoun in the Ablative absolute should not refer to the subject or object of the clause on which it depends.

Nunn §50

◊   Ablative absolutes may be used to replace a temporal, causal, concessive, or conditional clause. Examples:

Remota causa, removetur effectus.
If the cause is removed, the effect is removed.

Et cum haec dixisset, videntibus illis, elevatus est.
And when he had said this, while they were watching, he was taken up.   Acts 1:9.

...admirantur non concurrentibus vobis in eandem luxuriae confusionem.
...they are surprised when you do not run with them into the same flood of dissipation...   1 Pet. 4:4.

Readings

1. Indivíduum Est Incommunicábile. Non quidem *effectíve*; nam hac ratióne potest áliquid communicári *secúndum participatiónem uníus et eiúsdem rei secúndum númerum*[72]; puta hic ignis aquae suum calórem, hic pater suo fílio própria bona, hic praecéptor discípulis suam doctrínam commúnicat, et unum exémplar <u>sese</u> quasi commúnicat multis, quae ad eíus imitatiónem fiunt: item hac ratióne « **ópera satisfactória uníus álteri computántur... ex intentióne operántis áliquo modo dirécta ad ipsum** [73]». Ítaque indivíduum est *incommunicábile attributíve*, et *respéctu inferiórum*; habet enim natúram singulárem, ideóque nec ulli infra se communicári potest, seu attríbui; ita enim fíeret universále. Neque id infirmátur ex eo quod Natúra Divína est *número* una, et tamen *.attributíve* communicátur tribus Persónis. Natúra enim Divína non communicátur tribus Persónis, tamquam supérius inferióribus, sed tamquam aequále aequáli, singuláre singulári, seu, ut natúra suppósitis, in quibus ipsa neque ab illis, neque a <u>seípsa</u> divíditur, quia, ut s. Damascénus inquit, *indivísa est in divísis*[74], nempe tota est in síngulis, et in ómnibus simul *indistíncta* ab illis.

2. Substántia prima — secúnda. *Primae* substántiae vocántur indivídua, ut Petrus etc. *Secúndae* substántiae vo-

sese = se

seipsa = se + ipsa

---

72 *In lib. IV Sent.*, Dist. XLIX, q. 1, a. 1 sol. 1 ad 3
73 *In lib. IV Sent.*, Dist. XX, q. 1 a. 4, sol. 1 c
74 *De Fide orthod., lib. II, c. 8*

cántur génera, et spécies, quia pendent a primis substántiis; universália enim a singuláribus cogitándo eliciúntur. Cum autem spécies propínquior sit singuláribus, ídeo dícitur *magis substántia*. Porro substántia *prima* neque in subiécto est, neque de áliis enunciátur; sed tantum praedicári potest praedicatióne *praeter órdinem*. Substántia *secúnda* autem in subiécto non est, sed de subiécto dícitur; ut patet in genéribus et speciébus. Monéndum autem est cum s. Thoma, « **quod cum divíditur substántia in primam, et secúndam, non est divísio géneris in spécies, cum nihil contineátur sub secúnda substántia, quod non sit in prima; sed est divísio géneris secúndum divérsos modos esséndi. Nam secúnda substántia signíficat natúram géneris secúndum se absolútam; prima vero substántia signíficat eam ut individuáliter subsisténtem. Unde magis est divísio análogi, quam géneris** [75] ».

3. **Verum Et Bonum Convertúntur.** Tum enim bonum, tum verum convértitur cum ente. Ergo ipsum bonum convértitur cum vero, seu bonum et verum idem sunt *secúndum rem*. Ea tamen differre *ratióne* patet ex eo quod *bonum* réspicit appetítum, *verum* autem cognitiónem. Hinc séquitur ut verum *secúndum ratiónem* sit prius quam bonum; cognítio enim naturáliter praecédit appetítum [76]. Circa hoc effátum s. Bonaventúra advértit ipsum intelligéndum esse *circa idem*. « **Unde si res est vera, est bona; et si signum est verum, est**

---

75 *Qq. dispp., De Pot., q. IX, a. 2 ad 6*
76 I, q. XVI, a. 4 c

bonum; sed tamen non séquitur quod, si signum sit verum, signátum, sive res sit bona; et ídeo hic est fallácia accidéntis: omne verum est bonum; sed illud furári est verum; ergo illud furári est bonum: ex variatióne minóris extremitátis. Verum enim praedicátur de illo dicto ratióne compositiónis, cum sit díctio modális, bonum verum ratióne attributiónis [77]».

---

77   *In lib. I Sent. Dist. XLVI, a. I, q. 4 ad arg.*

Chapter 16

Vocabulary

cognitivus, -a, -um, adj., *related to knowing; cognitive*
falsitas, falsitatis, f., *falsehood, untruth*
assigno, assignare, assignavi, assignatus, *assign, distribute, allot; award*
falsus, falsa, falsum, adj., *wrong, false*
verus, vera -um, adj., *true, real*
veritas, veritatis, f., *truth*
expóstulo -áre, *ask, demand vehemently, require, dispute*
amótio -ónis, f., *removal, removing*

Grammar

◊   A sizable group of nouns are derived from adjectives by the addition of the suffixes:

    -tās,-tātis

    -tūdō,-tūdinis

    -ia,-iae and -itia,-itiae [for abstract nouns denoting qualities]

    Examples:

        bonitās, *goodness*

        celeritās, *swiftness*

        vēritās, *truth*

        magnitūdō, *greatness*

        fortitūdō, *bravery*

        audācia, *boldness*

        amīcitia, *friendship*

◊   Some adjectives are derived from Verbs:

    -idus, a, um denotes a state, as **timidus** *timid* **cupidus** *eager*

    -ilis and -bilis denote capacity or ability, usually in a passive sense, as **fragilis,** *fragile* (i. e. capable of being broken), **docilis,** *docile,* **intelligibilis,** *intelligible*

Readings

1. Falsum Fundátur In Vero. Huius ratiónem s. Thomas ita assígnat: « Áliquid exístens extra ánimam pro tanto dícitur falsum, quia natum est de se fácere falsam existimatiónem, quando movet virtútem cognitívam; unde opórtet quod illud, quod falsum dícitur, áliquod ens sit: unde cum omne ens, in quantum <u>huiúsmodi</u>, sit verum, opórtet falsitátem in rebus existéntem supra veritátem fundári: unde dicit Augustínus, in lib. *Solil.*, c. X, quod <u>tragáedus</u>, qui repraeséntat veras persónas in theátris, non esset falsus, nisi esset verus tragáedus; simíliter equus pictus non esset falsus equus, nisi esset pura pictúra. Non tamen séquitur contradictória esse vera, quia affirmátio et negátio, secúndum quod dicunt verum et falsum, non referúntur ad idem [78] ».

2. Actus primus—Actus secúndus. 1° *Actus primus* dícitur tum prima forma, seu esséntia rei, tum eíus intégritas. *Actus secúndus* est eíus operátio: « Actus primus est qui dat esse et spéciem et ratiónem ei, cuius est actus. Actus vero secúndus non est princípium operatiónis, sed ipsa operátio [79] ». Hoc sensu malum phýsicum consístere docétur in amotióne *actus primi*, uti cáecitas in animáli, quia est privátio perfectiónis, quae requíritur ad integritátem rei; malum autem culpae in amotióne *actus secúndi*, quia est privátio per-

---

huiusmodi
cf. Nunn §71

tragaedus
an actor

---

78 *Qq. dispp., De Ver., q. I, a. 10 ad 5*
79 Alb. M., De Hom., tract. I, q. IV, a. 2. Vid. s. Thom, I, q. XXVIII, a. 5

fectiónis, quam recta operátio expóstulat. 2° *In actu* primóres ita, vel non ita dícitur esse respéctu capacitátis, quam ad áliquod habet, vel non; puta qui dormit, videt *actu primo*, id quod de caeco ásseri nequit. In *actu secúndo*, si iam póssidet illud, a quo denominátur, uti Túllius *actu secúndo* fuit orátor. 3° *Actus primus* accípitur pro ipsa poténtia; sic volúntas *actus primus* vocári solet: *Actus secúndus* pro ipsa operatióne. 4° *Actu primo* res dícitur operári, si conditiónes in ea adsint, quae ad operándum requiríntur, ita ut si hae omnes in ea concúrrant, *actus primus* dicátur *próximus*, sin áliqua desit, *remótus*, e. g., ignis <u>stupae</u> admótus est in *actu primo próximo* eum uréndi, illi nondum admótus est in *actu primo remóto*: *Actu secúndo*, si iam operétur

stupae
cotton, or the coarse part of flax used to kindle fires in times past

Page intentionally left blank

Chapter 17

Vocabulary

distinctio, distinctionis, f., *distinction, difference*
praedico, praedicare, praedicavi, praedicatus, *to pro-claim, preach*
soleo, solere, solitus sum, *to be in the habit of, to be accus-tomed to*
nemo, neminis, n., *no one, nobody*
dúplex -icis, adj., *twofold, double, insincere*
intercedo, intercedere, intercessi, intercessus, *to inter-vene, intercede*
invólvo -ere -vólvi -volútum, *wrap up, roll up, cover, envelop*
linea, lineae, f., *a line*
obliquitas, obliquitatis, f., *a sidelong or slanting direction*
óbeo -íre, *die, fulfill, perform*
nugatorius, -a, -um, adj., *frivolous, trifling*

Grammar

◊ **Enclitic particles:** can be added to the ends of words to give emphasis or a special meaning.

-ce is attached to demonstrative pronouns and some adverbs for extra emphasis. E.g. **hisce,** *by these,* **huiusce,** *of this,* **sicce,** *thus, so,* **hincce,** *hence,* **illicce,** *there,* **hicce,** *here*

-nam is added to pronouns for emphasis. E.g. **Qui-snam?** *Who the heck?,* **Quanam?** *Where the heck?* **Cuiu-snam modi est?** *What the heck sort of thing is it?*

-ne can be added to the first word of a sentence to indicate a question. E.g. **Nonne sic est?** *Is it not so?*

-ci- can be used as an infix preceeding *-ne* for extra emphasis. E.g. **Haeccine vera sunt?** *Are these things true?,* **Siccine semper erit?** *Will it always be thus?*

Some enclitics function as conjunctions: **-que,** *and,* **-ve,** *or*

Readings

1.   **Formáliter—Reáliter—Ratióne.** De váriis *distinctió-num* speciébus haec praedicári solent. Reáliter distinguúntur

ea, quae, némine cogitánte, non sunt una et eádem res. Duplex autem est huiúsmodi distínctio, *maíor* nempe, et *minor*.
Distínctio *reális maíor* est distínctio rei a re, atque intercédit
inter duas res, quarum áltera vel ab áltera separátim exístit,
ut inter Pompeíum et Cáesarem; vel ab ea separári potest, ut
inter ánimam et corpus; vel relatiónis oppositiónem ad illam
invólvit, ut in Divínis inter Patrem, et Fílium. Distínctio *reális*
minor est ea, quae intercédit inter rem áliquam, et ipsíus modum; e. g., inter dígitum et eíus inflexiónem; inter líneam et
eíus obliquitátem. *Distínctio ratiónis* est ea, quae a mente ex-
cogitátur in iis, quae révera unum idémque sunt; iterúmque
duplex est, scílicet *ratiónis ratiocinántis*, et *ratiónis ratiociná-*
tae. Prima, quae propter suam inanitátem *nugatória* appellátur, est ea, quae fit sine fundaménto in re; e. g., cum Petrus in
hac propositióne, *Petrus est Petrus*, ita a nobis considerátur,
quasi per áliud habéret ratiónem subiécti, per áliud vero munus obíret praedicáti. Áltera est ea, quae fit cum áliquo fundaménto in re, cum nempe mens in una eadémque re plura
cóncipit, proptérea quod res ipsa eíus sit natúrae, ut plúribus
aequiváleat, vel várias prodúcat efféctus; huiúsmodi est ea
quae intercédit inter absolúta attribúta Dei; illa enim váriis et
distínctis concéptibus cogitámus, atque huius concéptuum
varietátis fundaméntum in ipsa Divínae perfectiónis emi-
néntia est; síquidem Divína Attribúta, etsi in ipso Deo una res
sint, tamen res illa plúribus aequiválet perfectiónibus creátis

reáliter distínctis, et divérsos prodúcit efféctus, qui a causis reípsa distínctis prodúci solent. Quocírca haec distínctio appellátur étiam *virtuális*, quia res, quae per eam distínguitur, licet sit una, tamen multis *virtúte* aequiválet; e. g., misericórdia et iustítia Dei, quae sunt una et eádem res, nempe Deus ipse, duábus virtútibus révera distínctis aequiválent.

2.   Praeter has distinctiónis spécies Scotus tértiam in Scholis invéxit, quam *formálem* ex *natúra rei* nuncupávit. Huiúsmodi distínctio, ex eíus senténtia, ea est, quae intercédit inter plura, quae in se reáliter non distinguúntur, neque a se ínvicem separári queunt, sed eíus sunt natúrae, ut, seclúsa mentis operatióne, divérsas definitiónes éxigant, diversósque concéptus exhíbeant, quia unum, quátenus tale, álterum a sui concéptu exclúdit, atque uni, quátenus tali, áliquid convénit, quod álteri, quátenus tali, non convénit. E. g., *animálitas* et *rationálitas* in hómine non distinguúntur *reáliter*, quia una nequit esse sine áltera; neque tantum *ratióne*, quia ante omnem intelléctus actiónem *animálitas* non est *rationálitas*; sed distinguúntur *formáliter*, quia habent divérsos concéptus obiectívos, síquidem *animálitas* sine *rationalitáte* cóncipi potest, atque per illam, secus ac per istam, convénit hómini similitúdo cum brutis. At praeter distinctiónem *reálem* et *ratiónis* nullum áliud distinctiónis genus excogitári posse céteri philósophi docent. Et sane, omnis distínctio vel praecédit mentis óperam, vel non. Iam, si praecédat, est *reális*; secus,

est *ratiónis*; quocírca ubi non est res distíncta, nequit esse distínctio extra mentem. Ínsuper per distinctiónem *virtuálem* ea explicári possunt, quae distinctióni *formáli* assignántur; nam eo ipso, quod res plúribus aequiválet, definitiónes várias, variósque concéptus admíttit, quorum unus eam apprehéndit, secúndum quod aequiválet uni, et álius, secúndum quod aequiválet álteri.

Chapter 18

Vocabulary

táliter, adv., *thus, so, in such manner*
lignum, ligni, n., *wood*
dependenter, adv., *dependently*
inhaeréntia -ae, f., *inherent quality*
interim, adv., *meanwhile, sometimes*
obsto, obstare, obstiti, obstatum, *oppose, hinder*
perpendo, perpendere, perpendi, perpensus, *weigh carefully; assess carefully*

Grammar

◊ **Relative clause of characteristic:** Such clauses require the subjunctive mood.

1. The relative clause of characteristic most commonly is required due to the presence of an indefinite or negative antecedent (e.g. **res quasdam,** *certain things,* **nihil,** *nothing,* **unus,** *one, someone,* **solus,** *only*). Example:

Nihil dicunt quod velimus audire.
They say nothing which we wish to hear.

Res quasdam fecit, quas non laudare possim.
He has done certain things, which I cannot praise.

2. The relative clause of characteristic may have an unexpressed or definite antecedent but be use to indicate that the person or thing denoted is capable or likely to have the characteristic or perform the action described in the relative clause.

Nunn §150

Quia adversarius vester diabolus tamquam leo rugiens circuit, quaerens quem devoret.

Because your adversary the devil goes around like a roaring lion seeking whom he may devour.   1 Pet. 5:8.

quem devoret
the sort of person whom (rather than any specific individual)

Readings

1.   **Áccidens est entis ens; et, Accidéntis esse est inésse.** [80] Primum apud Arist. [81]ita habétur: « **Cétera vero éntia dicúntur eo quod táliter entis, etc.** »Sénsus est; sola substántia est ens ratióne sui[82]: nam quando quáeritur, quid est? Respondétur per solam substántiam, dicéndo, est homo, vel lignum, etc. Accidéntia dicúntur éntia, ratióne substántiae [83]vel dependénter a substántia, quátenus illi inháerent [84]. Et sic dicúntur entis ens, in génere causae materiális, etc., vel quia definiúntur in órdine ad substántiam[85]; et non habent esse *simplíciter*, nempe ita perféctum, sicut substántia vel quia sunt dispositiónes substántiae [86]. Ínterim nihil obstat quo minus áccidens absolúte étiam ens dici possit [87].

non...sensus
nonsense

     Álterum dictum ex prióri séquitur, et non est sensus, quod inhaeréntia sit de esséntia accidéntis, ut áliqui volunt apud Zimárram, nam de actuáli inhaeréntia certum est, quod non, ut patet ex S. Eucharístia [88]. Sensus ítaque est, áccidens

Zimara, Marco Antonio; Italian humanist and philosopher; b. 1460; d. 1523

---

80   from GEORG REEB and GIOVANNI MARIA CORNOLDI, *Thesaurus philosophorum seu distinctiones et axiomata philosophica*, P. Lethielleux, 1891, p. 166-167.
81   7. met. t. 2
82   Fons. in explic. cit. t
83   Fons. ibidem
84   Zabar. de nat. scientiae, cap. 10
85   Zimar. theor. 3. ubi pluribus hoc explicat. Niphus in explic, cit. text. S. Thom. 1. 2. quaest. 13. art. 2. ad 3 hunc ordinem pulchre declarat
86   Alex. de Ales 7. met. t. 2
87   Suar. d. met. 52. sect. 2. n. 18. pluribus hoc probat, sicut et Zimar. loc. cit
88   Suar. d. 37. sect. 2. a num. 7

natúra sua petit inésse álii [89], et récipi in subiécto sibi propor-tionáto. Et hinc: « **Quántitas potest esse extra subiéctum.** »

2. *Schólion.* Perpénde id quod hac de re dicit S. Thomas, IV Dist. 42. art. 1 et 2. « **Causa prima est vehementióris im-pressiónis supra causátum causae secúndae quam ipsa causa secúnda. Unde quando causa secúnda rémovet in-fluéntiam suam a causáto, adhuc potest remanére influén-tia causae primae in causátum illud. Cum ergo causa prima accidéntium et ómnium existéntium Deus sit; causa autem secúnda accidéntium sit substántia, quia accidéntia ex princípiis substántiae causántur, póterit Deus accidéntia in esse conserváre, remóta étiam causa secúnda, scílicet substántia. Et ídeo absque omni dubitatióne dicéndum est, quod Deus potest fácere áccidens esse sine subiécto. Pri-ma accidéntia consequéntia substántiam sunt quántitas et quálitas; et haec duo proportionántur duóbus princípiis essentiálibus substántiae, scílicet formae et matériae, sed quálitas ex parte formae.** » Osténdit autem, art. 2. posse sic étiam accidéntia ágere. « **In actiónibus naturálibus formae substantiáles non sunt immediátum actiónis princípium, sed agunt mediántibus qualitátibus actívis et passívis, si-cut própriis instruméntis, et ídeo qualitátes non solum agunt in virtúte própria, sed étiam in virtúte formae sub-**

---

89 S. Thom. 1. 2. quaest. 101. art. 2. ad 3. et sic accidens dicitur ens ideo quia eo. aliquid est, seu quia est in illo, quod est, ut colligitur etiam in eadem p. q. 56. art. 4. ad 1. et in I. p. q. 90. art. 2, vide etiam Valent. tom. 3. d. 3. q. 2. pu. 3

stantiális. Unde áctio eárum non solum terminátur ad formam accidentálem, sed étiam ad formam substantiálem; et propter hoc generátio est términus alteratiónis. Huiúsmodi autem virtútem *instrumentálem* recípiunt eo ipso quo a princípiis essentiálibus causántur. Unde sicut remótis substántiis remánet accidéntibus idem esse secúndum spéciem virtúte divína, ita étiam remánet eis eádem virtus quae et prius; et ídeo, sicut ante póterant immutáre ad formam substantiálem ita et nunc. »

Chapter 19

Vocabulary

áttamen, adv., *nevertheless, nonetheless*
fundo, fundare, fundavi, fundatus, *to establish, found*
consisto, consistere, constiti, constitus, *to stand firmly; to consist*
suscípio -ere -cépi -céptum, *to take, receive*
contíngo (contínguo) -ere -tigi -táctum, *to touch, to concern; to pertain to*
dispositio, dispositionis, f., *disposition, providence, layout, orderly arrangement*

Grammar

◊   **Concessive clauses:** These clauses are introduced by **cum, quamvis, etsi, licet, quamquam,** and **ut** and in can be translated as *although, though, even if,* and *notwithstanding.* The verb in such clauses is usually in the Subjunctive mood (the exception being clauses introduced by **quamquam,** which more commonly stand in the Indicative). Examples:

cf. Nunn §166

> *Sed licet nos, aut angelus de caelo evangelizet vobis praeterquam quod evangelizavimus vobis, anathema sit.*
>
> But although we, or an angel from heaven preach to you any other gospel than that which we have preached to you, let him be accursed.   Gal. 1:8.
>
> *Etsi omnes scandalizati fuerint: sed non ego.*
>
> Although all shall be offended in you: yet I will not be offended.   Mk. 14:29.
>
> *Quamquam Jesus non baptizaret, sed discipuli ejus.*
>
> Although Jesus did not baptize, but his disciples. Jn. 4:2.

Readings

1.   **Véritas Non Súscipit Magis Et Minus.** Nempe, si accipiátur véritas prout est *adaequátio* rei et intelléctus, non datur una véritas áltera maíor; nam rátio aequalitá-

tis non súscipit magis et minus [90]. Attámen si consideré-tur ipsum *esse* rei, in quo véritas fundátur, exístit una vé-ritas áltera maíor; quae enim sunt magis éntia, sunt magis vera: « **Cum véritas consístat in adaequatióne intelléctus et rei, si considerétur véritas secúndum ra-tiónem aequalitátis, quae non récipit magis et minus, sic non contíngit esse áliquid magis et minus verum; sed si considerétur ipsum esse rei, quod est rátio veri-tátis, eádem est disposítio rerum in esse et veritáte; unde quae sunt magis éntia, sunt magis vera; et prop-ter hoc étiam in sciéntiis demonstratívis magis cre-dúntur princípia, quam conclusiónes [91]** ».

magis...quam
cf. Nunn §204

2. **Contraríorum Contrária Sunt Consequéntia.** E. g., quia virtus consequítur fortitúdinem, étiam contrárium virtútis, nempe vítium, consequítur contrárium fortitúdinis, nempe ignáviam. Iam hoc effátum accipiéndum est 1° de iis, in quibus utrínque idem modus repugnántiae exístit; e. g., contrárium eíus, quod consequítur calórem, consequítur fri-gus, dúmmodo calor et frigus secúndum eámdem gráduum intensiónem sumántur; 2° de contráriis, quátenus sunt con-trária; quocírca ex eo, quod timíditas consístit in deféctu, non consequítur fortitúdinem in excéssu consístere, nam fortitú-do et timíditas non velúti deféctus et excéssus, sed tamquam

---

90 « Una quippe est veritas, nec in partes divisa »; s. Ioann. Chrysost., *In Matlh. Hom.* XLVII, al. XLVIII, n. 2
91 *Qq. dispp., De Virtut.*, q. II, a. 9 ad 1

virtus et vítium sibi opponúntur; 3° de consequéntibus, quae prófluunt *per se* ex ipsa ratióne *contrarietátis*; uti, virtus est expeténda; ergo vítium est fugiéndum: contra, non valet, album est dulce; ergo nigrum est amárum; dulcédo enim *per áccidens* convénit albo, neque album ratióne dulcédinis est nigro contrárium.

3.　　**In Quale—In Quid—In Quale Quid.** Illud, quod esséntiam subiécti constítuit, atque de eo praedicátur ad modum substantívi, *in quid* praedicári dícitur; et quidem *in quid compléte*, si totam rei esséntiam, et *in quid incompléte*, si huius partem tantum ínnuat. Ex. gr., homo *in quid compléte* praedicátur de Petro, atque generátim sic praedicántur omnes spécies de inferióribus sibi subiéctis: Ánimal vero *in quid incompléte* praedicátur de hómine; atque generátim sic praedicántur ómnia génera de suis speciébus. *In quale* praedicári dícitur id, quod praedicátur ad modum adiectívi; hoc est ad modum qualitátis quasi adiacéntis, et non per se stantis. E. g., in hisce enunciatiónibus: Homo est liber, Petrus est doctus, praedicátio est *in quale*. Hoc modo de subiécto praedicántur próprium et áccidens, illud *in quale necessário*, istud *in quale* contingénter. Quod si vox adiectíva proprietátem éxprimit ad rei esséntiam pertinéntem, tunc praedicátio dícitur *in quale quid*. E. g., *rationále* praedicátur de hómine *in quale quid*, atque generátim sic quaecúmque differéntia praedicátur de spécie, quam constítuit.

Page intentionally left blank

Chapter 20

Vocabulary

defectus, defectus, m., *failure, absence*
superabundo, superabundare, superabundavi, supera-
   bundatus, *to be very abundant*
passio, passionis, f., *passion, suffering, a change which is*
   undergone, receptivity, passivity
dirigo, dirigere, direxi, directus, *arrange, align, direct*
sane, adv., *reasonably, certainly, truly*
moralis, moralis, morale, adj., *moral, concerning ethics*
rectus, recta -um, adj., *right, proper, straight*
mensura, mensurae, f., *measure, length*
diligo, diligere, dilexi, dilectus, *to love, hold dear, favor*
excedo, excedere, excessi, excessus, *to exceed, go beyond*

Grammar

◊ **Noun clauses:**

Nunn §117

   1. Infinitive verbs and their clauses can be used as
the subject of a verb, especially of the verb *esse*. This is
also the case in English (e.g. To err is human; to forgive,
divine)

   Beatius est magis dare quam accipere.

   It is more blessed to give than to receive.   Acts
20:35.

   Mihi vivere Christus est, et mori lucrum.

   For me to live is Christ, and to die is gain.   Phil.
1:21.

   2. A clause introduced by *ut* (or by *quod, quia, quo-*
niam) can be used as the subject of an impersonal verb.

cf. Nunn §127

   Ascendit in cor ejus ut visitaret fratres suos, filios Israel.

   It came into his heart to visit his brothers the children of Israel.   Acts 7:23.

   Sic ergo patet quod multum utile est habere fidem.

   So then it is plain that it is very profitable to have
faith.   Thos. Aq. Symb. Ap. 1.

Readings

1. **Virtus Consistit In Médio.** « Hoc, quod vult Philó-

intelligendum es see Nunn §192

sophus, virtútem esse in médio, <u>intelligéndum est</u> de virtú-

tibus morálibus, non autem est verum de virtútibus theo-

lógicis [92]». Et sane, virtus morális consístit in médio *inter*

superabundántiam et deféctum [93]. Nam « **virtútes moráles**

sunt circa passiónes et operatiónes, quas opórtet dirígere

secúndum régulam ratiónis. In ómnibus autem regulátis

consístit rectum, secúndum quod régulae aequántur; ae-

quálitas. autem média est inter maíus et minus; et ídeo

opórtet, quod rectum virtútis consístat in médio eíus, quod

superabúndat, et eíus, quod déficit a mensúra ratiónis rec-

ta [94]». Virtútis autem *theológicae* « **mensúra et régula est ipse**

Deus. Fides enim nostra regulátur secúndum veritátem Di-

charitas = caritas

vínam; Cháritas autem secúndum bonitátem Eíus; Spes au-

tem secúndum magnitúdinem omnipoténtiae et pietátis

Eíus; et ista est mensúra excédens omnem humánam facul-

tátem; unde numquam potest homo tantum dilígere Deum,

quantum díligi debet, nec tantum crédere, aut speráre in

Ipsum, quantum debet; unde multo minus potest ibi esse

excéssas; et sic bonum talis virtútis non consístit in médio;

---

92 Vid. s. Thom., *Qq. dispp., De Viri.*, q. III, a. 2 ad 10
93 Vid. s. Thom., *Qq. dispp., De Viri.*, , q. I, a. 13 c
94 *In lib. III Sent.*, Dist. XXXIII, q. I, a. 3, sol. 1 c

sed tanto est mélius, quanto magis accéditur ad sum-mum [95]».

2.   Subdit autem sanctus Doctor, *quandóque áliquam ex virtútibus theológicis posse esse in médio per áccidens*; scíli-cet « ratióne eíus, quod ordinátur ad principále obiéctum; sicut fides non potest habére médium, et extréma in hoc quod innitátur Primae veritáti, cui nullus potest nimis ín-niti; sed ex parte eórum, quae credit, potest habére médium et extréma, sicut unum verum est médium inter duo falsa. Et simíliter spes non habet médium, et extréma ex parte principális obiécti, quia Divíno auxílio nullus potest nimis ínniti, sed quantum ad ea, quae confídit áliquis adeptú-rum, potest esse ibi médium, et extréma, in quantum vel praesúmit ea, quae sunt supra suam proportiónem, vel dé-sperat de his, quae sunt sibi proportionáta [96]»; vel étiam *per áccidens* virtútes *theológicae in médio* consístunt[97], quátenus exercéndae sunt secúndum mensúram conditiónis natúrae, et nostri ingénii vires, non vero nímio conátu, ádeo ut cor-pus laedátur, aut nímium debilitétur. Síquidem, aiénte s. Ber-nárdo, « cum nullum finem, vel términum habére débeat devótio amántis, tamen términos suos et fines, et régulas habére debet áctio operántis [98]»

---

95   la 2ae, q. LXIV, a. 4 c
96   2a 2ae, q. XVII, a. 5 ad 2
97   *Qq. dispp., De Virtut.*, q. IV, a. 1 ad 7
98   *Serm. ad Fratres, De Monte Dei*

Page intentionally left blank

Chapter 21

Vocabulary

dignus, digna -um, adj., *appropriate, suitable, worthy*
brutum, bruti, adj., *beast, animal*
confero, conferre, contuli, collatus, *bring together, carry, compare, add, bestow, assign*
equus, equi, m., *horse*
infans, infantis, m. or f., *child, infant*
convenio, convenire, conveni, conventus , *be appropriate to, fit, be correctly shaped/consistent; harmonize, agree*
absum, abesse, abfui, abfuturus, *to be absent, to be lacking*
destituo, destituere, destitui, destitutus, *to leave without, to make destitute, render void*
ínstar, (indeclinable), n., *image, likeness, resemblance, kind, appearance; w. gen.: like to, after the fashion of*
superaddo, superaddere, superaddidi, superadditus, *to add to, to add over and above*
superadditio, -tionis, f., *a further addition*

Grammar

◊ **Periphrastic tenses**: The use of periphrastic constructions for expressing the tenses is a characteristic of Late Latin and paved the way for constructions in the Romance languages. Periphrastic tenses are formed from using a tense of *esse* as a helping verb along the present participle.

cf. Nunn §§90-93

Caution: do not confuse the general phenomena of periphrasis with the very specific case of the future passive periphrastic (e.g. *Cartago delenda est*)

Present periphrastic:

Non enim <u>sumus</u> sicut plurimi <u>adulterantes</u> verbum Dei.

For <u>we are</u> not as many <u>adulterating</u> the word of God. 2 Cor. 2:17.

<u>Esto consentiens</u> adversario tuo cito dum es in via cum eo.

<u>Agree</u> with thine adversary quickly while thou art in the way with him. Mt. 5:25.

Periphrastic Imperfect:

Et <u>erat</u> plebs <u>expectans</u> Zachariam.

And the people <u>was awaiting</u> Zachariah.   Lk. 1:21.

Et <u>erat</u> tribus diebus non <u>videns</u>, et non manducavit neque bibit.

And he was three days without sight, and did neither eat nor drink.   Acts 9:9.

Periphrastic Future.

Noli timere: ex hoc jam homines <u>eris capiens</u>.

Fear not: from henceforth you <u>will be catching</u> men. Lk. 5:10.

◊   **Periphrastic tenses formed with** *habere*: The usage of *habeo* with an infinitive verb in Ecclesiastical Latin typically has a sense of future necessity. From this phenomenon, the Future tenses in French and Italian eventually developed (e.g. in Italian the infinitive *credere + ho => crederò;* French is parallel where *croire + ai => croirai*)

Baptismo autem <u>habeo baptizari</u>.

But I have a baptism with which I must be baptized. Lk. 12:50.

<u>Habes</u>, homo, imprimis aetatem <u>venerare</u> aquarum, quod antiqua substantia.

First, O man, you must venerate the age of water; because it is an ancient substance.   Tert. de Bapt. 3.

Readings

Substántia Non Súscipit Magis Et Minus.   Licet enim quaedam substántiae sint áliis dignióres, ut hómines brutis, tamen in eo, quod sunt substántiae, non est una magis substántia, quam ália; neque eádem substántia, si conferátur cum seípsa, est magis, vel minus substántia. Hinc homo, si conferátur cum equo in eo, quod est substántia, non potest dici magis substántia, quam equus; neque vir adúltus magis est substántia, quam infans [99]. Item, una substántia potest esse magis substántia, quam ália, ratióne eórum, quae substántiis, non quátenus sunt substántiae, sed *per áccidens* convéniunt; e. g., quátenus una est singuláris, ália universális, una

---

[99] Vid. s. Thom., I, q. LXXVI, a. 4 ad 4; et q. XCIII, a. 3 ad 3

ad primas própius accédit, ália lóngius ab iis abest; sed in ratióne natúrae et esséntiae, nulla una substántia magis est
substántia, quam ália [100]. Rátio autem huius effáti perspícitur
ex eo, quod substántia, immo quaelíbet esséntia habet *esse*

ex eo quod
from the fact that

indivisíbile, et in puncto constitútum, ideóque grádibus destitúitur, quorum respéctu *magis et minus* dícitur. Unde esséntiae rerum dicúntur esse instar numerórum, quibus nihil
addi, aut détrahi potest, sine mutatióne speciéi. Ex hoc séquitur étiam, ut nulla *forma substantiális* recípiat *magis* et *minus*.
Nam, « **superaddítio maióris perfectiónis facit áliam spéciem, sicut addítio unitátis facit áliam spéciem in númeris.
Non est autem possíbile, ut una, et eádem forma número
sit diversárum specíerum** [101]». Unde in formis « **per hoc,
quod una perféctior exístit, quam ália** [102]», differéntia invenítur. Illud autem patet, quod s. Bonaventúra monet, quod
nempe, « **quamvis forma substantiális secúndum se non recípiat magis, et minus, habet tamen inténdi et remítti secúndum esse ipsíus in matéria** [103]».

3.   **Relátio Non Facit Compositíonem.** Hoc intellígitur
de relatióne, quátenus habet *esse ad áliud*, seu quátenus *dicit
ad*. « Relátio, secúndum ratiónem suam non habet quod sit
áliquid, sed solum quod ad áliud referátur; unde secúndum

---

100   « Eadem et in hoc, et in illo substantiae ratio est »; s. Greg. Nyss.,
Contr. Eunom., lib. I
101   I, q. CXVIII, a. 2 ad 2
102   *Contr. Gent.*, lib. III, c. 97
103   *In lib. II Sent.*, Dist. XIII, a. II, q. 2 ad arg.

ratiónem suam non ponit áliquid in subiécto [104]». At relátio,

prout *dicit in,* compónit cum subiécto cui inháeret: « **Relátio**

quae habet esse in creatúra, habet áliud esse, quam sit esse

sui subiécti, unde est áliquid áliud a suo subiécto [105]».

---

104 *In lib. I Sent., Dist. XX, q. I, a 1 sol.*
105 « *Dictura estin creatura, quia* « *in Deo nihil est, quod habet esse aliud ab Ipso; esse enim sapientiae est ipsum Esse Divinum, et non superadditura; et similiter esse Paternitatis* », *In lib. I Sent., Dist. XX, q. I, a 1 sol.*

Chapter 22

Vocabulary

ablativus, a, um, adj., *that which pertains to taking away something*

aúfero -férre, ábstuli, ablátum, *take away, remove*

appetibilis, appetibilis, appetibile, adj., *desirable, sought after*

rabio, rabere (also, rabo, rabare), *to be furious, to rage, to rave*

copulo, copulare, copulavi, copulatus, *connect, join physically, couple, unite*

compertum, comperti, n., *proven or verified fact, a certainty*

dúbius -a -um, adj., *doubtful, uncertain;* as a neuter noun: *doubt, hesitation*

verto, vertere, verti, versus, *to turn, to incline toward (a thing or idea)*

districtus, districta -um, adj., *strict, severe*

aliter, adv., *otherwise, differently*

labefacto, labefactare, labefactavi, labefactatus, *to shake; cause to waver, loosen*

vito, vitare, vitavi, vitatus, *to avoid, shun*

Grammar

◊ **Independent uses of the Subjunctive:** When the main verb of a sentence stands in the subjunctive mood it can have one of the following uses.

cf. Nunn §§101-103

1. **Jussive and Hortatory Subjunctives** express a command in the third person and an exhortation in the first person. E.g. *Transeamus usque Bethleem, et videamus hoc verbum quod factum est.* Let us go to Bethlehem and see this thing which has come to pass.   Lk. 2:15

2. **The Optative (or Volitive) Subjunctive** expresses a wish or unfulfilled desire. E.g. *Adveniat regnum tuum.* Your kingdom come.

3. **The Deliberative Subjunctive** is used in questions of uncertainty, deliberation, or anger. E.g. *Quid faciamus?* What are we to do?

Readings

1. **Esse Est Absólute Mélius Quam Non Esse.** Síquidem *esse* perfectiónem, seu *realitátem*; *non esse* autem deféctum cuiuscúmque *realitátis* signíficat. Inde fit, ut « **unumquódque naturáliter suo modo** *esse* **desíderet** [106]», Dícitur *absolúte*; nam *non esse* aliquándo *per áccidens* existimátur bonum, quátenus per *non esse* áliquod malum aufértur. Hinc s. Thomas: « **Dicéndum, quod non esse potest duplíciter considerári. Uno modo secúndum se, et sic nullo modo est appetíbile, cum non hábeat ratiónem boni, sed sit boni pura privátio. Álio modo potest considerári in quantum est ablatívum poenális vitae, vel misériae, et sic non esse áccipit ratiónem boni, cárere enim malo est quoddam bonum, ut dicit Philósophus in quinto Ethicórum; et per hunc modum mélius est damnátis non esse, quam míseros esse; unde Matth. XXVI, v. 24, dícitur,** *Bonum erat ei, si natus non fuísset homo* **ille** [107]».

2. **Essentiáliter. Accidentáliter. Integráliter.** [108] Ánima humána essentiáliter est forma córporis humáni quamquam non essentiáliter matériae córporis humáni copulétur.

Schólion. Dicéndam esse ánimam humánam *essentiáliter* formam córporis humáni non minus philósophis quam theólo-

---

106   *Contr. Gent.*, lib. II, c. 79
107   3, q. XCVII, a. 3 c
108   from GEORG REEB and GIOVANNI MARIA CORNOLDI, *Thesaurus philosophorum seu distinctiones et axiomata philosophica*, P. Lethielleux, 1891, p. 50-52.

gis est in compérto. Rabémus ex Concílio Later. V sub Leóne X. « **Hoc sacro approbánte concílio damnámus et reprobámus omnes asseréntes ánimam intellectívam mortálem esse, aut únicam in cunctis homínibus; et haec in dúbium verténtes; cum illa non solum** *vere per se* **et** *essentiáliter* **humáni córporis forma exístat, sicut in canóne felícis recordatiónis Cleméntis Papae V praedecessóris nostri in generáli Viennénsi Concílio édito continétur; verum et immortális et pro córporum quibus infúnditur, multitúdine singuláriter multiplicábilis et multiplicáta et multiplicánda sit. Cumque verum vero mínime contradícat, omnem assertiónem veritáti illuminátae fídei contráriam, omníno falsam esse defínimus, et ut áliter dogmatizáre non líceat districtius inhibémus: omnésque huiúsmodi erróris assertiónibus inhaeréntes, velut damnatíssimas háereses seminántes, per ómnia ut detestábiles et abominábiles haeréticos et infidéles, cathólicam fidem labefactántes vitándos et puniéndos fore decérnimus.** »

Matéria prima uníus córporis terréstris non differt essentiáliter a matéria prima altérius, sed accidentáliter, quamquam eádem córpora sint divérsae speciéi, v. gr. aquae, et oxigénei, et hydrogénei. Id étiam ex eo patet quod matéria prima oxygénei et hydrogénei ope substantiális transmutatiónis fit matéria prima aquae.

Page intentionally left blank

APPENDIX 1: ECCLESIASTICAL LATIN GRAMMAR

selected from

AN INTRODUCTION

TO ECCLESIASTICAL LATIN

BY
H. P. V. NUNN

Page intentionally left blank

THE ORIGIN AND CHARACTER OF ECCLESIASTICAL LATIN

The points in which Ecclesiastical Latin differs from Classical Latin are principally the following:

The use of a great number of abstract and compound nouns and of nouns denoting an agent and ending in *or*.

The use of diminutives. The use of words transliterated from Greek.

The extended use of prepositions where in Classical Latin a simple case of the noun would have sufficed.

The disappearance of long and elaborate sentences with many dependent clauses. Clauses are often connected simply by *et*, or no conjunction is used at all.

The disappearance to a great extent of the Oratio Obliqua and the Accusative with Infinitive construction.

The substitution therefor of a new construction imitated from the Greek and introduced by *quod, quia*, or *quoniam*.

The gradual extension of this construction even in clauses where *ut* would be used in Classical Latin especially in noun clauses.

The Infinitive used to express purpose or result, as in Greek, and also to express dependent commands.

The Subjunctive is used where it would not be used in Classical Latin and vice versa.

The use of periphrastic forms of verbs, especially forms made up with *esse* or *habere*.

In a word we see the process at work which turned the Latin of the Empire into the modern Romance languages.

SYNTAX

SENTENCES

1. Syntax deals with the methods by which words are combined to form **sentences.**

A sentence is a group of words expressing a statement, a question, or a desire. (Under the term *desire* commands, entreaties and wishes are to be included.)

2. Every sentence must consist of at least two parts, either expressed or understood:

(1) **The Subject**—the word or group of words denoting the person or thing of which the predicate is said.

(2) **The Predicate**—the word or group of words denoting all that is said about the subject; or the word or group of words which expresses the assertion that is made, the question that is asked, or the desire that is expressed about the subject. The predicate is not necessarily identical with the verb. It includes the complements and extensions of the verb and also the object.

If a verb is transitive it must have an object.

The Object is the word or group of words denoting the person or thing towards which the action of the verb is directed.

The verb agrees with its subject in number and person.

3. Verbs which require a complement to complete their meaning are called **Copulative verbs.** The most important copulative verb is the verb *to be*.

Verbs which signify *to become, to appear, to be chosen, to be named,* and the like are also copulative.

If the complement of a copulative verb is a noun, it agrees with the subject of the verb in number and case; if it is an adjective, it agrees with the subject of the verb in number, gender and case.

This rule is sometimes put in the following form:

The verb 'to be' takes the same case after it as before it.

Examples:

Caesar imperator est. *Caesar is general.*
Metelli facti sunt consules. *The Metelli have been made consuls.*
Rex magnus est. *The king is great.*
Regina magna est. *The queen is great.*
Reges magni sunt. *The kings are great.*
Regnum magnum fit. *The kingdom becomes great.*
Felices appellamur. *We are called happy.*

4. A Simple sentence is a sentence which contains a single subject and a single predicate.

Multiple and Complex sentences are sentences which contain more than one subject and predicate.

In dealing with sentences it will be found convenient to keep carefully to the following terminology:

The name *sentence* should be applied only to a complete statement, command, or question occurring between two full stops.

Groups of words forming part of a multiple or complex sentence, and having a subject and predicate of their own should be called *clauses.*

Groups of words forming an equivalent to some part of speech, and not having a subject and predicate of their own, should be called *phrases.*

5. A Multiple sentence is a sentence which consists of two or more clauses none of which depends on any of the others, but which all make equally important and independent statements. These clauses are said to be combined by co-ordination.

In the Hebrew language such co-ordinated clauses are very common, and this peculiarity is faithfully reflected in the Vulgate Old Testament, and, to a certain extent, in the New Testament In Latin, uninfluenced by Hebrew, clauses are more generally combined into complex sentences.

Example:

Et egressus est rursus ad mare: omnisque turba veniebat ad eum, et docebat eos. *And he went out again to the sea, and all the crowd came to him, and he taught them.*   Mk. 2:13.

6. A Complex sentence is a sentence which consists of a principal or main clause and one or more subordinate clauses depending on it, or on one another as noun, adjective, or adverb equivalents. These clauses are said to be combined by subordination.

Example:

Si quis voluerit voluntatem ejus facere, cognoscet de doctrina, utrum ex Deo sit, an ego a meipso loquar. *If any man willeth to do his will, he shall know of the teaching, whether it is of God, or whether I speak of myself.*
Jn. 7:17.

7. Subordinate clauses are divided into three classes:

(1) **Noun** or **Substantival clauses** that take the place of a noun.

(2) **Adjectival clauses** that take the place of an adjective.

(3) **Adverbial clauses** that take the place of an adverb.

NOUNS

8. Cases and their meanings. Inflection is a change made in the form of a word to denote a modification of its meaning, or to show the relationship of the word to some other word in the sentence.

Examples: *bird* becomes *birds* in the Plural and *man* becomes *men*.

The pronoun *he* is used when it is the subject of a sentence; but it is changed into *him* when it is the object. There are however few inflections left in English.

Latin nouns, pronouns and adjectives have inflections to show number and case; adjectives and some pronouns have inflections to show gender as well.

To give a list of these inflections is called *giving a declension*, or *declining a word*, because the cases other than the Nominative were considered by the old grammarians to fall away (*declinare*) from the form of the Nominative. For the same reason cases other than the Nominative are sometimes called Oblique cases.

Hence also the origin of the name *Case* from the Latin *casus* = falling.

The cases actually in use are seven in number.

(1) The Nominative, used to express the subject of a finite verb.

(2) The Vocative, used in addressing a person or thing.

(3) The Accusative, used to denote motion towards and to express the object of a transitive verb.

(4) The Genitive, used to limit the meaning of another noun like an adjective and to denote various relations most of which are expressed in English by the use of the preposition *of* or by the possessive case.

(5) The Dative, used to express that to or for which anything is done. This includes the dative of the indirect object after transitive verbs.

(6) The Ablative, used to express separation or motion from and in many other senses.

(7) The Locative, which is not given in the tables of declensions in grammars, used to denote the place at which anything happens in certain expressions.

9. The Nominative Case is the case of the **Subject** of a sentence or clause in all sentences or clauses in which the verb is not in the Infinitive mood.

Tunc discipuli ejus, relinquentes eum, omnes fugerunt. *Then all his disciples forsook him and fled.*   Mk. 14:50.

10. The Vocative Case is used in **addressing** a person or a personified thing.

Bone Pastor, Panis vere, *Good Shepherd, true Bread,*

Jesu, nostri miserere. *Jesus, have mercy on us.*

11. The Accusative Case denotes **motion towards** or **extension**.

It is therefore the case of the **Direct Object**, because the object is the name of that towards which the action of the verb goes forth.

So the Accusative is used with or without a preposition to denote **motion towards**.

The Accusative denotes the **time during which** anything happens and also **extent of space**.

12. The Accusative is used to express the direct object of a transitive verb.

>Qui videt me, videt eum qui misit me. *He that seeth me, seeth him that sent me.*Jn. 12:45.

The same verbs are not necessarily transitive in Latin as in English, hence many verbs which are followed by an Accusative in English are followed by a Genitive, Dative, or Ablative in Latin.

13. Motion towards is generally expressed by a preposition such as *ad* or *in* followed by a noun in the Accusative case.

The preposition is omitted in Classical Latin before the names of towns and small islands and before certain words such as *domum, rus, foras.*

In the Vulgate a preposition is generally used before *domum,* and it is also found before the names of towns.

>Non relinquam vos orphanos: veniam ad vos. *I will not leave you orphans: I will come to you.*   Jn. 14:18.

>Sed cum Romam venisset, sollicite me quaesivit. *But when he came to Rome, he sought me out diligently.*   2 Tim. 1:17.

>Venit ergo iterum in Cana Galilaeae.... *He came therefore again to Cana of Galilee....*   Jn. 4:46.

14. The Accusative may denote **extent of time or space,** but in Ecclesiastical Latin the Ablative is often used for extent of time. See section 55.

>Et mansit ibi duos dies. *And he remained there two days.*   Jn. 4:40.

15. Cognate Accusative. Any verb whose meaning permits it may take after it an Accusative of cognate or kindred meaning.

>Bonum certamen certavi. *I have fought a good fight.* 2 Tim. 4:7.

>Nolite judicare secundum faciem, sed justum judicium judicate. *Do not judge after the appearance, but judge a righteous judgment.*   Jn. 7:24.

>See also Lk. 2:8; 1 Tim. 6:12; 1 Pet. 3:14.

16. Certain verbs meaning to teach, to ask, to conceal are followed by **two Accusatives,** one of the person and another of the thing.

If a verb of this kind is used in the Passive voice the object noun denoting the thing is retained in the Accusative case.

>Ille vos docebit omnia. *He shall teach you all things.* Jn. 14:26.

>Aut quis est ex vobis homo, quem, si petierit filius suus panem, numquid lapidem porriget ei? *Or what man is there of you whom, if his son ask him for a loaf, will he give him a stone?*   Mt. 7:9.

>Hic erat edoctus viam Domini. *He was instructed in the way of the Lord.* Acts 18:25.

17. Two Object Accusatives are rarely used, in imitation of Greek, after verbs meaning *to put on.*

This is not Classical The Classical construction is to use the Accusative of the person and the Ablative of the thing put on.

>Calcia te caligas tuas. *Put on thy sandals.*   Acts 12:8.

>Induite vos armaturam Dei. *Put on yourselves the armour of God.*   Eph. 6:11.

>Induti loricam fidei. *Clad with the breastplate of faith.*   1 Thess. 5:8.

So in one instance with a verb meaning *to put off:*

>Expoliantes vos veterem hominem. *Putting off from yourselves the old man.* Col. 3:9.

18. The Accusative is sometimes used after **Passive** verbs to denote an action done to oneself. This seems to be an imitation of the Greek Middle voice. This construction is rare in prose, but common in Latin poetry, where it is used with great freedom.

> State ergo succincti lumbos vestros in veritate: et induti loricam justitiae, et calciati pedes in praeparatione evangelii pacis. *Stand therefore with your loins girt about with truth, and having put on the breastplate of righteousness, and with your feet shod with the preparation of the gospel of peace.* Eph. 6:14.
>
> Abluti corpus aqua munda. *With our body washed with pure water.* Heb. 10:22.

19. The Genitive Case is an **adjectival** or **descriptive** case. A noun in the Genitive case is generally connected with another noun which it qualifies very much in the same way as an adjective.

The Genitive case can generally be translated into English by the use of the preposition *of* or by the Possessive case.

The name *Genitive case* means the case of kind or origin; but the case is most frequently used to denote possession.

20. Possessive Genitive denoting possession.

> Justorum autem animae in manu Dei sunt. *But the souls of the righteous are in the hand of God.* Wisdom 3:1.

21. The Genitive may express **authorship, source,** or **material**, or almost any relationship that can exist between two persons or things.

> Inter natos mulierum. *Among those born of women.* Mt. 11:11.
>
> Periculis fluminum, periculis latronum. *In perils of rivers, in perils of robbers...* (i.e. *arising from rivers or robbers*). 2 Cor. 11:26.
>
> Ergo evacuatum est scandalum crucis. *Therefore the reproach of the cross has ceased.* Gal. 5:11.
>
> Prae gaudio illius. *For joy thereof.* Mt. 13:44.

So the Genitive is used to denote **personal relationship** such as that of son and father, mother and son, or even husband and wife

> Dicebat autem Judam Simonis Iscariotem. *But he spake of Judas the son of Simon the Iscariot.* Jn. 6:71.
>
> Stabant autem juxta crucem Jesu...Maria Cleophae et Maria Magdalene. *But Mary the wife of Cleophas and Mary Magdalene were standing by the cross of Jesus.* Jn. 19:25.

22. The Partitive Genitive expresses the whole after words denoting a part.

> Magister bone, quid boni faciam, ut habeam vitam aeternam? *Good Master, what good thing shall I do that I may have eternal life?* Mt. 19:16.
>
> See also Mt. 25:19; Acts 5:15; Rom. 15:26; Acts 24:21.

23. The Subjective Genitive. The Genitive is said to be used subjectively when the noun which is in the Genitive case is the name of the subject of the action denoted by the noun with which it is connected.

> Quis nos separabit a caritate Christi? *Who shall separate us from the love of Christ?* (i.e. *from the love that Christ feels for us*). Rom. 8:35.
>
> Propter quod tradidit illos Deus in desideria cordis eorum. *Wherefore God gave them up to the desires of their own heart.* Rom. 1:24.
>
> See also 2 Cor. 5:14; 1 Tim. 4:1.

The Subjective Genitive is also found in the Vulgate after adjectives and participles in imitation of the Greek.

Et erunt omnes docibiles Dei. *And they shall all be taught of God.* Jn. 6:45.

Quae et loquimur non in doctis humanae sapientiae verbis.... *Which also we speak, not in words taught by human wisdom....* 1 Cor. 2:13.

24. The Objective Genitive. The Genitive is said to be used objectively when the noun which is in the Genitive case is the name of the object of the action denoted by the noun with which it is connected.

The objective Genitive is used much more freely in the Vulgate than in Classical Latin, in imitation of the Greek. It is often used with nouns which express the action of an intransitive verb.

Dedit illis potestatem spirituum immundorum. *He gave them power (to cast out) unclean spirits.* Mt. 10:1.

Sicut dedisti ei potestatem omnis carnis. *As thou hast given him power over all flesh.* Jn. 17:2.

Et erat pernoctans in oratione Dei. *And he was spending all the night in prayer to God.* Lk. 6:12.

Si nos hodie judicamur in benefacto hominis infirmi.... *If we are judged to-day for a good deed done to an impotent man....* Acts 4:9.

Quidam autem conscientia usque nunc idoli, quasi idolothytum manducant.... *For some men with the consciousness even now of the idol eat it as a thing offered to an idol....* 1 Cor. 8:7.

Spiritus autem blasphemia non remittetur. *But blasphemy against the Spirit shall not be forgiven.* Mt. 12:31.

See also Mk. 11:22; Jn. 2:17; Rom. 10:2, 15:8; 2 Cor. 10:5; Col. 2:12; 1 Tim. 3:5.

25. The Possessive Pronoun may be used in the sense of an objective Genitive

Hoc facite in meam commemorationem. *Do this in remembrance of me.* Lk. 22:19.

Quaecumque enim scripta sunt, ad nostram doctrinam scripta sunt. *For whatsoever things were written were written for our learning—*(i.e. *to teach us*). Rom. 15:4.

Neque veni Hierosolymam ad antecessores meos apostolos. *Nor did I go to Jerusalem to the apostles who were before me.* Gal. 1:17.

Ita et isti non crediderunt in vestram misericordiam. *So they also did not believe that mercy might be shown to you.* Rom. 11:31.

Quotidie morior per vestram gloriam, fratres, quam habeo in Christo Jesu Domino nostro. *I die daily, brethren, I protest by the glorying in you which I have in Christ Jesus our Lord.* 1 Cor. 15:31.

The question whether a Genitive is subjective or objective can only be decided by the context. Sometimes the decision is not easy.

26. The Descriptive Genitive is used to give a description or explanation of the noun with which it is connected.

In Classical Latin a descriptive Genitive is always qualified by an adjective; but this is not always the case in Ecclesiastical Latin

In the Vulgate the use of this Genitive is widely extended in imitation of the Construct state in Hebrew There are few adjectives in Hebrew, and a noun in the Construct state is connected with another noun where an adjective would be used in Latin or Greek.

Et facti estis judices cogitationum iniquarum. *And ye become judges with evil thoughts* (i.e. *unfair judges*).   Jas. 2:4.

Quia propter te mortificamur: tota die aestimati sumus ut oves occisionis. *Because we are put to death for thy sake: all the day we are counted as sheep for the slaughter.*   Rom. 8:36, quoted from Ps. 43:22.

In odorem suavitatis. *For a sweet smelling savour.*   Eph. 5:2.

Annorum enim erat amplius quadraginta homo, in quo factum erat signum istud sanitatis. *For the man was more than forty years old on whom this sign of healing was done.*   Acts 4:22.

See also Mt. 8:26; Mk. 1:4; Lk. 2:14; Jn. 5:29, 7:35; Rom. 15:5; Phil. 3:21.

27. The descriptive Genitive may also be used **predicatively.**

Nescitis cujus spiritus estis. *Ye know not of what spirit ye are.* Lk. 9:55.

Nam ut impudentis est clamoribus strepere, ita congruit verecundo modestis precibus orare. *For as it is the mark of a shameless person to make a disturbance with his cries, so it befits a modest person to pray with restraint.* Cyprian, *De Oratione Dominica.*

28. The Genitive of price or value. The Genitive of some neuter adjectives such as *magni, parvi, tanti, quanti*, is used to denote the price at which a thing is valued, bought or sold.

Dixit autem ei Petrus: Dic mihi, mulier, si tanti agrum vendidistis? *But Peter said to her: "Tell me, woman, if you sold the field for so much?"* Acts 5:8; Lk. 12:24.

29. The Genitive is used **after certain verbs** which are not transitive in Latin as they are in English.

Most verbs meaning to pity, to remember, to forget, are followed by a Genitive case in Classical Latin

In the Vulgate the usage varies. A Dative is found after *misereor* and sometimes *super* with an Accusative Ps. 102:13; Prov. 21:10; Mt. 9:36; Mk. 8:2.

Recordor is very rarely followed by an Accusative   Hos. 7:2; Ez. 23:19.

Memini is also rarely followed by an Accusative   Is. 46:8; 1 Macc. 7:38.

Obliviscor is followed by an Accusative   Ps. 9:18, 49:22; Heb. 13:2.

The following are examples of the normal use.

Misertus autem dominus servi illius, dimisit eum. *But the lord taking pity on that slave, forgave him.*   Mt. 18:27.

Omnia ostendi vobis, quoniam sic laborantes oportet suscipere infirmos, ac meminisse verbi Domini Jesu, quoniam ipse dixit: Beatius est magis dare quam accipere. *I have shown you all things, that so labouring ye ought to support the weak, and to remember the word of the Lord Jesus, how he said: "It is more blessed to give than to receive."* Acts 20:35.

Non enim injustus Deus, ut obliviscatur operis vestri.... *For God is not unjust that he should forget your work....*   Heb. 6:10.

30. The following uses of the Genitive which are not found in Classical Latin, but which are found in the Vulgate, in imitation of Greek, should be noted.

Verbs meaning to rule and to fill are followed by a Genitive and also the adj. *plenus,* full.

Reges gentium dominantur eorum. *The kings of the nations rule over them.* Lk. 22:25.

Et impletae sunt nuptiae discumbentium. *And the wedding was filled with guests.*   Mt. 22:10.

See also Acts 19:16; Rom. 14:9.

31. The Genitive Absolute is found

Qui ostendunt opus legis scriptum in cordibus suis, testimonium reddente illis conscientia ipsorum, et inter se invicem cogitationum accusantium, aut etiam defendentium. *Who show the work of the law written in their hearts, their own conscience bearing testimony to them, and their thoughts accusing them, or even defending them to themselves.*   Rom. 2:15.

This is the reading of Wordsworth and White. The SC text reads *cogitationibus accusantibus*, etc.

See also Acts 1:8; 2 Cor. 10:15.

At first sight it might seem that these passages might be explained differently, more in accordance with Latin usage; but the original Greek shows that the construction is meant for the Genitive Absolute.

32. The Genitive is used after the **comparative of an adjective.**

Qui credit in me, opera quae ego facio et ipse faciet: et majora horum faciet.... *He that believes in me, the works that I do he shall do also; and greater than these shall he do...*   Jn. 14:12.
See also Mk. 12:31; Acts 17:11; Heb. 3:3, 6:16; 3 Jn. 4.

33. The Genitive may be used to express **space within which.**

Et videtis, et auditis, quia non solum Ephesi, sed paene totius Asiae, Paulus hic suadens avertit multam turbam.... *And ye see and hear that not only at Ephesus, but throughout almost all Asia, this Paul persuades and turns away much people.* Acts 19:26.

34. The Dative Case denotes that to or for which anything is done. It is generally translated into English by the use of the prepositions *to* or *for*.
N.B. The Dative does not denote motion to.

35. The Dative of the **Indirect Object** is used after many verbs which are also followed by a direct object in the Accusative case.

Pecuniam copiosam dederunt militibus.... *They gave large money to the soldiers....*   Mt. 28:12.

36. When verbs which are followed by an indirect object in the Dative as well as by a direct object in the Accusative are used in the Passive voice, the direct object becomes the subject of the sentence and the Dative remains.

Auferetur a vobis regnum Dei, et dabitur genti facienti fructum ejus. *The kingdom of God shall be taken from you and given to a nation bringing forth the fruit thereof.*   Mt. 21:43.

37. The Dative is used after many verbs which are not transitive in Latin as they are in English.
The most important of these verbs are:
imperare, *to command.*
ignoscere, *to pardon.*
remittere, *to pardon.*
parcere, *to spare.*
credere, *to believe.*
obedire, *to obey.*

suadere, *to persuade.*
servire, *to serve.*
placere, *to please.*
displicere, *to displease.*
nocere, *to injure.*
resistere, *to resist.*
confiteri, *to confess, give honour to.*
evangelizare, *to preach the gospel.*

Some verbs that are followed by a Dative in Classical Latin are followed by an Accusative in Ecclesiastical Latin

Credere is often followed by *in* with the Accusative, *benedicere* and *maledicere* are followed either by the Dative or the Accusative

Many verbs compounded with a preposition are followed by a Dative, especially compounds of *esse.*

Etenim Christus non sibi placuit. *For even Christ pleased not himself.* Rom. 15:3.

Hujuscemodi enim Christo Domino nostro non serviunt, sed suo ventri. *For men of this kind do not serve Christ our Lord, but their own belly.* Rom. 15:18.

Et obtulerunt ei omnes male habentes. *And they brought to him all that were sick.* Mt. 14:24.

Quid mihi prodest, si mortui non resurgunt? *What doth it profit me if the dead rise not?* 1 Cor. 15:32.

38. If a verb which is followed by the Dative as its sole object is used in the Passive voice, it is always used impersonally.

Si enim aliquis diceret aliquid de aliqua terra remota, et ipse non fuisset ibi, non crederetur ei sicut si ibi fuisset. *For if anyone should say anything about some distant land, and he himself had not been there, he would not be believed, as he would be, if he had been there.* Thomas Aquinas.

39. The Dative may denote the person **in whose interest, or against whose interest** anything takes place.

Et ecce aperti sunt ei caeli.... *And behold the heavens were opened for him...* Mt. 3:16.

Quomodo aperti sunt tibi oculi? *How were thine eyes opened for thee?* Jn. 9:10.

Tibi soli peccavi, et malum coram te feci. *Against thee only have I sinned, and done evil in thy sight.* Ps. 51:4.

See also Mt. 21:2, 5, 27:21.

40. The Dative is used with *esse* to denote **possession.**

Quod tibi nomen est? *What is thy name?* Lk. 8:30.

Argentum et aurum non est mihi. *Silver and gold have I none.* Acts 3:6.

41. The Dative of certain nouns (in Ecclesiastical Latin these are generally nouns denoting emotions) is used, especially with *esse* to denote **result** or **purpose**. This Dative is generally accompanied by another noun or pronoun in the Dative denoting the person interested.

Et eritis odio omnibus gentibus propter nomen meum. *And ye shall be hated of all nations for my name's sake.* Mt. 24:9.

Et nihil eorum Gallioni curae erat. *And Gallio cared for none of these things.*   Acts 18:17.
See also Col. 4:11; 1 Thess. 2:7.

42. The Dative is regularly used to express the **Agent** after a gerundive participle and rarely after a perfect participle.

Audistis quia dictum est antiquis.... *Ye have heard that it was said by them of old time....*   Mt. 5:21.

Novissime autem omnium tanquam abortivo, visus est et mihi. *And last of all he was seen by me also, as by one born out of due time.*   1 Cor. 15:8.

Et ecce nihil dignum morte actum est ei. *And behold nothing worthy of death has been done by him.*   Lk. 23:15.

43. A quite exceptional instance of the Dative being used to express motion towards is found in Rev. 1:11.

Et mitte septem ecclesiis. *And send it to the seven churches.*
This is, as usual, an exact translation of the Greek.

44. The Ablative Case may be described as an **adverbial** case, because a noun in the Ablative case generally qualifies a verb, adjective or adverb in the same way as an adverb.

The name *Ablative case* means the *taking away case*. It is a very unsuitable name, as it covers only a small number of the uses of the case.

The meanings of the Ablative case, as we find it in Latin, are derived from the meanings of three different cases which existed in the primitive form of the language:

1. A true **Ablative** case, denoting separation, or the place from which anything is taken.

2. An **Instrumental**, or **Sociative** case, denoting the instrument by means of which anything is done, or the accompanying circumstances of the action.

3. A **Locative** case, denoting the place where, or the time when anything happens.

The particular kind of meaning denoted by a noun standing **in** the Ablative case depends partly on the **meaning of the noun itself** and partly on the **meaning of the word with which it is connected**.

Thus in the sentence *Roma abiit*, He went from Rome, *Roma* is obviously used in the proper Ablative signification of separation from.

In the sentence *Baculo puerum percussit*, He struck the boy with a stick, *Baculo* is Instrumental.

In the sentence *Proximo anno rediit*, He returned next year, *anno* is Locative.

The student must always consider the **context** in which a word in the Ablative case is found before attempting to translate it.

The meanings of the case are so various, that it is not well to attach too definite a meaning to it in the mind.

In many instances, especially in late Latin, a preposition is placed before a noun in the Ablative case to make its meaning more precise.

45. The Ablative of Separation, generally translated '*from.*' In Classical Latin the Ablative is used without a preposition to denote motion from a place when the place spoken of is a town or small island.

The Ablative of certain words such as *domo* is used in the same way.

In Ecclesiastical Latin a preposition may be used with nouns of this kind; with all other nouns a preposition is used to denote motion from.

> Et alia die cum exirent a Bethania, esuriit. *And on another day when they came out from Bethany he was hungry.*   Mk. 11:12.
> See also Acts 18:1, 25:1.

46. The Ablative is used with verbs and adjectives denoting **separation, deprivation, release** or **want** and also with words denoting **descent** or **origin**.
In Ecclesiastical Latin a preposition is often used after such words.

> Qui veritate privati sunt. *Who are deprived of truth.*   1 Tim. 6:5.

47. The Instrumental Ablative and the Ablative of Attendant Circumstances, generally translated '*with.*'
The Ablative of the Instrument. The word that denotes the means by which anything is done is put in the Ablative without a preposition.

> Occidit autem Jacobum fratrem Johannis gladio. *But he killed James the brother of John with a sword.* Acts 12:2.

In the Vulgate the prepositions *a* or *in* are sometimes found before a word denoting the Instrument in imitation of Hebrew, or of Greek influenced by Hebrew

> Et commota sunt superliminaria cardinum a voce clamantis. *And the posts of the door were moved by the voice of him that cried.*   Isa. 6:4.
> Ego baptizo in aqua ... *I baptize with water...*   Jn. 1:26.
> Domine, si percutimus in gladio? *Lord, are we to strike with the sword?* Lk. 22:50.
> See also James 3:4.

48. The Ablative of Manner. The word which denotes the manner in which anything takes place is put in the Ablative, without a preposition if it is qualified by an adjective: if it is not qualified by an adjective, the preposition *cum* is used before it.

> At illi instabant vocibus magnis postulantes ut crucifigeretur. *But they were urgent with loud voices demanding that he should be crucified.* Lk. 23:23.
> Qui autem supra petrosa seminatus est, hic est qui verbum audit, et continuo cum gaudio accipit illud. *But he that was sown on the stony places, this is he who hears the word, and immediately with joy receives it.* Mt. 13:20.

The preposition is used in Ecclesiastical Latin even when the noun denoting manner is qualified by an adjective.

> Qui susceperunt verbum cum omni aviditate.... *For they received the word with all eagerness....*   Acts 17:11.

49. Verbs and adjectives denoting **filling** or **equipping** may be followed by a word in the Ablative denoting that with which the filling or equipping is done.
In the Vulgate such verbs and adjectives may be followed by a word in the Genitive in imitation of Greek

> O plene omni dolo, et omni fallacia.... *O full of all guile and all deceit....* Acts 13:10.
> Et impletae sunt nuptiae discumbentium. *And the wedding was furnished with guests.*   Mt. 22:10.
> Plenum gratiae et veritatis. *Full of grace and truth.* Jn. 1:14.

50. The Ablative of Price. The word which denotes the price at which anything is bought, sold or hired, is put in the Ablative case.

Quare hoc unguentum non veniit trecentis denariis? *Why was not this unguent sold for three hundred pence?*   Jn. 12:5.

See also Mk. 6:37; Acts 22:28.

51. The Ablative Absolute. A noun or pronoun in the Ablative case with a predicative participle, or adjective, or even another noun agreeing with it, is used to denote an incident that accompanies or explains the action of the verb on which it depends like an adverbial clause. This construction is very common in Latin, and is called the Ablative Absolute, because it is independent of, or loosed from (*absolutus*), the main structure of the sentence.

The Ablative in this construction is an Ablative of accompanying circumstances. A phrase of this kind is generally best translated into English by an Adverbial clause. The kind of Adverbial clause most suitable for the translation of any particular instance of this construction is determined by the context; generally speaking it will be either a clause of Time, a clause of Cause, or a clause of Concession. See sections 153, 156, 166.

The noun in the Ablative Absolute construction should not denote the same person or thing as the subject or object of the clause on which it depends.

This rule is however frequently violated in Ecclesiastical Latin

In English there is a similar construction which is called the Nominative Absolute.

It is seen in the following sentence:

This done, he went home.

In Latin this sentence would be:

Hoc facto domum abiit.

A closer parallel is seen in the colloquial use of a phrase beginning with *with*: "With things being so dear I shall never be able to manage it."

Examples of the Ablative Absolute:

1. Equivalent to a clause of **Time.**

Et ejecto daemone, locutus est mutus. *And when the devil was driven out, the dumb man spake.*   Mt. 9:33.

Et cum haec dixisset, videntibus illis, elevatus est. *And when he had said this, as they were looking on, he was taken up.*   Acts 1:9.

2. Equivalent to a clause of **Cause.**

In quo admirantur non concurrentibus vobis in eandem luxuriae confusionem. *In which they wonder, because you do not run with them into the same slough of debauchery.*   1 Pet. 4:4.

The following are examples of the ungrammatical use of the Ablative Absolute, where the noun in the Ablative refers to the same person as the object of the clause with which the Ablative Absolute is connected.

Et ascendente eo in naviculum, secuti sunt eum discipuli ejus. *And when he went up into a ship, his disciples followed him.*   Mt. 8:23.

Paulo autem volente intrare in populum, non permiserunt discipuli. *But when Paul wished to go in to the people, the disciples suffered him not.* Acts 19:30.

See also Mt. 8:34, 9:27; Acts 7:21, 10:19, 20:1.

Rarely a participle stands in the Ablative by itself in this sense:

Videntes autem Petri constantiam et Johannis, comperto quod homines essent sine litteris et idiotae... *But seeing the boldness of Peter and John, and finding out that they were unlettered and ordinary men. ...*   Acts 4:13.

The following is a very harsh example of an Ablative Absolute used to translate a Greek active participle agreeing with the subject of the main clause.

Quo statim cognito Jesus spiritu suo quia sic cogitarent intra se.

This is untranslatable as it stands. It is meant to translate the Greek καὶ εὐθέως ἐπιγνοὺς ὁ'Ἰησοῦς τῷ πνεύματι αὐτοῦ ὅτι οὕτως διαλογίζονται ἐν ἑαυτοῖς   Mk. 2:8.

52. Locative Ablative, or Ablative of Place or Time, generally translated '*in*' or '*at*.'

Ablative of Place. The Ablative case is used to denote the place in which, or the time at which anything happens.

In Ecclesiastical Latin it is often preceded by a preposition where one would not be used in Classical Latin

The way in which the place at which anything happens is expressed in Classical Latin is somewhat peculiar.

Generally speaking the preposition *in* is used followed by a noun in the Ablative case; but if the place spoken of is a town or small island the name of the town or small island is put in the so-called Locative case. This ends in *ae* in singular nouns of the 1st declension and in *i* in singular nouns of the 2nd declension. In the plural of these declensions, and in the 3rd declension, the ending of the Locative case is the same as the ending of the Ablative

Examples:

Romae, *At Rome.* Corinthi, *At Corinth.* Athenis, *At Athens.*

The Locative case is also found in the words *domi* at home: *rure* in the country: *foris* out of doors.

In Ecclesiastical Latin the Locative is sometimes found in the names of towns: sometimes *in* with the Ablative is used.

Erat autem quidam discipulus Damasci.... *But there was a certain disciple at Damascus....*   Acts 9:10.

Paulus autem, cum Athenis eos expectaret.... *But Paul, when he was waiting for them at Athens....*   Acts 17:16.

Et erat vir in Lystris infirmus pedibus.... *And there was a man in Lystra lame in his feet....*   Acts 14:7.

53. A kind of Locative Ablative is used to express **the thing in respect of which** a statement is made, especially in words denoting a part of the body or mind. This is sometimes called the Ablative of Respect.

Vir infirmus pedibus.... *A man lame in his feet....*   Acts 14:7.

Beati pauperes spiritu. *Blessed are the poor in spirit.* Mt. 5:3.

Fratres, nolite pueri effici sensibus: sed malitia parvuli estote. *Brethren, do not become children in sense: but in malice be ye babes.*   1 Cor. 14:20.

Sed ad sua desideria coacervabunt sibi magistros, prurientes auribus. *But at their desire they will heap up to themselves teachers: itching in the ears.*   2 Tim. 4:3.

Mattheum nomine. *Matthew by name.*   Mt. 9:9

See also Acts 7:51.

54. Ablative of Time. The time at which anything happens is denoted by the Ablative when the noun denotes a period of time.

In Ecclesiastical Latin a preposition may be used.

Quinta autem vigilia noctis venit ad eos, ambulans supra mare. *But in the fifth watch of the night he came to them, walking on the sea.*   Mt. 14:25.

In diebus autem illis venit Johannes Baptista, praedicans in deserto Judaeae. *But in those days John the Baptist came preaching in the desert of Judea.* Mt. 3:1.

55. The Ablative of nouns denoting a period of time may be used to denote the **time within which anything happens**.

This use is widely extended in the Vulgate to denote the time during which anything takes place, which is denoted in Classical Latin by the Accusative case.

Quadraginta et sex annis aedificatum est templum hoc, et tu tribus diebus excitabis illud? *Forty and six years was this temple in building, and wilt thou raise it up in three days?* Jn. 2:20.

Tanto tempore vobiscum sum? *Have I been so long with you?* Jn. 14:9.

Quid hic statis tota die otiosi? *Why stand ye here all the day idle?* Mt. 20:6.

Et erat tribus diebus non videns. *And he was three days without sight.* Acts 9:9.

56. The **Adjectival Ablative** or **Ablative of Description** describes a person or thing. The noun in the Ablative generally denotes a feature of the body or mind and is always qualified by an adjective.

Patres, nolite ad indignationem provocare filios vestros, ut non pusillo animo fiant. *Fathers, do not provoke your children to wrath, that they may not become of feeble mind.* Col. 3:21.

Beati mundo corde. *Blessed are the pure in heart.* Mt. 5:8.

57. Ablatives used with verbs. The Ablative is used after certain verbs which are not transitive in Latin as they are in English.

The commonest of these verbs are:

    utor, *I use.*
    fruor, *I enjoy.*
    fungor, *I perform.*
    potior, *I get possession of.*
    careo, *I am without.*
    egeo, indigeo, *I need.*

Ego autem nullo horum usus sum. *But I have used none of these things.* 1 Cor. 9:15.

Pro Christo ergo legatione fungimur. *We therefore perform the office of ambassador on behalf of Christ.* 2 Cor. 5:20.

Et civitas non eget sole neque luna, ut luceant in ea. *And the city needs not the sun or moon to shine in it.* Rev. 21:23.

Egeo is used with a Genitive in imitation of Greek in Rev. 3:17.

58. The adjectives *dignus* and *indignus* are generally followed by a noun in the Ablative

In the Vulgate they are sometimes followed by a noun in the Genitive in imitation of Greek

Dignus est operarius cibo suo. *The workman is worthy of his food.* Mt. 10:10.

Amplioris enim gloriae iste prae Mose dignus habitus est. *For he was thought worthy of more glory than Moses.* Heb. 3:3.

PRONOUNS

59. A **Pronoun** is a word used instead of a noun to point out or enumerate persons or things without naming them.

Many words classed as pronouns can be used as adjectives to define or point out nouns.

Personal and Reflexive pronouns can only be used in place of nouns. Possessive, Demonstrative, Relative, Interrogative and Indefinite pronouns can be used either in place of nouns or adjectivally.

When a pronoun can be used adjectivally it should be called an Adjectival Pronoun.

As a rule pronouns agree in gender and number with the noun in place of which they are used, but sometimes they agree only in sense with the noun and not with its grammatical number and gender.

Thus a plural pronoun may be used with reference to a collective noun, a neuter plural pronoun may be used with reference to two feminine nouns denoting things without life, a plural pronoun may be used with reference to a country because the thought is directed rather towards its inhabitants.

> Euntes ergo docete omnes gentes, baptizantes eos.... *Go therefore and teach all nations, baptizing them....*   Mt. 28:19.
>
> Possessiones et substantias vendebant, et dividebant illa omnibus.... *They sold their possessions and goods and divided them all....*   Acts 2:45.
>
> Et circumibat Jesus totam Galilaeam, docens in synagogis eorum. *Jesus went about all Galilee, teaching in their synagogues.*   Mt. 4:23.
>
> Sed habes pauca nomina in Sardis, qui non inquinaverunt vestimenta sua. *But thou hast a few names in Sardis, who have not defiled their garments.* Rev. 3:4.
>
> See also Rom. 9:24.

60. Personal Pronouns. As the ending of a Latin verb shows what person and number its subject is, the Nominative of personal pronouns is seldom used, except when special emphasis is desired.

> Nos audivimus ex lege quia Christus manet in aeternum; et quomodo tu dicis: Oportet exaltari filium hominis? *We have heard out of the law that Christ abideth for ever; and how sayest thou: "The Son of man must be lifted up"?*   Jn. 12:34.
>
> Ille erat lucerna ardens et lucens. Vos autem voluistis adhoram exultare in luce ejus. *He was a burning and a shining light. But you were willing for a season to rejoice in his light.* Jn. 5:35.

There are no personal pronouns of the third person in Latin except the Reflexive *se*. Demonstrative and Relative pronouns are used to take the place of the missing personal pronoun.

Ille, ipse, iste and *hic* are all used as personal pronouns of the third person in the Vulgate quite commonly, as well as *is.*

See Jn. 9:8, 12, 18, 21, 36; Lk. 9:9.

61. Reflexive Pronouns may be treated as a branch of personal pronouns. They are used when the subject of the verb is described as acting on himself, or in his own interest, or as saying or thinking something about himself.

In the first and second persons reflexive pronouns are identical in form with the oblique cases of the personal pronouns: in the third person both singular and plural the forms *se, sui, sibi, se* are used.

> Nihil feceris tibi mali. *Do thyself no harm.* Acts 16:28.

> Et abiens laqueo se suspendit. *And going away, he hanged himself.* Mt. 27:5.

When reflexive pronouns are used in a subordinate clause they sometimes refer to the person denoted by the subject of the main clause. This is seldom the case where any ambiguity is likely to be caused.

The use of reflexive pronouns is rather loose in Ecclesiastical Latin

> Et cadens in terra audivit vocem dicentem sibi.... *And falling to the earth he heard a voice saying to him....* Acts 9:4.

> Dispersit superbos mente cordis sui. *He hath scattered the proud in the imagination of their hearts.* Lk. 1:51.

> See also Acts 28:16; Mt. 7:11.

Rarely a demonstrative pronoun is used in the Vulgate where a reflexive pronoun would have been more correct.

> Exinde coepit Jesus ostendere discipulis suis, quia oporteret eum ire Hierosolymam.... *From that time Jesus began to show to his disciples that he must go to Jerusalem.* Mt. 16:21.

> See also Mk. 10:32; Rom. 3:26.

62. Possessive Pronouns are used adjectivally and are equivalent to the Genitive case of the personal or reflexive pronoun.

In the first and second persons the Genitive of the personal pronoun is rarely found in the sense of a possessive pronoun. Phil. 2:12.

In the third person *suus* is used reflexively, that is when the person or thing to which it refers is the subject of the sentence or clause in which it stands.

> Propterea ergo magis quaerebant eum Judaei interficere: quia non solum solvebat Sabbatum, sed et Patrem suum dicebat Deum. *On this account therefore the Jews sought the more to kill him, because he was not only breaking the Sabbath, but also because he said that God was his Father....* Jn. 5:18

When the person or thing referred to by the pronoun is not the subject of the sentence or clause in which it stands, the Genitive of a demonstrative pronoun (generally *ejus* or *eorum* etc.) is used as the possessive pronoun of the third person.

> Princeps autem sacerdotum Ananias praecepit adstantibus sibi percutere os ejus. *But the chief of the priests Ananias commanded those that stood by him to smite his mouth* (i.e. Paul's mouth). Acts 23:2.

Sometimes where no ambiguity is likely to be caused *suus* is used in a subordinate clause when the person or thing to which it refers is denoted by the subject of the main clause.

> Idem cum Johanne ad nonam horam ad templum adibat, ubi paralyticum sanitati reformavit suae. *He went with John to the temple at the ninth hour, where he restored the paralytic to his health.* Tertullian *de Oratione* xxv.

N.B. In Latin, as in French, the gender of a possessive pronoun does not depend on the gender of the word denoting the possessor; but possessive pronouns agree with the nouns which they qualify in gender, number and case, like adjectives.

> Sua mater, *His mother.* Suus pater, *Her father.*

63. Demonstrative Pronouns are used to point out some person or thing.

114

In Classical Latin *hic, haec, hoc* denotes that which is near to the speaker and is generally translated *this.*

Ille, illa, illud denotes that which is more remote, and is generally translated *that.*

I ste, ista, istud denotes that which belongs to the person spoken to; it is sometimes used contemptuously and translated *that of yours.*

Is, ea, id is an unemphatic word, generally used as a personal pronoun of the third person and translated *he, she, it.*

Ipse, ipsa, ipsum is emphatic, and may be translated *himself, herself, itself.*

It is often used in speaking of a famous person, and so it is often used of God and Christ in the Vulgate: it is used with other pronouns to give emphasis and also to show that they are reflexive. See examples below.

Idem, eadem, idem means *the same.*

64. In Ecclesiastical Latin the demonstrative pronouns are not strictly used in the senses given above: *iste* is often used where *hic* or *ille* would be used in Classical Latin

> Ipsi scitis: quoniam ad ea quae mihi opus erant, et his qui mecum sunt, ministraverunt manus istae. *Ye yourselves know that these hands have ministered to those things that were needful for me and for those that were with me.* Acts 20:34.

> Omnes vos scandalum patiemini in me in ista nocte. *All ye shall be caused to stumble because of me this night.* Mt. 26:31.

For an example of *hic* and *iste* used in exactly parallel senses:

> Vos ascendite ad diem festum hunc: ego non ascendo ad diem festum istum. *Go ye up to this feast: I go not up to this feast.* Jn. 7:8.

See also Rom. 11:30, 31.

Hic and *ille* are sometimes used to translate the Greek definite article. See Jn. 9:30: respondit ille homo (ὁ ἄνθρωπος). Ps. 112:2: ex hoc nunc (ἀπὸ τοῦ νῦν).

The following are examples of the use of *ipse.*

Emphatic use.

> Omnia per ipsum facta sunt. *All things were made through him.* Jn. 1: 3.

> Johannes testimonium perhibet de ipso. *John bears witness about him.* Jn. 1:15.

> Deus ipse Dominus; ipse fecit nos, et non ipsi nos. *God Himself is the Lord; He has made us, and not we ourselves.* Ps. 99:3.

> Ego scio eum, quia ab ipso sum, et ipse misit me. *I know him, because I am from him, and he sent me.* Jn. 7:29.

Reflexive use.

> Tu de te ipso testimonium perhibes. *Thou bearest witness of thyself.* Jn. 7:13, 28; Rom, 12:16.

Ipse is also used in the sense of *the same:*

> Ex ipso ore procedit benedictio et maledictio. *Out of the same mouth proceedeth blessing and cursing.* Jas. 3:10.

See also Heb 13:8.

Idipsum is used in the sense of *the same* to translate Greek τὸ αὐτό.

> Idipsum autcm latrones improperaverunt ei. *But the robbers cast the same reproach at him.* Mt. 27:44; 1 Cor. 1:10; Heb. 4:11.

In idipsum is used in the sense of *together* to translate Greek ἐπί τό αὐτό.

> Dominus autem augebat, qui salvi fierent quotidie in idipsum. *But the Lord increased daily those who should be saved into one body.* Acts 2:47.

> Et iterum revertimini in idipsum. *And come together again.* 1 Cor. 7:5.

Magnificate Dominum mecum: et exaltemus nomen ejus in idipsum. *O magnify the Lord with me: and let us exalt his name together.*   Ps. 33:4.

Hierusalem quae aedificatur ut civitas, cujus participatio ejus in idipsum. *Jerusalem which is built as a city that is at unity in itself.*   Ps. 121:3.

See also Pss. 61:10, 73:6.

65. The Relative Pronoun is used like a conjunction to connect two clauses in a sentence: the second of the two connected clauses may be either subordinate to, or co-ordinate with the first.

The relative pronoun always refers back to some noun or pronoun (expressed or implied) in the clause which it connects to the clause in which it stands. This noun or pronoun is called its Antecedent. In Latin, relative pronouns agree with their antecedent in gender, number and person, but **not** in case.

The **case** of a relative pronoun depends on the **function** which it performs in the clause in which it stands.

The relative pronoun can never be omitted in Latin as it often is in English. Examples:

Accepistis illud...sicut verbum Dei, qui operatur in vobis, qui credidistis. *You received it...as the word of God who works in you who believe.*   1 Thess. 2:13.

Discedite a me, qui operamini iniquitatem. *Depart from me ye that work iniquity.*   Mt. 7:23.

66. A relative pronoun often stands at the beginning of a sentence and must then be translated into English by *and* followed by a personal pronoun[1].

It is often used in the Vulgate to translate the Greek ὁ δέ.

Qui cum recedissent, ecce angelus Domini apparuit in somnis Joseph...qui consurgens accepit puerum. *And when they had departed, behold an angel of the Lord appeared to Joseph in a dream...and he arose and took the child.*   Matt. 2:13.

Quorum fidem ut videt, dixit.... *And when he saw their faith, he said....*   Lk. 5:20.

A very harsh example is found in Acts 17:11:

Hi autem erant nobiliores eorum qui sunt Thessalonicae, qui susceperunt verbum cum omni aviditate.... *But these were more noble than those who are at Thessalonica, for they received the word with all eagerness....*

See also Mt. 15:23; Jn. 1:38; Acts 7:2.

67. Attraction of the Antecedent. The antecedent may be attracted into the case of the relative and at the same time be placed in the relative clause. When this happens a personal pronoun in the right case may take the place of the antecedent in the clause to which it properly belongs.

Quem ego decollavi Johannem, hic a mortuis resurrexit. *John whom I beheaded is risen from the dead.* Mk. 6:16.

Omne verbum otiosum quod locuti fuerint homines, reddent rationem de eo in die judicii. *Every idle word that men shall speak, they shall give account thereof in the day of judgment.*   Mt. 12:36.

See also Mt. 21:42: Dan. 4:17.

---

1 An unsuccessful attempt to introduce this construction into English is to be noted in several places in the A.V., especially in Acts. See Acts 14:14.

An example of inverse attraction, that is of the relative being attracted into the case of the antecedent, is found in Ps. 9:23: *Comprehenduntur in consiliis quibus cogitant.*

68. A Demonstrative Pronoun in the same number, gender and case as the relative pronoun may be inserted in a relative clause in imitation of the Hebrew The Hebrew relative אֲשֶׁר is invariable in form and has a personal pronoun in apposition to it to show its relationship to the sentence.

> Beatus vir, cujus est nomen Domini spes ejus.... *Blessed is the man whose hope is in the name of the Lord....* Ps. 39:5.

> Quem Dominus Jesus interficiet spiritu oris sui, et destruet illustratione adventus sui eum. *Whom the Lord Jesus will slay with the breath of his mouth, and destroy with the brightness of his coming.* 2 Thess. 2:8.

> See also Pss. 18:4, 32:12, 73:2, 145:5.

69. The Interrogative Pronoun *quis* may take the place of either a noun or an adjective.

When it is a true pronoun it has the form *quis (qui), quae, quid.*

When it is a pronominal adjective it has the form *qui (quis), quae, quod.*

In the Vulgate it may be used in place of the Interrogative *uter* = which of two.

> Quem vultis vobis de duobus demitti? *Which of the two do ye wish to be released for you?* Mt. 27:21.

> See also Mt. 9:5, 21:31; 1 Cor. 4:21; Lucan, *Pharsalia* i, 126. *Quid* may be used like the Greek τί to ask a question.

> Quid hic statis tota die otiosi? *Why do ye stand here idle all the day?* Mt. 20:6.

Ut quid is used to translate the Greek ἵνα τί or εἰς τί.

> Ut quid enim libertas mea judicatur ab aliena conscientia? *For why is my liberty judged of another man's conscience?* 1 Cor. 10:29.

> See also Mt. 9:4, 26:8.

69a. The Indefinite Pronoun *quis, quae* or *qua, quid* may be used to take the place of either a noun or an adjective.

It is used by itself in the Vulgate to translate the Greek τις.

> Infirmatur quis in vobis? *Is any among you sick?* Jas. 5:14.

> See also Acts 10:47, 26:31; Rom. 5:7; 1 Cor. 4:2.

The Relative pronoun is used instead of the Indefinite *quisquis* in imitation of Greek ὅς ἄν.

> Qui ergo solverit unum de mandatis istis minimis, et docuerit sic homines, minimus vocabitur in regno caelorum. *Whosoever shall break one of these least commandments and shall teach men so, shall be called least in the kingdom of heaven.* Mt. 5:19.

Ne alicui is used Lk. 8:56 instead of the usual *ut nulli.*

70. The Reciprocal Pronoun which is expressed in English by *one another,* and in Classical Latin by *alius alium, alter alterum, inter se* is generally expressed in the Vulgate by *invicem* which is treated as an indeclinable pronoun.

It may also be expressed by *alterutrum.*

> Estote autem invicem benigni, misericordes, donantes invicem. *But be ye kind to one another, pitiful, forgiving one another.* Eph. 4:32.

> Nolite murmurare in invicem. *Do not murmur one to another.* Jn. 6:43.

> Orate pro invicem. *Pray for one another.* Jas. 5:16.

Non ergo amplius invicem judicemus. *Let us not therefore judge one another any longer.* Rom. 14:13.

See also Jn. 13:35, 15:17; Acts 15:39; Rom. 12:16, 16:16.

Confitemini ergo alterutrum peccata vestra. *Confess your sins one to another.* Jas. 5:16.

Dicebant ad alterutrum. *They were saying one to another.* Mk. 4:40.

Id ipsum sapere in alterutrum. *To think the same thing one with another.* Rom. 15:5.

See also Mk. 4:40; Acts 7:26.

71. *Hujusmodi* and *ejusmodi* are used in the Vulgate with an ellipse of the noun which they should qualify, which makes them almost equivalent to a pronoun.

Hujusmodi enim Christo Domino nostro non serviunt. *For such men do not serve Christ our Lord.* Rom. 16:18.

Pro hujusmodi gloriabor.... *For such a one will I glory....* 2 Cor. 12:5.

Adversus hujusmodi non est lex. *Against such there is no law.* Gal. 5:23.

See also Jn. 8:5; Acts 22:22; Rom 16:18; 1 Cor. 7:28.

VERBS

Mood

72. Moods are forms which verbs assume to show the way in which the action or state denoted by the verb is to be regarded, i.e., if it is to be regarded as a statement, a command, a desire, or a thought.

The **Indicative** Mood (generally) makes a statement or asks a direct question.

The **Imperative** Mood gives a command, or expresses a wish.

The **Subjunctive** Mood expresses a thought rather than a fact.

It is used to give a command or express a wish directly in the third person and is often used in prohibitions and in hesitating or polite statements or wishes.

It is generally used in indirect commands and questions and in many kinds of subordinate clauses, especially those that express purpose or result.

The uses of the Subjunctive are so various and its use in Latin is often so different from its use in English, that it is inadvisable to learn any English equivalent for it such as *I may love*, or *I might love*.

Very often it is translated by the English Indicative. The student must learn to translate it by observing its use in Latin.

The **Infinitive** Mood is really the dative or locative case of a verbal noun. It gets its name, which means "un-bounded," from the fact that it is not bounded like other parts of the verb by number and person.

The **Participle** is a verbal adjective.

The **Gerund** and **Supine** are verbal nouns.

Tense

73. The action denoted by a verb may be defined both as regards its **time** and as regards its **state** or progress.

Its time may be defined as past, present, or future.

Its state or progress may be regarded as

continuous or incomplete,

perfect or complete,
simple or indefinite.

The combination of these ideas of time and state should produce nine different tenses.

Past continuous *I was loving.*   Present continuous *I am loving.*

Past perfect *I had loved.*   Present perfect *I have loved.*

Past simple *I loved.*   Present simple *I love.*

Future continuous *I shall be loving.*
Future perfect *I shall have loved.*
Future simple *I shall love.*

Different forms to express all these combinations exist in English, but not in Latin.

The Latin tenses are arranged below in the same order as the English tenses in the table above. The names commonly given to them in grammars are printed in capitals.

IMPERFECT *amabam.*   (missing)

PLUPERFECT *amaveram.*   PERFECT *amavi.*

PERFECT *amavi.*   PRESENT *amo.*

(missing)
FUTURE PERFECT *amavero.*
FUTURE *amabo.*

It should be noticed that the tense called the Perfect in Latin has to do the work of two dissimilar tenses:—the Past Simple and the Present Perfect.

If continuous action in present or future time has to be expressed in Classical Latin the Simple Present or Future must be used.

In Ecclesiastical Latin we see the development of tenses formed by a participle and part of the verb *esse* which are very similar in meaning and form to the English Present Continuous and Future Continuous. See section 90.

74. The Present tense denotes either an action or state in progress in present time, or customary or repeated action in present time.

Filius hominis traditur in manus peccatorum. *The Son of man is being betrayed into the hands of sinners.*   Mt. 26:45.

Domine, salva nos, perimus. *Lord, save us, we are perishing.* Mt. 8:25.

Lampades nostrae extinguuntur. *Our lamps are going out.*   Mt. 25:8.

Corrumpunt mores bonos conloquia mala. *Evil communications corrupt good manners.*   1 Cor. 15:33.

Omnis arbor, quae non facit fructum bonum, exciditur et in ignem mittitur. *Every tree that bringeth not forth good fruit is hewn down and cast into the fire.*   Mt. 7:19.

See also Mt. 9:17.

75. Conative Present. As the Present tense denotes action in progress which is not necessarily complete, it may be used to denote action which is attempted or desired, but not performed.

Multa bona opera ostendi vobis ex Patre meo: propter quod eorum opus me lapidatis? *I have shown you many good works from my Father: because of which of these do ye desire to stone me?* Jn. 10:32.

Evacuati estis a Christo, qui in lege justificamini; a gratia excidistis. *Ye are separated from Christ, ye who desire to be justified by the law: ye have fallen from grace.* Gal. 5:4.

See also 1 Cor. 7:28.

76. Historic Present. The Present tense is used in narrative to denote events in past time for the sake of vividness.

Et veniunt rursus Hierosolyma. *And they come again to Jerusalem.* Mk. 11:27.

77. The Present used for the Future. The Present is sometimes used colloquially in a Future sense.

Tempus meum prope est: apud te facio Pascha cum discipulis meis. *My time is at hand: I will eat the Passover at thy house with my disciples.* Mt. 26:18.

Descendat nunc de cruce, et credimus ei. *Let him now come down from the cross, and we will believe him.* Mt. 27:42.

See also Lk. 19:8; Jn. 21:23.

78. The Present of ἔρχεσθαι which is used in a Future sense in the New Testament with reference to the Messiah, especially in the participle, is sometimes translated by the Future in the Vulgate or even by the Perfect. It may also be translated by a Present.

See Mt. 11:3; Jn. 6:14, 11:27, 14:3.

A very curious use of the Present among several Futures is found in Acts 28:6. There is nothing to suggest it in the Greek

79. The Imperfect tense denotes an action or state in progress in past time, or customary or repeated action in past time.

The Imperfect is a descriptive tense and denotes an action in progress or a state of things actually observed. Hence in many instances it does not differ in meaning from the Perfect. This is especially the case with the verb *esse*:

Dux erat and *Dux fuit* may mean practically the same thing, the former describes the condition, the latter only states it.

Et multi divites jactabant multa. *And many rich men were casting in much.* Mk. 12:41.

Ecce quomodo amabat eum. *Behold how much he loved him.* Jn. 11:36.

Petrus autem et Johannes ascendebant in templum ad horam orationis nonam. *But Peter and John used to go up to the temple at the hour of prayer, the ninth hour.* Acts 3:1.

In Acts 12:4–7 there are several examples of the use of the Imperfect tense and the contrasted use of the Perfect tense.

See also Mt. 8:2; Lk. 3:10, 15:16, Eph. 4:28.

80. Conative Imperfect. The Imperfect is sometimes used to denote an action in past time which was attempted or desired, but not performed.

Et vocabant eum nomine patris ejus Zachariam. *And they wished to call him by the name of his father Zacharias.* Lk. 1:59.

See Acts 7:26, 26:2.

81. The Imperfect is also used to express a **polite** or **hesitating wish** which the speaker does not like to express directly.

Volebam et ipse hominem audire. *I should like to hear the man myself.* Acts 25:22.

Optabam enim ipse ego anathema esse a Christo pro fratribus meis. *I could wish myself accursed from Christ for the sake of my brethren.* Rom. 9:3.

82. The Future tense denotes an action or state which is expected to take place in future time.

The context decides whether the action denoted by the verb is simple or continuous.

Pariet autem filium: et vocabis nomen ejus Jesum. *For she shall bring forth a son: and thou shalt call his name Jesus.* Mt. 1:21.

Et in hoc gaudeo, sed et gaudebo. *And in this I rejoice, yea I will continue to rejoice.* Phil. 1:18.

83. The Future may have the force of an **Imperative**.

Relinque ibi munus tuum ante altare, et vade, prius reconciliare fratri tuo: et tunc veniens offeres munus tuum. *Leave there thy gift before the altar, and go first and be reconciled to thy brother, and then come and offer thy gift.* Mt. 5:24.

Et cum oratis, non eritis sicut hypocritae. *And when ye pray, be not as the hypocrites.* Mt. 6:5.

See also Mk. 12:31.

84. The Perfect tense in Latin performs the functions of two tenses which are quite distinct in English and Greek. These are the tenses which are commonly called the **Past Simple** (or Preterite) and the **Perfect** (or Present Perfect) in English, and the **Aorist** and **Perfect** in Greek.

The translation of the tenses in the Vulgate is generally very careful: the Imperfect represents the Greek Imperfect and the Perfect the Greek Aorist or Perfect in the Indicative mood.

The Aorist is used in Greek far more frequently than the Perfect. The Perfect in Greek denotes completed action. The Aorist Indicative generally denotes action in past time, but must often be translated into English by the form which is called the Perfect (the tense form made with the auxiliary verb *have*).

It would be impossible and confusing to go into the reasons for this here. Those who wish for further information on the point will find it in the author's *Syntax of New Testament Greek.*

The point to be remembered by the Latin student is that the Latin Perfect may be translated by either the English Past Simple or by the Perfect.

The most suitable form to use is decided by the context in all cases. The Greek original is not a safe guide.

Example of the Latin Perfect denoting simple action in past time.

Et veniens ad discipulos suos, vidit turbam magnam circa eos. *And when he came to his disciples he saw a great crowd round them.* Mk. 9:14.

Examples of the Latin Perfect denoting that the action of the verb is regarded as complete[2] at the time of speaking, and that its results are regarded as still existing.

---

2 When it is said that the action is regarded as *complete* this does not mean that it is regarded as ended, but only that it is regarded as brought to its appropriate conclusion in such a way that its effects still remain in action. The tense when used in this sense has as much to do with present as with past time, as it describes the present result of a past action. It may sometimes be translated by an English Present.

Bonum certamen certavi, cursum consummavi, fidem servavi. *I have fought the good fight, I have finished the course, I have kept the faith.* 2 Tim. 4:7.

Sed potius ite ad oves quae perierunt domus Israel. *But rather go to the sheep that have perished (or the lost sheep) of the house of Israel.* Mt. 10:6.

Omnium autem finis appropinquavit. *But the end of all things is at hand.* 1 Pet. 4:7.

85. The Perfect is used to translate the **Greek Timeless Aorist** and expresses a general truth, an habitual action, or action at a time not defined. When so used it must be translated by the Present tense in English.

Exortus est enim sol cum ardore, et arefecit faenum, et flos ejus decidit, et decor vultus ejus deperiit. *For the sun arises with its burning heat, and dries up the grass, and its flower falls, and the beauty of its shape perishes.* Jas. 1:2.

See also 1 Pet. 1:24 and the curious imitation of the Greek in Wordsworth and White's text in Jn. 15:6.

Tu es filius meus dilectus, in te complacui. *Thou art my beloved son, in thee I am well pleased.* Mk. 1:11.

Calendas vestras, et sollemnitates vestras, odivit anima mea: facta sunt mihi molesta, laboravi sustinens. *Your festivals and feasts my soul hateth: they are a trouble to me, I am weary to bear them.* Isa. 1:14.

86. The Pluperfect tense denotes an action or state completed in past time, or an action which took place before some point in past time referred to in the context, or which the speaker has in mind.

Et descendit pluvia, et venerunt flumina, et flaverunt venti, et irruerunt in domum illam, et non cecidit: fundata enim erat super petram. *And the rain descended, and the floods came, and the winds blew, and they fell upon that house, and it fell not: for it had been founded upon a rock.* Mt. 7:25.

Venit enim filius hominis salvare quod perierat. *For the Son of man came to save that which had been lost.* Mt. 18:11.

The force of the Perfect, Pluperfect and Imperfect tenses is seen in the following example:

Et vidit duas naves stantes secus stagnum: piscatores autem descenderant, et lavabant retia. *And he saw two ships standing by the lake: for the fishermen had come down out of them, and were washing their nets.* Lk. 5:2.

87. The Future Perfect tense denotes an action or state which is regarded as completed at some point in future time which the speaker has in mind or which is referred to in the context.

It is used very frequently in Latin where in English we use a Simple Future, a Present, or a Perfect.

His autem expletis, proposuit Paulus in Spiritu, transita Macedonia et Achaia, ire Hierosolymam, dicens: Quoniam postquam fuero ibi, oportet me et Romam videre. *When this was ended Paul purposed in the Spirit, after he had passed through Macedonia and Achaia, to go to Jerusalem, saying: "After I have been there I must also see Rome."* Acts 19:21.

Nisi abundaverit justitia vestra plus quam Scribarum et Pharisaeorum, non intrabitis in regnum caelorum. *Unless your righteousness exceed that of the Scribes and Pharisees, ye shall not enter into the kingdom of heaven.* Mt. 5:20.

Si fuerint alicui centum oves, et erraverit una ex eis, nonne relinquet nonaginta novem in montibus...? *If any man has a hundred sheep and one of them goes astray, does he not leave the ninety and nine in the mountains...?.* Mt. 18:12.

88. It is used in **indefinite relative clauses** and in **indefinite clauses of time and place,** referring to future time. See sections 154, 155.

Et in quamcumque domum intraveritis, ibi manete, et inde ne exeatis. *And into whatever house ye enter, there remain, and go not forth from thence.* Lk. 9:4.

Qui enim voluerit animam suam salvam facere, perdet illam: nam qui perdiderit animam suam propter me, salvam faciet illam. *For whoso wishes to save his soul shall lose it: but whoso shall lose his soul for my sake shall save it.* Lk. 9:24.

Et beatus est qui non fuerit scandalizatus in me. *And blessed is he who is not offended in me.* Mt. 11:6.

See also Mt. 26:13; Rom. 15:24.

89. It is also used like the Future with the force of an **Imperative**. Nihil tuleritis in via. *Take nothing for the way.* Lk. 9:3.

See also Mt. 27:4; Acts 18:15.

90. Periphrastic forms of tenses are formed in Ecclesiastical Latin as in English, by joining the appropriate tense of *esse* to the present participle.

Periphrastic Present formed from the Present tense of *esse* and the Present Participle.

Non enim sumus sicut plurimi adulterantes verbum Dei. *For we are not as many adulterating the word of God.* 2 Cor. 2:17.

Esto consentiens adversario tuo cito dum es in via cum eo. *Agree with thine adversary quickly while thou art in the way with him.* Mt. 5:25.

Periphrastic Imperfect.

Et erat plebs expectans Zachariam. *And the people was expecting Zacharias.* Lk. 1:21.

Et erat tribus diebus non videns, et non manducavit neque bibit. *And he was three days without sight, and did neither eat nor drink.* Acts 9:9.

Periphrastic Future.

Noli timere: ex hoc jam homines eris capiens. *Fear not: from henceforth thou shalt be catching men.* Lk. 5:10.

91. A Future tense is also formed from the **Future Participle** of *esse* with a clause introduced by *ut* as its subject.

Futurum est enim ut Herodes quaerat puerum ad perdendum eum. *For Herod will seek the young child to destroy him.* Mt. 2:13.

A Future Subjunctive is formed from the Future Participle and the Present Subjunctive of *esse*.

Nolite putare quia ego accusaturus sim vos apud Patrem. *Do not think that I shall accuse you to the Father.* Jn. 5:45.

92. Periphrastic tenses formed with *habere* and *facere*.

The beginning of the periphrastic formation of tenses which resulted in the forms now used for the **Future** tenses in French and Italian is to be discerned in Ecclesiastical Latin

The use began in the employment of the verb *habere* in its ordinary sense with an explanatory Infinitive. This is found in the Classics.

Adhuc multa habeo vobis dicere. *I have yet many things to say to you.* Jn. 16:12.

Quia non habent retribuere tibi. *Because they have not (anything) whence to pay you back.* Lk. 14:14.

Hence arises a sense of future necessity:

Baptismo autem habeo baptizari. *But I have a baptism with which I must be baptised.*   Lk. 12:50.

Habes, homo, imprimis aetatem venerare aquarum, quod antiqua substantia. *First, O man, you must venerate the age of water; because it is an ancient substance.*   Tertullian *de Bapt. 3.*

Aquas video quas videbam quotidie: istae me habent mundare in quas saepe descendi, et nunquam sanatus sum. *I see water which I was used to see every day: it has got to cleanse me, though I have often gone down into it, and I have never been cleansed.* Ambrose, *de Mysteriis,* IV, 19.

93. *Habere* is also found as an auxiliary verb with a **past participle**—a construction which became the normal way of expressing the pluperfect tense in Italian and French.[3]

Tantum autem auditum habebant.... *Only they had heard....* Gal. 1:23.

94. The Infinitive is used with the verb *facere* in the sense of **causation.**

Et adduxerunt asinam et pullum, et imposuerunt super eos vestimenta sua, et eum desuper sedere fecerunt. *And they brought the ass and the colt and put on them their clothes, and they made him sit thereon.* Mt. 21:7.

95.. **The sequence of tenses**. The Present, Future, Future Perfect and Perfect (when translated by the English Perfect formed with the auxiliary *have*) are called **Primary** tenses.

The Imperfect, Pluperfect and Perfect (when translated by the English Past) are called **Secondary** tenses.

When the verb in a principal clause is in a Primary tense, a verb in the Subjunctive mood in a subordinate clause is in a Primary tense in certain kinds of clauses.

When the verb in a principal clause is in a Secondary tense, a verb in the Subjunctive mood in a subordinate clause is in a Secondary tense in certain kinds of clauses. This rule is not strictly observed in Ecclesiastical Latin

VOICE

96. The **Active** voice is used when the subject of the verb is spoken of as acting or doing something.

The **Passive** voice is used when the subject of the verb is spoken of as suffering or being acted upon. Only Transitive verbs can have a passive voice.

There are certain verbs such as *to fall* and *to die* which do not speak of the subject as acting, but which are regarded as being in the active voice because they are Intransitive.

---

3 Compare "De numero eorum omnia se habere explorata," Caesar, *B.G.*, 2. 4. 1.

97. Certain verbs in Latin are passive in form, but active in meaning. These are called **Deponent** verbs because the old grammarians thought that they had laid aside a passive and assumed an active meaning.

A few verbs such as *gaudeo, -ere, gavisus sum* have the deponent form only in the Perfect, Pluperfect and Future Perfect tenses. These are called Semi-deponent verbs.

THE IMPERATIVE AND SUBJUNCTIVE MOODS IN PRINCIPAL CLAUSES

98. The Imperative Mood is used to express commands and entreaties in the second person singular or plural, and has forms which may be used to express a command given in the third person.

> Sed, si quid potes, adjuva nos. *But, if thou canst do anything, help us.* Mk. 9:22.

> Dixit ergo Jesus: Facite homines discumbere. *Therefore Jesus said: Make the men sit down.* Jn. 6:10.

In Ecclesiastical Latin the second person of the Present Subjunctive is used to express a command or entreaty.

> Nec doleas, quod talem amiseris, sed gaudeas, quod talem habueris. *Do not grieve because you have lost such a man, but rejoice because you had him.* Jerome, *Ep. 60.*

The Present Subjunctive is generally used to express a command or entreaty in the first or third person. This use of the Subjunctive is called the **Jussive Subjunctive**.

> Nam Deus dixit: Honora patrem et matrem; et: Qui maledixerit patri vel matri morte moriatur. *For God said: Honour thy father and mother; and: If any curse his father or his mother, let him surely die.* Mt. 15:4.
> Sometimes *sine* or *sinite = allow* is prefixed to the Subjunctive.

> Sine ejiciam festucam de oculo tuo. *Let me cast out the mote out of thine eye.* Mt. 7:4.

99. Prohibitions are negative commands or entreaties. The Imperative is not used in prohibitions, except in poetry.

Prohibitions are expressed in prose:

(1) By *noli* or *nolite* followed by an Infinitive.

(2) By *ne* (or *non* in Ecclesiastical Latin) followed by the Perfect Subjunctive.

(3) By *ne* or *non* followed by the Present Subjunctive.

(4) By *vide* followed by a negative and the Present or Perfect Subjunctive.

The first two methods are regularly used in Classical prose. The last two are often found in Ecclesiastical Latin

(1) Noli vexare illum. *Trouble him not.* Lk. 8:49.

> Nolite dare sanctum canibus, neque mittatis margaritas vestras ante porcos. *Do not give that which is holy to the dogs, and do not cast your pearls before swine.* Mt. 7:6.

(2) In viam gentium ne abieritis, et in civitates Samaritanorum ne intraveritis. *Go not into the way of the Gentiles, and into the cities of the Samaritans enter ye not.* Mt. 10:5.

> Nihil feceris tibi mali. *Do thyself no harm.* Acts 16:28.

(3) Nec vocemini magistri. *Be not ye called masters.* Mt. 23:10.

Non mireris quia dixi tibi: Oportet vos nasci denuo. *Marvel not that I said to thee: Ye must be born again.* Jn. 3:7.

Qui furabatur, jam non furetur, magis autem laboret. *Let him that stole steal no more, but rather let him labour.* Eph. 4:28.

(4) Videte ne contemnatis unum ex his pusillis. *See that ye despise not one of these little ones.* Mt. 18:10.

Vide nemini dixeris. *See thou tell no man.* Mt. 8:4.

100. An emphatic and absolute prohibition may be expressed by *omnis* and a verb in the Present Subjunctive negatived by *non* in imitation of Hebrew

Omnis sermo malus ex ore vestro non procedat. *Let no corrupt speech proceed out of your mouth.* Eph. 4:29.

101. Hortatory Subjunctive. Besides expressing commands the Subjunctive may express an exhortation or a wish.

Transeamus usque Bethleem, et videamus hoc verbum quod factum est. *Let us go to Bethlehem and see this thing which has come to pass.* Lk. 2:15.

In expressing a wish the Present Subjunctive denotes that the wish is **still possible**, the Imperfect Subjunctive or Pluperfect Subjunctive that it is **unaccomplished in present time**, or in certain cases that it is **impossible**. *Utinam* is often used before the Past tenses of the Subjunctive when they express an unaccomplished wish.

Sanctificetur nomen tuum: adveniat regnum tuum. *Hallowed be thy name: thy kingdom come.* Mt. 6:9.

Utinam fuisset dominus meus ad prophetam, qui est in Samaria. *Would that my master were with the prophet who is in Samaria.* 2 Kings 5:2.

Utinam frigidus esses aut calidus. *Would that thou wert cold or hot.* Rev. 3:15; 1 Cor. 4:8.

102. Deliberative Subjunctive. In Classical Latin the Subjunctive is used in deliberative questions when a person asks himself or another what he is to do.

In Ecclesiastical Latin the Future or the Present Indicative is also often used in this sense.

Subj. Euntes emamus denariis ducentis panes? *Are we to go and buy two hundred pennyworth of bread?* Mk. 6:37.

Fut. Quid faciemus et nos? *What shall we do?* Lk. 3:14.

*Pres. Ind*icative. Tu es qui venturus es, an alium expectamus? *Art thou he that should come, or are we to look for another?* Mt. 11:3.

103. Potential Subjunctive. The Subjunctive is used to express an action which is not regarded as actual, but only as possible or conceivable. Expressions of this kind may be regarded as the apodoses[4] of conditional sentences where the condition is not expressed. The Subjunctive is rarely used in this sense in the Vulgate

Profecto curasset eum a lepra, quam habet. *Surely he would cure him of the leprosy which he has.* 2 Kings 5:2.

Vix enim pro justo quis moritur: nam pro bono forsitan quis audeat mori. *For scarcely for a just man does one die, but perhaps for a good man one would dare to die.* Rom. 5:7.

---

4 See section 167.

Vellem autem esse apud vos modo, et mutare vocem meam. *But I should like to be among you now and to change my tone.* Gal. 4:20.
See also Mt. 25:27.

The above uses of the Subjunctive are the only ones which occur in independent sentences and principal clauses.

NOUN CLAUSES

THE IMPORTANCE OF DISTINGUISHING BETWEEN DIFFERENT SENSES OF THE SAME WORD

104. Many of the difficulties that beginners find in mastering a foreign language arise from the fact that they do not consider the meaning of some of the words that most frequently occur, but look only at their form.

Some of these words which are in common use are employed in several totally different senses.

Take for example the English word *that*. It may be

(1) A Demonstrative Pronoun or Adjective trans. by the Latin *ille*, etc.

Give me that. *Da mihi illud.*

I see that woman. *Illam mulierem video.*

(2) A Relative Pronoun trans. by Latin *qui*, etc.

I have the book that you bought. *Librum, quem emisti, habeo.*

I see the man that sent for me. *Virum, qui me arcessivit, video.*

(3) A Conjunction introducing a clause of purpose trans. by Latin *ut*.

I came that I might see you. *Ut te viderem, veni.*

(4) A Conjunction introducing a clause of consequence trans. by Latin *ut* or *ita ut*.

The storm was so great that the ship was wrecked. *Tanta erat procella, ut navis demergeretur.*

(5) A Conjunction introducing a noun clause which is trans. either by the Accusative and Infinitive construction, or by a clause introduced by *ut*, or in Ecclesiastical Latin by *quod, quia* or *quoniam*.

He said that my brother had come. *Fratrem meum venisse dixit.*

It is expedient that I should do this. *Expedit ut hoc faciam.*

He prayed that the Lord would send labourers into the harvest. *Rogavit ut Dominus operarios in messem ejiceret.*

We know that you speak the truth. *Scimus quia vera dicis.*

The constructions mentioned in sub-section 5 are explained in the following pages. The object of the above paragraph is to warn the student not to confuse the noun clauses, now to be described, with the adverbial clauses described in sections 157–165.

As the English word *that* is used in so many entirely distinct senses, it is obviously most essential to be certain of its meaning before trying to translate it into Latin.

Take for example the sentences:

I know that that that that man says is true. *Vera esse scio ea, quae ille dicat.*

He told me that he went to Rome that he might see Caesar. *Dixit mihi se Romam adivisse, ut Caesarem videret.*

The great difference between English and Latin is obvious from these examples.

105. While this question of words with similar forms having widely different meanings is being discussed, it will be well to refer to the Latin words which present a similar difficulty.

These are *ut, cum, quod*.

Ut when it introduces a clause with the verb in the **Indicative** mood means either *as, when* or *where* according to the context.

The clause that it introduces is either a clause of comparison, a clause of time, or a clause of place. See sections 153–155, 175.

When *ut* introduces a clause with the verb in the **Subjunctive** mood the clause may be:

      (1) A clause of purpose. See sections 157, 158.

      (2) A clause of consequence. See section 163.

      (3) A noun clause. See sections 116–127, 142, 145.

In all these cases *ut* is translated by *that* in English.

Example:

      Et factum est ut discesserunt ab eis angeli in caelum, pastores loque-bantur ad invicem.... *And it came to pass when the angels were gone away from them into heaven, the shepherds were saying one to another....*
Lk. 2:15.

In the following example *ut* is first used to introduce a clause of purpose and secondly a clause of comparison.

      Non ut confundam vos haec scribo, sed ut filios meos carissimos mo-neo. *I do not write these things that I may confound you, but as my beloved sons I warn you.* 1 Cor. 4:14.

In the following example *ut* is used first to introduce a noun clause, in the second place to introduce a clause of consequence, in the third place to introduce a clause of comparison.

      Orantes simul et pro nobis, ut Deus aperiat nobis ostium sermonis ad loquendum mysterium Christi, propter quod etiam vinctus sum, ut man-ifestem illud ita ut oportet me loqui. *Praying at the same time for us also, that God would open to us a door of utterance to speak the mystery of Christ, for which also I am bound, that I may make it manifest as I ought to speak.* Col. 4:3.

Cum may be either a preposition meaning *together with* or a conjunction introducing a clause of time, a clause of cause, or a clause of concession and trans. *when, since, although.* See sections 153, 154, 156, 166, 210.

In old Latin books *cum* when used as a conjunction is generally spelt *quum*. In books recently printed it is spelt *cum* or *quom*.

Quod may be either the neuter singular of the relative pronoun or a conjunction introducing a clause of cause and trans. *because*, or (in Ecclesiastical and late Latin only) a conjunction introducing a noun clause. See section 156. A careful study of the context is often needed to find out whether *quod* is a relative pronoun or a conjunction.

THE INFINITIVE MOOD AND ITS EQUIVALENTS

106. The so-called **Infinitive Mood** had its origin in the Dative or Locative case of a verbal noun. *Habere* meant originally *for having* or *in having*. In early Latin the Dative sense of the Infinitive was still obvious, for it was used to express purpose.

      Reddere hoc, non perdere, erus me misit. *My master sent me to return (for returning) this, not to lose it.* Plautus, *Ps.* 642.

Nec dulces occurrent oscula nati
Praeripere. *Nor will your sweet children run to you to snatch your kisses.* Lucretius III, 895.

This usage apparently held its ground in vernacular Latin, and appears occasionally in the Augustan poets who would be encouraged to use it by the analogy of the use of the Infinitive in Greek to express purpose.

Nos numerus sumus, et fruges consumere nati. *We are a mere collection of nonentities, born to devour the fruits of the earth.* Horace, *Ep.* I, II, 27.

This use of the Infinitive never occurs in Classical Latin prose. Its place is taken by a clause introduced by *ut*, or by one of the other const. mentioned in sections 157–162.

In Ecclesiastical Latin the Infinitive is frequently used to express purpose.

107. In Classical Latin the Infinitive is treated as the Nom. or Accusative case of a verbal noun. Its Dative sense is generally ignored.

In the same way, although the English Infinitive is generally found with the preposition *to* in front of it, this preposition is no part of the Infinitive, and is omitted after certain verbs such as *may, can, shall, bid, let, make.*

Examples: *I can do this. Let me go. Make him stay. I will say what I like. I bid you come here.*

Contrast these with: *I am able to do this. Allow me to go. Force him to stay. I intend to say what I like. I command you to come here.*

The omission or insertion of the preposition *to* before the Infinitive is quite arbitrary: it contributes nothing to the meaning of the phrase.

In such a sentence as: *To err is human, to forgive divine*, the Infs. are treated exactly as if they were verbal nouns standing as the subjects of the clauses: the preposition *to* is absolutely without meaning.

The preposition only has its proper force when the Infinitive is used to express purpose or result, or is used in an explanatory sense. Examples: *I came here to fish. I am tall enough to look over your head. It is time to go home.* Even in this use the force of the preposition is so little felt that another preposition may be inserted in front of it. Example: *What went ye out for to see?*

108. The Infinitive partakes of the nature both of a verb and a noun.

As a verb it has a subject, expressed or understood; if it is the infinitive of a transitive verb, it has an object: it governs the same case as the verb from which it is derived; it is qualified by adverbs: it has tense and voice.

As a noun it can be used as the subject or object of a sentence, or it may stand in apposition to another noun: but in Latin it cannot be governed by a preposition.

The subject of an Infinitive is in the **Accusative Case**. The reason for this will be explained later.

The fact that the Infinitive is a verbal noun caused it to be used in noun clauses.

109. In Classical Latin the Infinitive with its subject in the Accusative (called the **Accusative and Infinitive Construction**) is regularly used in object clauses standing as objects of verbs denoting saying and thinking.

There are however two other constructions that are in some sense equivalent to the Accusative Infinitive construction in noun clauses.

These are

(1) A clause introduced by *ut* with the verb in the Subjunctive (called **ut with the Subjunctive construction**).

(2) A clause introduced by *quod, quia, quoniam* with the verb in the Indicative or Subjunctive (called **quod, quia, quoniam construction**).

This latter construction only occurs in Ecclesiastical Latin with very few exceptions mentioned below.

The use of these constructions is described in the following sections. A few words may be said here about their origin.

110. The *ut with the Subjunctive* construction is most frequently found in object clauses depending on verbs meaning to command, to request, to bring about, etc.

Examples:

Ut hoc facias tibi impero.
Te rogo ut mihi subvenias.
Effecit ut ex urbe exirent.

It is easy to see that there is something of a sense of *purpose* or *desired result* in the clauses introduced by *ut*.

The meaning of these sentences might be expressed as follows:

I give a command to you *in order that* you may do this.
I make a request to you *in order that* you may help me.
He brought it about *with the result that* they went out of the city.

As is explained in sections 157, 163 clauses introduced by *ut* with a verb in the Subjunctive mood denote both purpose and result.

111. The *ut with the Subjunctive* construction is however found in other noun clauses, especially in clauses which are the subjects of impersonal verbs or of the verb *to be*.

In some of these no sense of purpose or result can be discovered. It seems as if this construction were used as a substitute for the Infinitive, just as the ἵνα *with a Subjunctive* construction is used in later Greek.

Example:

Expedit vobis ut ego vadam. *It is expedient for you that I go away.*
Jn. 16:7.
συμφέρει ὑμῖν ἵνα ἐγὼ ἀπέλθω.

This construction is quite Classical, and goes back to the beginning of the language, as far as we know it.

112. The *quod, quia, quoniam* construction however is not Classical It seems to have taken its rise during the decadence of the language, and it is quite certain that its prevalence is due to slavish imitation of the Greek original on the part of those who translated the Septuagint and the New Testament into Latin.

It is so common in Ecclesiastical Latin, and so characteristic of it, that its origin must be treated at length.

113. Clauses introduced by the neuter relative *quod* referring to a noun or pronoun (expressed or understood) in the main clause, are used in Classical Latin in a sense approximating to that of a noun clause in apposition. Although these clauses serve to explain the signification of the noun or pronoun to which they refer, just like a noun in apposition, they do not necessarily agree with it in case or gender.

Haec res mihi curae est, quidnam hoc sit negoti, quod filia repente expetit ex me, ut ad se irem. *This is what worries me, what can be the reason that my daughter suddenly asks me to go to her.*   Plaut. *Men.* 762.

Accidit perincommode, quod eum nusquam vidisti. *It happens most awkwardly that you have never seen him.* Cic. *Ep. ad Att.* 1:17.

Hoc scio quod scribit nulla puella tibi. *This I do know that no girl writes to you.* Mart. XI, 64.

Hoc uno praestamus vel maxime feris, quod exprimere dicendo sensa possumus. *In this one thing we surpass the beasts most of all, namely that we can express our thoughts in speech.* Cic. *Or.* I, 8.

There are two examples in early Latin where a clause introduced by *quod* stands as the object of a verb of saying or feeling. The verb is in the Subjunctive.

Equidem scio jam filius quod amet meus istanc meretricem. *Truly I know now that my son loves that harlot.* Plaut. *As.* 52.

The other example is in Cato the Elder.

This construction also occurs in the book on the Spanish war, written by a follower of Caesar in an uncultivated style, in Suetonius, Apuleius and Tacitus, but only very rarely.

In later writers it becomes more and more common.

Examples:

Renuntiaverunt quod Pompeium in potestate haberent. *They announced that they had Pompey in their power.* Bell. Hisp. 36.

Titus, recordatus quondam super cenam quod nihil cuiquam toto die praestitisset.... *Titus, remembering once during supper that he had given nothing to anyone during the whole day....* Suetonius, *Titus.*

Qui puellae nuntiaret quod eam juvenis vocaret ad se.... *Who was to tell the girl that the young man called her to him....* Apuleius 10.

See also Tacitus, *Ann.* XIV, 6.

The usual opinion about this construction is that it is a vernacular idiom, ignored by the Classical writers, which came into common use during the decay of the language.

Madvig however thinks that, if this had been a vernacular idiom, it would have occurred more frequently in Plautus. He prefers to connect it with the use of *quod* in apposition mentioned above, and regards the passages in Plautus and Cato as possibly corrupt.

114. However this may be, the use of this construction received a great extension in the Old Latin version of the Bible and is quite common there as well as in the Ecclesiastical writers, who were naturally much influenced in their style by the version of the Bible which they used.

In the Bible and in these writers both the Indicative and Subjunctive moods are used indifferently in this construction.

The reason why the translators of the Bible made so much use of this construction is that there is in Greek an alternative construction to the Accusative and Infinitive construction used after verbs of saying or thinking. This consists of a clause introduced by ὅτι with the verb in the Indicative mood. In certain of its uses ὅτι corresponds to the Latin *quod*, and the translators, who strove to translate the Greek as literally as possible, eagerly seized upon the construction with *quod* which was coming into use in Latin to translate clauses introduced by ὅτι.

They also kept the mood of the Greek original in some cases, although this was quite contrary to Latin usage.

They did even more than this. ὅτι also means *because* in Greek, and there are two Latin words that can be used to translate it literally in this sense, namely *quia* and *quoniam.*

These words were therefore used to translate ὅτι when introducing an object clause after a verb of saying or thinking exactly as *quod* was used.

There seems to be a certain approximation to this use in the lines of Catullus:

> Id gratumst mihi, me quoniam tibi dicis amicum,
> Muneraque et Musarum hinc petis et Veneris.
> *This is pleasing to me, that you call me your friend and seek the gifts of Venus and the Muses from me.*   68:8.

where *quoniam* picks up and explains *id* just as *quod* did in the examples in section 113.

Some usage of this kind in familiar speech may have served to help the introduction of this form of expression; but it must have made the early versions of the Bible sound very strangely to educated ears.

However this usage spread from these versions to all Ecclesiastical writers, even to Tertullian and Cyprian, although they employ it sparingly. Generally speaking this construction is employed by the early Fathers in those parts of their writings which were intended for partly educated people, or which deal directly with the Bible.

Jerome retained it in his revised version of the Bible, which we call the Vulgate, even in the Old Testament which he translated anew from the Hebrew, although he modified some of the extreme literalness of the old versions.

115. The use of clauses introduced by *quod* was widely extended in later Latin to cover most of the senses that had been expressed in Classical Latin, and even in the early Fathers, by an Accusative Infinitive or a clause introduced by *ut*.

From these uses descend the many uses of *que* in French and *che* in Italian.

It should be noticed how much nearer the general construction of English is to the style of Ecclesiastical Latin than to that of Classical Latin

English is not derived from Latin except in respect of a great part of its vocabulary; but there is no doubt that the general structure of English has been largely modified by the style of the English Bible of 1611, the style of which was in its turn influenced by the Vulgate

Examples of noun clauses introduced by *quod, quia, quoniam* are given in section 135.

THE INFINITIVE OR ITS EQUIVALENTS USED AS THE SUBJECT OR COMPLEMENT OF A VERB

116. The Simple Infinitive, an Accusative and Infinitive, a clause introduced by *ut*, or (in Ecclesiastical Latin only) a clause introduced by *quod, quia, quoniam* is used as the subject of impersonal verbs and in many expressions containing the verb *esse*.

The usage varies with different periods of the language and with different writers; the student must learn the construction of the various verbs by experience.

In English the syntax of sentences of this kind is confused by the fact that they are written in the following forms:

> It is more blessed to give than to receive.
> It is expedient that one man should die for the people.

The real subject of the first of these sentences is *to give than to receive*.

The real subject of the second sentence is *that one man should die for the people*.

The word *it* in each sentence is the Preparatory Subject, and the sentences are written in this way in English, because, in that language, the subject is nearly always put first in the sentence.

Indeed, this is the only way in which the subject can be distinguished from the object in English owing to the absence of case endings. The Preparatory Subject serves to give notice that the real subject is coming afterwards.

In many Latin grammars impersonal verbs are said *to take an Infinitive, or a clause with* ut *and the Subjunctive after them.*

This confuses the student who may think that these clauses come after the verbs as objects, whereas they are really subjects.

117. A Simple Infinitive may be used in Latin, as in English, as the subject of a verb, especially of the verb *to be.*

As Subject:

Beatius est magis dare quam accipere. *It is more blessed to give than to receive.* Acts 20:35.

Mihi vivere Christus est, et mori lucrum. *To me to live is Christ, and to die is gain.* Phil. 1:21.

117a. A Simple Infinitive may be used in Latin as in English as the complement of a verb, especially of the verb *to be.*

Hoc est praeceptum Dei facere, hoc est voluntatem Patris adimplere. *This is to perform the commandment of God: this is to fulfil the will of the Father.* Cyprian.

See the whole selection *Quid est voluntas Dei* in the Appendix, p. 119, for examples of the use of the Simple Infinitive.

118. The verb *oportet* generally has an Accusative and Infinitive as its subject.

Illum oportet crescere, me autem minui. *He must increase, but I must decrease.* Jn. 3:30.

Oportet Deo obedire magis quam hominibus. *It is necessary for us to obey God, rather than men.* Acts 5:29.

But it may take a clause introduced by *quod* in Ecclesiastical Latin

Oportet quod verbum Dei in nobis manens continue meditemur. *We ought continually to meditate on the word of God which abides in us.* Thomas Aquinas *de Symb. Ap.*

119. We may here notice a peculiar idiom which is also found in Classical Latin, namely to use a Past tense of the verb *oportere* with a Present Infinitive as its subject to express an unfulfilled duty. This is expressed in English by the use of a Past Infinitive.

Haec oportuit facere, et illa non omittere. *These ye ought to have done, and not to have left the other undone.* Mt. 23:23.

Oportuit ergo te mittere pecuniam meam nummulariis, et veniens ego recepissem utique quod meum est cum usura. *Thou oughtest to have put my money to the bankers, and then at my coming I should have received my own with usury.* Mt. 25:27.

See Acts 24:20.

A Past tense of *oportere* may have however simply a past sense without any idea of unfulfilled duty.

Oportebat autem eum transire per Samariam. *But he had to go through Samaria.* Jn. 4:4; Lk. 15:32.

120. Other impersonal verbs may have either a clause introduced by *ut* or an Accusative Infinitive for subject. In some cases *ut* is omitted and a Simple Subjunctive with its subject, etc. forms the noun clause. The use of Ecclesiastical writers varies much from that of Classical writers and no exact rule can be laid down.

121. The expression *factum est* to represent the Greek ἐγένετο, which in its turn represents the Hebrew וַיְהִי, is very frequent in the Vulgate and is generally translated *it came to pass.* It is not Classical

It generally has for its subject a clause introduced by *ut*, but it may have an Accusative and Infinitive or even a clause with the verb in the Indicative and no connecting particle.

>Factum est autem et in alio Sabbato, ut intraret in synagogam, et doceret. *And it came to pass on another Sabbath that he entered into a synagogue and taught.* Lk. 6:6.

>Factum est autem revertenti mihi in Hierusalem, et oranti in templo, fieri me in stupore mentis. *And it came to pass that when I had returned to Jerusalem and was praying in the temple, I was in a trance.* Acts 22:17.

>See Acts 16:16.

>Factum est autem in illis diebus, exiit in montem orare. *And it came to pass in those days that he went out into a mountain to pray.* Lk. 6:12.

122. *Accidit, contigit, expedit, pertinet.* In Classical Latin the subject clause is constructed with *ut*.

The Accusative and Infinitive construction is found in the Vulgate, or the Subjunctive with *ut* omitted, or *quia* with Indicative.

>Accidit autem ut sacerdos quidam descenderet eadem via. *But it happened that a certain priest was going down by the same way.* Lk. 10:31.

>Et cum iter faceret contingit ut adpropinquaret Damasco. *And when he was travelling it happened that he drew near to Damascus.* Acts 9:3.

>Expedit vobis ut ego vadam. *It is expedient for you that I go away.* Jn. 16:7.

>Contigit autem patrem Publii...jacere. *But it happened that the father of Publius lay sick.* Acts 28:8.

>Et contigit, dum iret, a turbis comprimebatur. *And it happened that while he went he was pressed by the crowds.* Lk. 8:42.

123. *Necesse est, decet.* The subject clause is constructed either with the Accusative and Infinitive or with *ut*.

>Unde necesse est et hunc habere aliquid quod offerat. *Whence it is necessary that he should have something to offer.* Heb. 8:3.

>Necesse est enim ut veniant scandala. *It must needs be that offences come.* Mt. 18:7.

>1 Thess. 1:8; Heb. 7:12; Heb. 9:16: (*ut* omitted).

>Sine modo, sic enim decet nos implere omnem justitiam. *Suffer it to be so now, for thus it becomes us to fulfil all righteousness.* Mt. 3:16.

>Talis enim decebat ut esset nobis pontifex. *For it was befitting that there should be such a high priest for us.* Heb. 7:26.

124. *Licet* and *placet* have a Simple Infinitive for subject with a dative of the person to whom the action is allowable or pleasing. The *ut* clause is also used.

>Non licet mittere eos in corbanan. *It is not lawful to put them into the treasury.* Mt. 27:6.

>See also Mt. 22:17.

Placuit nobis remanere Athenis solis. *It pleased us to remain in Athens alone.* 1 Thess. 3:1.

Cum placuit ei...ut revelaret Filium suum in me. *When it pleased him... to reveal his Son in me.* Gal. 1:15.

125. *Interest* is only used once in the New Testament and has its peculiar construction of an Ablative feminine of the possessive pronoun to express the person in whose interest the action takes place.

Quales aliquando fuerint, nihil mea interest. *Whosoever they were makes no matter to me.* Gal. 2:6.

The following are examples of the use of *quod* and *quia* in subject clauses:

Non ad te pertinet quia perimus? *Doth it not matter to thee that we perish?* Mk. 4:38.

Latet enim eos hoc volentes, quod caeli erant prius. *For this they are willingly ignorant of, that the heavens were of old.* 2 Pet. 3:5.

126. An impersonal predicate made up of a neuter adjective and the verb *esse* may have either a Simple Infinitive or Accusative and Infinitive or a clause introduced by *ut* (or in Ecclesiastical Latin by *quod*, etc.) as its subject.

Non est vestrum nosse tempora vel momenta, quae Pater posuit in potestate sua. *It is not yours to know times and seasons which the Father put in his own power.* Acts 1:7.

Facilius est enim camelum per foramen acus transire, quam divitem intrare in regnum Dei. *For it is easier for a camel to go through the eye of a needle than for a rich man to enter into the kingdom of God.* Lk. 18:25.

Bonum est enim mihi magis mori, quam ut gloriam meam quis evacuet. *For it is better for me to die than that anyone should make my glory vain.* 1 Cor. 9:15.

Reliquum est, ut et qui habent uxores, tanquam non habentes sint. *It remains that those that have wives should be as if they had none.* 1 Cor. 7:29.

Manifestum est quod regnum mundi non est per multos deos, sed per unum tantum. *It is plain that the government of the world is not through many gods, but through one only.* Thos. Aq. *Symb. Ap.* 4.

127. A clause introduced by *ut* (or in Ecclesiastical Latin by *quod*, etc.) may form the subject of any verb used impersonally whether in the Active or the Passive voice.

Ascendit in cor ejus ut visitaret fratres suos, filios Israel. *It came into his heart to visit his brothers the children of Israel.* Acts 7:23.

Hic jam quaeritur...ut fidelis quis inveniatur. *Here it is expected that a man be found faithful.* 1 Cor. 4:2.

Sic ergo patet quod multum utile est habere fidem. *So then it is plain that it is very profitable to have faith.* Thos. Aq. *Symb. Ap.* 1.

The infinitive or its equivalents used to complete the meaning of verbs

128. Certain verbs which are generally the same in Latin as in English are followed by an Infinitive to complete their meaning. These are sometimes called **Modal verbs** because they add new modes of expression or moods to the verbs to which they are attached.

The most important are *possum, volo, nolo, malo*, and also verbs denoting beginning or ceasing, habit, continuance, desire, purpose, aim or duty.

If the subject of the principal verb is the same as that of the Infinitive the subject of the Infinitive is often not expressed, it is however generally speaking in the Nominative case and any adjectives that agree with it must be in that case; see example 2.

If the subject of the Infinitive is not the same as the subject of the principal verb, the subject of the Infinitive is in the Accusative case; see example 3.

In Ecclesiastical Latin a clause introduced by *ut* with the Subjunctive, or a Subjunctive without *ut*, or even an Indicative may take the place of the Infinitive after *volo*.

Quomodo potest homo nasci, cum senex sit? *How can a man be born when he is old?* Jn. 3:4.

Si vis perfectus esse, vade, vende quae habes. *If thou wishest to be perfect, go and sell what thou hast.* Mt. 19:21.

Volo ergo viros orare in omni loco. *I wish therefore men to pray in every place.* 1 Tim. 2:8.

Omnia ergo quaecumque vultis ut faciant vobis homines, et vos facite eis. *Whatsoever things therefore that ye wish men should do unto you, do ye also unto them.* Mt. 7:12.

See also Jn. 17:24; Mt. 20:32.

Ubi vis paremus tibi comedere Pascha? *Where dost thou wish us to prepare for thee to eat the Passover?* Mt. 26:17.

Vis imus et colligimus ea? *Dost thou wish us to go and gather them up?* Mt. 13:28.

Et iterum coepit docere ad mare. *And he began again to teach by the sea.* Mk. 4:1.

Ut cessavit loqui, dixit ad Simonem.... *When he ceased to speak, he said to Simon....* Lk. 5:4.

Per diem autem festum dimittere solebat illis unum ex vinctis. *On the feast day he was wont to release to them one of the prisoners.* Mk. 15:6.

The infinitive or its equivalents used as the object of a verb.

129. The Simple Infinitive may be used as the object of a verb, just like a noun.

Perficere autem non invenio. *But how to perform it I find not.* Rom. 7:18.

129*a*. The Infinitive may be used as one of two objects after certain verbs such as *docere, jubere,* and in Ecclesiastical Latin *rogare.*

Docuerunt enim linguam suam loqui mendacium. *For they taught their tongue to speak a lie.* Jer. 9:5.

Jussit milites descendere, et rapere eum de medio eorum. *He commanded the soldiers to go down and to take him from the midst of them.* Acts 23:10.

Propter quod rogo vos accipere cibum pro salute vestra. *Wherefore I ask you to take food for your health's sake.* Acts 27:34.

The Infinitive may be retained as object after a passive verb of this kind.

Ubi inventis fratribus rogati sumus manere apud eos dies septem. *Where having found brethren, we were asked to remain with them seven days.* Acts 28:14.

See also 2 Cor. 10:2, 9.

130. Out of this construction there arose a usage of the greatest importance in Latin. The Accusative and Infinitive, instead of being regarded as two separate objects of the main verb, combined together so as to form a single object clause in which the Infinitive acquired a predicative sense and the Accusative was regarded as its subject.

This usage is called the Accusative with the Infinitive construction, because the Accusative goes with the Infinitive as its subject and not with the main verb as its object.

Example:

Jussit eum duci in castra. *He commanded him to be led to the camp.* Acts 21:34.

This sentence does not state that the order was given to Paul: the whole clause *duci eum in castra* is the object of the main verb.

This construction is very common in Classical Latin in object clauses depending on verbs denoting saying or thinking (*verba declarandi vel sentiendi*).

Whole speeches are commonly reported in this way and are then given not in the words in which they were actually delivered, but in the words of a reporter. When applied to speeches this construction is called the **Oratio Obliqua**. It is very uncommon in the Vulgate, for in the Hebrew original of the Old Testament speeches are given in the words of the original speaker and not reported. In the New Testament the influence of Hebrew methods of expression causes the Oratio Obliqua to be equally rare and it is not common in Ecclesiastical writers.

It seems unnecessary to go into a long description of this complicated construction in a book intended as an introduction to Ecclesiastical Latin

It may suffice to say that in this construction all main verbs are in the Infinitive mood, and all verbs in subordinate clauses in the Subjunctive mood. The latter half of this rule is not universally observed in Ecclesiastical Latin

131. Noun clauses standing as objects of verbs are of three kinds.

1. **Dependent statements**, or object clauses depending on verbs denoting saying or thinking (*verba declarandi vel sentiendi*).

2. **Dependent commands**, or object clauses depending on verbs denoting entreaty, command, exhortation, or bringing about (*verba imperandi vel efficiendi*).

3. **Dependent questions**, or object clauses depending on verbs meaning to ask a question, or clauses introduced by an interrogative word depending on verbs of various meanings.

132. Dependent statements. In English these nearly always take the form of a clause introduced by *that* with the verb in the Indicative mood. The tense of the verb in these clauses is always one stage further in the past than the tense used by the original speaker, if the verb on which the clause depends is in a past tense.

Thus:

He said that he was pleased to be in London.
The original words used by the speaker were:
I am pleased to be in London.

He said that he had seen his brother.
The original words used by the speaker were:
I have seen my brother.

He said that he would go to London on Friday.
The original words used by the speaker were:
I will go to London on Friday.

N.B. In modern Grammars the tense formed with *would* and *should* is called the *Future in the past.*

This, as has been said, is the usual construction; but there are a few verbs in English that are followed by an Accusative Infinitive construction.

> The judge declared him to be a criminal.
>
> I believe them to be safe.
>
> I consider you to be incompetent.

But even in the case of these verbs a clause introduced by *that* may also be used.

> The judge declared that he was a criminal. (Notice the change of tense.)
>
> I believe that they are safe.
>
> I consider that you are incompetent.

133. In Classical Latin the **only** construction that is used in object clauses after verbs of *sentiendi vel declarandi* is the Accusative and Infinitive.

As has already been explained a clause introduced by *quod, quia* or *quoniam* can be used in Ecclesiastical Latin instead of the Accusative and Infinitive The verb in these clauses may be either Subjunctive or Indicative.

If the main verb is in the third person singular or plural and the subject of the Infinitive in the subordinate clause is the same as that of the main verb, the reflexive pronoun *se* is always used. Otherwise a demonstrative pronoun is used.

The use of the tenses of the Infinitive is not very exact in Ecclesiastical Latin, but, generally speaking, if the time of the action denoted by the main verb and that of the action denoted by the Infinitive is the same, the Present Infinitive is used.

> Dicitis in Beelzebub ejicere me daemonia. *You say that I cast out devils in Beelzebub.*   Lk. 11:18.

If the time denoted by the Infinitive is prior to that of the main verb the Perfect Infinitive is used.

> Aestimantes eum mortuum esse. *Thinking he was dead.*   Acts 14:19, 16:27; Phil. 3:13.

If the time denoted by the Infinitive is future to that of the main verb the Fut. Infinitive is used.

> Et responsum acceperat a Spiritu Sancto non visurum se mortem.... *And he had received a reply from the Holy Ghost that he should not see death....*   Lk. 2:26.

134. The tenses of verbs in subordinate clauses in dependent statements should follow the rule of the sequence of tenses; but sometimes the tense used when the words were actually spoken or the thought framed is retained, in imitation of Greek.

> Dicentes se visionem angelorum vidisse, qui dicunt eum vivere. *Saying that they saw a vision of angels, who say that he is alive.*   Lk. 24:23.

Notice the use of *se* and *eum* in this example and also the use of an Indicative in a subordinate clause.

> Huic omnes prophetae testimonium perhibent, remissionem peccatorum accipere per nomen ejus omnes qui credunt in eum. *To him all the prophets bear witness that all who believe in him receive remission of sins through his name.*   Acts 10:43.

The normal Classical construction is seen in the example below:

> Et respondebant se nescire unde esset. *And they answered that they did not know whence he was.*   Lk. 20:7.

135. The following are examples of the construction of object clauses with *quod, quia* and *quoniam,* the origin of which is explained in sections 113–115.

The verb may be in the Indicative or Subjunctive mood without any difference in meaning.

> De escis autem quae idolis immolantur, scimus quia nihil est idolum in mundo, et quod nullus Deus nisi unus. *With regard to meats offered to idols, we know that an idol is nothing in the world, and that there is no God but one.* 1 Cor. 8:4.

> Credere enim oportet accedentem ad Deum quia est, et inquirentibus se remunerator fit. *For one that cometh to God ought to believe that he is, and that he becomes a rewarder of those that seek him.* Heb. 11:6.

Sometimes the tense of the original thought is retained as in Greek.

> Et nesciebat quia verum est, quod fiebat per angelum. *And he did not know that what was done by the angel was true.* Acts 12:9.

The following is an example of the use of the *quod, quia, quoniam* construction from Tertullian, showing how soon this construction was adopted even by an educated writer:

> Adeo postea in Actis Apostolorum invenimus, quoniam, qui Johannis baptismum habebant, non accepissent Spiritum Sanctum. *De Bapt.* 10.

In the following examples the subject of the dependent clause is pleonastically repeated in the principal clause:

> Dominus novit cogitationes sapientium quoniam vanae sunt. *The Lord knoweth the thoughts of the wise that they are vain.* 1 Cor. 3:20, cited from Ps. 93:11.

> Christus praedicatur quod resurrexit a mortuis. *Christ is preached that he rose from the dead.* 1 Cor. 15:12.

See also Acts 9:20.

In Acts 21:29 the object of the dependent clause is repeated in the main clause:

> Viderant enim Trophimum Ephesium in civitate, quem aestimaverunt quoniam in templum introduxisset Paulus. *For they had seen Trophimus an Ephesian in the city, whom they thought that Paul had brought into the temple.*

136. Here may be noticed the very peculiar imitation of the Greek idiom found in the New Testament and the LXX by which ὅτι is used to introduce the actual words of a speaker. *Quod, quia* or *quoniam* are employed to translate ὅτι in this sense quite indifferently. They must not be translated into English. The only English equivalent to them when used in this way is the use of inverted commas. The punctuation of the Vulgate is sometimes peculiar, as will be seen from the examples below. The introductory word is printed with a capital letter after a colon, as if it were part of the speech.

> Et mulieri dicebant: Quia jam non propter tuam loquellam credimus; ipsi enim audivimus, et scimus quia hic est vere salvator mundi. *And they kept saying to the woman, "We believe, not because of your talking; for we have heard him ourselves, and we know that this is truly the saviour of the world."* Jn. 4:42.

> Scriptum est enim quod Angelis suis mandabit de te, ut conservent te: et quia In manibus tollent te.... *For it is written "He shall give his angels charge concerning thee, that they may preserve thee": and "In their hands they shall bear thee up...."* Lk. 4:10, 11.

> Si quis dixerit quoniam diligo Deum, et fratrem suum oderit, mendax est. *If any man say "I love God," and hateth his brother, he is a liar.* 1 Jn. 4:20.

For the use of *quod, quia*, etc. see Jn. 4:46–54.

137. Special forms of dependent statements.

In Classical Latin verbs denoting *to promise, to hope, to swear*, and similar verbs which relate to the future are followed by the Accusative with a Future Infinitive.

In Ecclesiastical Latin a Present Infinitive may be used, or a clause introduced by *quia*, etc. or *ut*.

> Devotione devovimus nos nihil gustaturos, donec occidamus Paulum. *We have bound ourselves by a great curse that we will eat nothing until we have killed Paul.*Acts 23:14.

> Spero autem in Domino Jesu, Timotheum cito me mittere ad vos. *But I hope in the Lord Jesus that I may send Timothy to you shortly.* Phil. 2:19.

> Quibus autem juravit non introire in requiem ipsius, nisi illis qui increduli fuerunt? *But to whom did he swear that they should not enter into his rest, except to those that were unbelieving?* Heb. 3:18; Acts 2:30.

> Simul et sperans quia pecunia daretur a Paulo. *At the same time hoping that money would be given by Paul.* Acts 24:26.

> Juravit ut non transirem Jordanem. *He swore that I should not pass over Jordan.* Deut. 4:21 and 1:8.

137a. In imitation of Hebrew the verb *jurare* may be followed by *si* to express a strong negative, and by *nisi* to express a strong affirmative.

> Sicut juravi in ira mea: Si introibunt in requiem meam. *As I sware in my wrath: "They shall not enter into my rest."* Heb. 3:11.

> Juravit per semetipsum, dicens: Nisi benedicens benedicam te, et multiplicans multiplicabo te. *He sware by himself, saying: "Surely I will bless thee and multiply thee exceedingly."* Heb. 6:13.

In Mk. 8:12 a construction of the same character is found after *dicere*.

> Amen dico vobis, si dabitur generationi isti signum. *Verily I say to you, no sign shall be given to this generation.*

The Hebraic form of adjuration *Vivo ego, dicit Dominus* is followed by *quoniam* or *quia*.

> Vivo ego, dicit Dominus, quoniam mihi flectet omne genu. Rom. 14:11, cited from Is. 45:23.

138. The verbs *audire* and *videre* may be followed by an Accusative and a participle in imitation of Greek, if they refer to something that was actually heard or seen when it was taking place.

> Et vidit omnis populus eum ambulantem et laudantem Deum. *And all the people saw him walking and praising God.* Acts 3:9.

> Et cadens in terram audit vocem dicentem sibi.... *And falling to the earth he heard a voice saying to him....* Acts 9:4.

Contrast with this:

> Audierunt autem de te quia discessionem doceas a Mose. *For they have heard of thee that thou teachest departure from Moses.* Acts 21:21.

> See also Mt. 6:16; Lk. 4:23; Acts 2:6.

139. Verbs meaning *to fear* are followed in Classical Latin by a clause introduced by *ne* (which is equivalent to *lest* or *that* in English) when the subordinate clause is affirmative, and by a clause introduced by *ut* when the subordinate clause is negative.

Vereor ne veniat. *I fear that he will come.*
Vereor ut veniat. *I fear that he will not come.*
Examples from the Vulgate:

Timens tribunus ne discerperetur Paulus ab ipsis.... *The tribune fearing that Paul would be torn in pieces by them....* Acts 23:10.

In the Vulgate an Infinitive is found after *timere*:

Timuit illuc ire. *He was afraid to go there.* Mt. 2:22.

140. In Classical Latin object clauses after verbs meaning *to refuse, to prevent,* etc. are introduced by *quominus* or *quin* and have the verb in the Subjunctive.

Quominus and *quin* are rare in the Vulgate A Simple Infinitive is found after verbs of this kind.

Non enim subterfugi quominus adnuntiarem.... *For I have not shrunk from announcing....* Acts 20:27.

Propter quod et impediebar...venire ad vos. *On account of which I was hindered from coming to you.* Rom. 15:22.

See also Acts 24:24; 1 Cor. 14:39.

141. *Mirari* and *admirari* are followed by a clause introduced by *quia* or *quod* and occasionally by *si* in imitation of Greek.

Non mireris quia dixi tibi: Oportet vos nasci denuo. *Wonder not that I said to you: Ye must be born again.* Jn. 3:7.

Nolite mirari, fratres, si odit vos mundus. *Do not wonder, brethren, if the world hates you.* 1 Jn. 3:13.

See also Mk. 15:44.

142. Dependent commands. In English object clauses after verbs meaning to entreat, to command, to exhort, to bring about etc. are generally expressed by the Accusative and Infinitive construction.

In Classical Latin they are nearly always expressed by a clause introduced by *ut* with its verb in the Subjunctive

This causes a great deal of difficulty to beginners unless they get the fact clearly in their minds that where Classical Latin uses an Infinitive, English generally uses a clause introduced by *that*, and where Classical Latin uses a clause introduced by *ut* English generally uses the Infinitive.

The verb *jubere, to command*[5], is followed by the Accusative Infinitive construction in Classical Latin

In Ecclesiastical Latin object clauses after verbs of commanding etc. are generally expressed by a clause introduced by *ut*. Sometimes *ut* is omitted. An Accusative and Infinitive construction may also be used after these verbs in imitation of Greek, or even a clause introduced by *quod*.

Rogate ergo Dominum messis ut ejiciat operariors in messem. *Pray ye therefore the Lord of the harvest to thrust out labourers into his harvest.* Mt. 9:38.

---

5 N.B. *Dicere* often means *to command* in Ecc. L. It is then followed by a clause introduced by *ut* or by an Infinitive.

Et dixit discipulis suis ut navicula sibi deserviret. *And he commanded his disciples that a little ship should wait on him.* Mk. 3:9.

See also Mt. 5:39; Mk. 5:43; Rom. 12:3.

Statuerunt ut ascenderent Paulus et Barnabas. *They determined that Paul and Barnabas should go up.* Acts 15:2.

Ecce faciam illos ut veniant, et adorent ante pedes tuos. *Behold I will make them come and worship before thy feet.* Rev. 3:9.

Notice the pleonastic repetition of the subject of the dep. clause as the object of the main clause.

Propter quod obsecro patienter me audias. *Wherefore I beseech thee to hear me patiently.* Acts 26:3.

See also Mt. 8:4.

The following are examples of the use of the Infinitive.

Ascendens autem in unam navem, quae erat Simonis, rogavit eum a terra reducere pusillum. *And going into one ship which was Simon's, he asked him to push out a little from the land.* Lk. 5:3.

Petistis virum homicidam donari vobis. *Ye asked for a murderer to be granted to you.* Acts 3:14.

Admone illos principibus et potestatibus subditos esse. *Warn them to be in subjection to princes and powers.* Tit. 3:1.

Itaque, fratres, aemulamini prophetare. *And so, brethren, desire earnestly to prophecy.* 1 Cor. 14:19.

Progenies viperarum, quis demonstravit vobis fugere a futura ira? *Offspring of vipers, who warned you to flee from the wrath to come?* Mt. 3:7.

See also Acts 3:12, 11:24, 26:29; 1 Cor. 5:11, 7:10; Phil. 4:2; Heb. 13:19; 1 Pet. 2:11.

The following is an example of a clause introduced by *quod* used as a dependent command.

Sed nos desideramus quod sicut voluntas Dei completa est in beatis, ita compleatur in nobis. *But we pray that as the will of God is fulfilled among the blessed so it may be fulfilled among us.* Thomas Aquinas.

A clause introduced by *si* may be used after a verb denoting requesting, to denote a request that seems unlikely to be fulfilled.

Obsecrans si quomodo tandem aliquando prosperum iter habeam in voluntate Dei veniendi ad vos. *Praying if by any means yet sometime I may have a prosperous journey by the will of God to come to you.* Rom. 1:10.

143. Dependent questions. Object clauses after verbs meaning *to ask a question* or clauses introduced by an interrogative word after other verbs are called Dependent Questions in Latin grammar. In English such clauses have the verb in the Indicative and present no difficulty; but in Classical Latin the verb is always in the Subjunctive in these clauses.

In Ecclesiastical Latin the verb in a Dependent Question is often in the Indicative.[6]

Examples of the ordinary Classical construction:

Et interrogabat quis esset, et quid fecisset. *And he asked who he was, and what he had done.* Acts 21:33.

Nescimus quid factum sit ei. *We know not what has become of him.* Acts 7:40.

Et annuntiaverunt eis quanta ad eos principes sacerdotum et seniores dixissent. *And they announced to them all that the chief priests and elders had said to them.* Acts 4:23.

---

6 This usage is also found in early and late Latin. Compare Lucan, *Pharsalia*, 1:126, 9:563.

Et quaerebant summi sacerdotes et scribae quomodo eum cum dolo tenerent et occiderent. *And the chief priests and scribes sought how they might take him with guile and kill him.*   Mk. 14:1.

Cognoscet de doctrina utrum ex Deo sit, an ego a me ipso loquar. *He shall know of the doctrine whether it is of God, or whether I speak of myself.* Jn. 7:17.

144. Examples of dependent questions with the verb in the Indicative:

Domine, nescimus quo vadis. *Lord, we know not whither thou goest.* Jn. 14:5.

Redi domum tuam, et narra quanta tibi fecit Deus. *Return to thy home, and tell all that God has done for thee.*   Lk. 8:39.

Quomodo autem nunc videat, nescimus: aut quis ejus aperuit oculos nos nescimus. *We know not how he now sees, nor do we know who opened his eyes.* Jn. 9:21.

Indirect questions are sometimes introduced by *si* in Ecclesiastical Latin This is not Classical

Observabant eum scribae et Pharisaei, si Sabbato curaret. *The scribes and Pharisees watched him if he would heal on the Sabbath.*   Lk. 6:7.

Noun Clauses in Apposition to a Noun or Pronoun

145. A noun clause is sometimes used in apposition to a noun or pronoun to explain the meaning of the noun or pronoun.

These clauses are generally expressed by *ut* with the Subjunctive or by an Infinitive.In Ecclesiastical Latin they may be expressed by a clause introduced by *quod, quia, quoniam.*

Meus cibus est ut faciam voluntatem ejus, qui misit me. *My meat is to do the will of him that sent me.*   Jn. 4:34.

Visum est Spiritui Sancto et nobis nihil ultra imponere vobis oneris quam haec necessario: ut abstineatis vos ab immolatis. ...,*It seemed good to the Holy Spirit and to us to lay no further burden on you than these things necessarily: that you should abstain from things sacrificed. ...*   Acts 15:28.

Quandoquidem recte mihi vivere puero id proponebatur, obtemperare monentibus. *Since this was set before me as the ideal of a boy's existence, namely to obey those that instructed me.* Augustine.

See also Jn. 6:39, 40, 16:32.

Hoc est autem judicium: quia lux venit in mundum, et dilexerunt homines magis tenebras quam lucem....*But this is the judgement: that light came into the world, and men loved darkness rather than light.*   Jn. 3:19.

Omnia ostendi vobis, quoniam sic laborantes oportet suscipere infirmos. *I have shown you all things, that so labouring ye ought to support the weak.* Acts 20:35.

See also Phil. 1:6.

146. The Infinitive used as an Imperative. The Pres. Infinitive is very rarely used in the sense of an Imperative in imitation of a rare use in New Testament Greek. This idiom is found in French and Italian, rarely in English.

Gaudere cum gaudentibus, flere cum flentibus. *Rejoice with them that do rejoice and weep with those that weep.*Rom. 12:15.

The Infinitive in Mt. 5:34, 39 may possibly be an Imperative Infinitive.

147. Explanatory Infinitive. The Infinitive (retaining somewhat of its original Dative sense) is used with certain adjectives and nouns, generally such as denote power, capacity, merit, fitness, in an explanatory sense.

Scio cui credidi, et certus sum quia potens est depositum meum servare in illum diem. *I know in whom I have believed and I am certain that he is able to keep that which I have deposited with him until that day.* 2 Tim. 1:12.

See also Lk. 5:24; 2 Cor. 9:8; Rev. 13:5.

Qui idonei erunt et alios docere. *Who shall be fit to teach others also.* 2 Tim. 2:2.

Non habent necesse ire. *They have no need to go away.* Mt. 14:16.

But we also find:

Et non necesse habetis ut aliquis doceat vos. *And ye have no need that anyone should teach you.* 1 Jn. 2:27.

Et jam non sum dignus vocari filius tuus. *And I am no longer worthy to be called thy son.* Lk. 15:19, 21:36.

A clause introduced by *ut* is also used with *dignus* in imitation of the Greek. Jn. 1:27. See also Mt. 8:8.

Et hoc scientes tempus: quia hora est jam nos de somno surgere. *And that knowing the time, that it is now the hour for us to awake out of sleep.* Rom. 13:2; Rev. 11:18.

Bonam voluntatem habemus magis peregrinari a corpore, et praesentes esse ad Dominum. *We have a good will rather to be absent from the body and to be present with the Lord.* 2 Cor. 5:8.

In Classical Latin prose such words would be followed by a Gerund or Gerundive with *ad*, by a Relative clause, or by a Genitive of the Gerund or Gerundive, as in this example:

Et hic habet potestatem a principibus sacerdotum alligandi omnes, qui invocant nomen tuum. *And here he has power from the chief priests to bind all that call on thy name.* Acts 9:14.

148. The Infinitive is used in an explanatory sense after verbs: sometimes it describes the purpose and sometimes the consequence of the verb on which it depends.

It is used in imitation of Greek, and would not be so used in Classical prose.

Esurivi enim et dedistis me manducare. *I was hungry and ye gave me to eat.* Mt. 25:35

Quomodo tu, Judaeus cum sis, bibere a me poscis, quae sum mulier Samaritana? *How is it that thou, although thou art a Jew, askest to drink of me who am a Samaritan woman?* Jn. 4:9.

Observabant autem scribae et Pharisaei si sabbato curaret, ut invenirent accusare illum. *And the scribes and the Pharisees watched him, whether he would heal on the Sabbath; that they might find how to accuse him.* Lk. 6:7.

Moram facit Dominus meus venire. *My lord delays to come.* Mt. 24:49.

Elegit Deus per os meum audire gentes verbum evangelii. *God chose that the Gentiles should hear through my mouth the word of the gospel.* Acts 15:7.

Nunc ergo quid temptatis Deum imponere jugum super cervicem discipulorum? *Now therefore why do ye tempt God to put a yoke upon the neck of the disciples?* Acts 15:10.

See also Mt. 7:5; Acts 16:14; Heb. 11:8.

The Vulgate is not at all consistent in this usage. *Ut* is used in Heb. 5:5, 6:10, and Col. 4:6, where an Infinitive is used in Greek.

ADJECTIVAL CLAUSES

149. An **Adjectival Clause** qualifies a noun or pronoun, which is called its antecedent, in the same way as an adjective.

Adjectival clauses are introduced by the relative pronouns *qui, quicumque,* or by the relative adverbs *quo, unde, quomodo,* etc.

When an adjectival or relative clause, as it is generally called, refers to an actual event or fact, it is called a Definite Relative Clause.

When a relative clause refers to a supposed event or instance and hence implies a condition, it is called an Indefinite Relative Clause.

The verb in a definite relative clause is in the Indicative mood, as it is in English; unless the clause comes under one of the classes specified below which have their verb in the Subjunctive.

Example:

> Nonne ecce omnes isti qui loquuntur Galilaei sunt? *Are not all these who speak Galilaeans?* Acts 2:7.

150. The verb in a definite relative clause is in the Subjunctive mood.

(1) To indicate that the person or thing denoted by the antecedent is capable of performing, or is of such a character as to be likely to perform or to suffer the action denoted by the relative clause.

Such clauses may be called Characterising Relative Clauses.

> Viri Ephesii, quis enim est hominum, qui nesciat Ephesiorum civitatem cultricem esse magnae Dianae? *Men of Ephesus, what man is there that does not know that the city of the Ephesians is a worshipper of great Diana?* Acts 19:35.
>
> Quia adversarius vester diabolus tamquam leo rugiens circuit, quaerens quem devoret. *Because your adversary the devil goeth about like a roaring lion seeking whom he may devour.* 1 Pet. 5:8.
>
> Neminem enim habeo tam unanimem, qui sincera affectione pro vobis sollicitus sit. *For I have no one so like minded who with sincere affection is likely to care for you.* Phil. 2:20.
>
> Filius autem hominis non habet ubi caput reclinet. *For the Son of man hath not where to lay his head.* Mt. 8:20.
>
> See also Acts 11:17, 13:11; Jn. 12:48; 1 Kings 18:26.

The following uses are akin to the above:

(*a*) A Subjunctive is sometimes found in a relative clause when the principal clause has for its predication the idea of existence.

> Ego autem non quaero gloriam meam: est qui quaerat et judicet.[7] *But I do not seek my own glory: there is one that seeks and judges.* Jn. 8:50.
>
> Omnes declinaverunt, simul inutiles facti sunt, non est qui faciat bonum, non est usque ad unum. *They have all gone out of the way, they have all together become profitless, there is not one that doeth good, no not one.* Rom. 3:12.

(*b*) A relative clause with the verb in the Subjunctive is sometimes found after the adjectives *dignus* and *indignus.*

---

7 This is the reading of SC. WW has Indicative in both verbs.

Et si in vobis judicabitur mundus, indigni estis, qui de minimis judicetis? *And if the world shall be judged by you, are you unworthy to judge the smallest matters?*   1 Cor. 6:2.

(2) The Subjunctive is used in a relative clause if the clause expresses purpose, consequence, or cause.

Purpose:

Et observantes miserunt insidiatores, qui se justos simularent. *And observing him they sent forth spies who should feign themselves to be just men.* Lk. 20:20.

Consequence:

Quis enim novit sensum Domini, qui instruat eum? *For who knows the mind of the Lord, so as to instruct him?*   1 Cor. 2:16.

Nam et Pater tales quaerit, qui adorent eum. *For the Father looks for such to worship him.*   Jn. 4:23.

(3) When a relative clause forms part of a sentence in an indirect statement or question, and generally when it depends on a clause with its verb in the Subjunctive, the verb in the relative clause is put in the Subjunctive in Classical Latin

This rule is not generally observed in the Vulgate

Et dum intra se haesitaret Petrus quidnam esset visio quam vidisset. ... *And while Peter doubted in himself what the vision was which he had seen ...* .   Acts 10:17.

In Mt. 27:15 there is an example of a relative clause of this kind. It expresses the wish of the people not directly, but indirectly. This construction is called *Virtual Oratio Obliqua.*

The following is an example of the Indicative used in a relative clause of this kind:

Venerunt dicentes se etiam visionem angelorum vidisse, qui dicunt eum vivere. *They came saying that they had also seen a vision of angels who say that he is alive.*   Lk. 24:23.

In Classical Latin this would be: *quid dicerent eum vivere.*

(4) In Ecclesiastical Latin the Subjunctive is used in relative clauses without any apparent reason.

Nec enim nomen aliud est sub caelo datum hominibus, in quo oporteat nos salvos fieri. *For there is no other name under heaven given to men whereby we must be saved.*   Acts 4:12.

151. The Future Perfect tense is generally used in indefinite relative clauses referring to future time.

Non occides: qui autem occiderit reus erit judicio. *Thou shalt not kill: but whosoever shall kill shall be guilty so as to be in danger of the judgement.* Mt. 5:21.

ADVERBIAL CLAUSES

152. Adverbial Clauses are clauses that stand in relationship of an adverb to some verb in another clause.

Adverbial clauses may be divided into eight classes.

(1) Clauses of Time. (Temporal Clauses.)
(2) Clauses of Place. (Local Clauses.)
(3) Clauses of Cause. (Causal Clauses.)

(4) Clauses of Purpose. (Final Clauses.)
(5) Clauses of Consequence. (Consecutive Clauses.)
(6) Clauses of Concession. (Concessive Clauses.)
(7) Clauses of Condition. (Conditional Clauses.)
(8) Clauses of Comparison. (Comparative Clauses.)

The names given in brackets are those given to these clauses in most grammars. They are not very satisfactory, as the words *temporal, final, consecutive* have quite a different sense in ordinary use to that which they have when used as grammatical terms. These names should however be known, as they are so commonly used.

The names given first are those suggested by the Committee on Grammatical Terminology.

153. (1) **Clauses of Time** denote the time of the action of the verb in the clause on which they depend.

They are introduced by the conjunctions

cum, ut[8], quando, ubi[9] = *when*;
antequam, priusquam = *before*;
postquam = *after*;
dum = *while, until*;;
donec, quando = *until*.

The Indicative mood is used in clauses of time introduced by *ut, quando, ubi* and *postquam*. (In Ecclesiastical Latin the Subjunctive is rarely found after *postquam*. Lk. 15:14; Rev. 22:8.)

Venit nox, quando nemo potest operari. *The night cometh, when no man can work.* Jn. 9:4.

Et ut cognovit vocem Petri, prae gaudio non aperuit januam. *And when she knew the voice of Peter, she did not open the door for joy.* Acts 12:14.

Postquam autem resurrexero, praecedam vos in Galilaeam. *But after I am risen, I will go before you into Galilee.* Mt. 26:32.

153a. A clause introduced by *cum* has the verb in the Indicative, if the clause only indicates the **time** of the action of the verb which it qualifies. If the clause introduced by *cum* denotes the **circumstances** that lead up to the condition or action of the verb which it qualifies, the verb in the clause introduced by *cum* is in the Subjunctive mood.

In Ecclesiastical Latin the verb in a clause introd. by *cum* is sometimes put in the Subjunctive mood without any apparent reason.

In the following examples the clause introduced by *cum* only indicates the time of the action of the verb which it qualifies.

In the first three the verb is in the Indicative mood in accordance with Classical usage: in the fourth the Subjunctive is used.

In veritate dico vobis, multae viduae erant in diebus Heliae in Israel, quando clausum est caelum annis tribus et mensibus sex, cum facta est fames magna in omni terra. *I tell you in truth there were many widows in the days of Elias in Israel, when the heaven was shut up for three years and six months, when a great famine took place in all the earth.* Lk. 4:25.

Et spiritus immundi, cum eum videbant, procidebant ei. *And the unclean spirits, when they saw him, used to fall down before him.* Mk. 3:11.

---

8 This use of *ut* must be carefully distinguished from the uses mentioned in sections 157, 158, 163.
9 *ubi* nearly always means *where* in the Vg., but see Gal. 4:4.

Cum ergo venerit, ille nobis annuntiabit omnia. *Whenever therefore he shall come, he will tell us all things.* Jn. 4:25.

Cum autem adpropinquaret portae civitatis, et ecce defunctus effere-batur. *But when he was drawing near to the gate of the city, behold a dead man was being borne out.* Lk. 7:12.

In the following examples the clause introduced by *cum* denotes not only the time of the action of the main verb, but also the attendant circumstances which explain it, or seem likely to hinder it.

Quod cum videret Simon Petrus, procidit ad genua Jesu. *And when Simon Peter saw it, he fell down at Jesus' knees.* Lk. 5:8.

(The clause explains why he fell down.)

Quomodo potest homo nasci cum senex sit? *How can a man be born when he is old?* Jn. 3:4.

(His age is likely to prevent his being born.)

Ne forte, cum aliis praedicaverim, ipse reprobus efficiar. *Lest per-chance, when I have preached to others, I myself may become reprobate.* 1 Cor. 9:27.

(The fact that he has preached to others ought to save him from be-coming reprobate; but will it?)

154. In clauses introduced by *antequam, priusquam, dum, donec, quoad*, either the Indicative or the Subjunctive mood may be used.

The Indicative mood is used in Classical Latin if the clause merely denotes the **time** of the action of the verb which it qualifies.

The Subjunctive mood is used if the clause refers to an action which is only in prospect and explains the **purpose** of the action of the verb which it qualifies.

Examples:

Clause simply denoting time.

Antequam abiit, hoc dixit. *He said this before he went away.*

Dum mecum eras, ille in Hispaniam properavit. *While you were with me, he hastened into Spain.*

Clause denoting expectation and purpose.

Num expectas donec testimonium dicat? *Are you waiting until he gives his evidence?* (i.e. *with a view to hearing him*).

Impetum hostium sustinuit donec ceteri scalas ad muros ponerent. *He sustained the attack of the enemy until the others could set ladders to the walls.*

Ad oppidum, antequam milites a terrore se reciperent, properavit. *He hastened to the town (so as to be there) before the soldiers should recover themselves from their terror.*

In Ecclesiastical Latin either the Indicative or the Subjunctive is used in claus-es introduced by *antequam, priusquam, dum, donec*, without any distinction of meaning. The Subjunctive is more frequently used than the Indicative.

Examples from the Vulgate:

Priusquam te Philippus vocaret, cum esses sub ficu, vidi te. *Before Philip called thee, when thou wast under the fig tree, I saw thee.* Jn. 1:48.

Dum autem irent emere, venit sponsus. *But while they went to buy, the bridegroom came.* Mk. 25:10.

Simile est regnum caelorum fermento, quod acceptum mulier abscon-dit in farinae satis tribus, donec fermentatum est totum. *The kingdom of heaven is like leaven which a woman took and hid in three measures of meal, until the whole was leavened.* Mt. 13:33.

Dico tibi, Petre, non cantabit hodie gallus, donec ter abneges nosse me. *I say to thee, Peter, the cock shall not crow this day until thou hast denied three times that thou knowest me.* Lk. 22:34.

See also Mt. 18:30; Lk. 8:42, 9:27, 29; Acts 21:26, 27.

Clauses of time may also be expressed by the Ablative Absolute or by a Participle: see sections 51, 183.

155. (2) **Clauses of Place** denote the place where the action of the verb in the clause on which they depend is said to happen.

They are introduced by the conjunctions

ubi, quo = *where, whither;*

unde = *whence.*

Mood: Indicative, as in English.

If the clause of place refers to an action which will take place in some indefinite place in future time, the verb is generally in the Future Perfect tense.

Nolite thesaurizare vobis thesauros in terra, ubi erugo et tinea demolitur. *Lay not up for yourselves treasures on the earth, where rust and moth do corrupt.* Mt. 6:19.

Ego semper docui in synagoga et in templo, quo omnes Judaei conveniunt. ... *I always taught in the synagogue and in the temple, whither all the Jews come together. ...* Jn. 18:20.

Amen dico vobis, ubicumque praedicatum fuerit hoc evangelium in toto mundo, dicetur et quod haec fecit in memoriam ejus. *Verily I say to you, wherever this gospel shall be preached in the whole world, this which she hath done shall be told for a memorial of her.* Mt. 26:13.

156. (3) **Clauses of Cause** denote the reason (real or alleged) given for the action of the verb in the clause on which they depend.

They are introduced by *quia, quoniam, quod, eo quod, cum, = since, because,* etc.

In Classical Latin the Indicative is generally used in clauses introduced by *quia, quoniam, quod,* if the clause states what was the real cause of the action of the main verb in the opinion of the speaker or writer.

If however the clause denotes the cause of the action of the main verb in the opinion of some one other than the speaker or writer, or gives an opinion as to its cause which the speaker or writer once held, but which he now does not hold, the Subjunctive is used.

Examples:

Judaei Apostolos, quod legem violaverant, persecuti sunt. *The Jews persecuted the Apostles because they had* (in point of fact) *broken the law.*

Judaei Apostolos, quod legem violavissent, persecuti sunt. *The Jews persecuted the Apostles, because* (in the opinion of the *Jews) they had broken the law.*

In the first example the writer states that the Apostles were persecuted because they had actually broken the law. In the second example the writer leaves it an open question as to whether the Apostles had broken the law, or not; but he states that the Jews persecuted them, because they thought the Apostles had broken the law.

In Ecclesiastical Latin clauses introduced by *quia, quoniam, quod, eo quod* may have the verb in the Subjunctive even when they imply that the cause given for the action of the main verb is the real cause in the opinion of the speaker or writer.

Exi a me, quia homo peccator sum, Domine. *Depart from me, for I am a sinful man, O Lord.* Lk. 5:8.

Serve nequam, omne debitum dimisi tibi, quoniam rogasti me. *Thou worthless slave, I forgave thee all thy debt because thou didst ask me.* Mt. 18:32.

Non quod ipse esset Pater et Filius. ... sed quod tam similes sint Pater et Filius, ut qui unum noverit, ambos noverit. *Not because the Father and the Son were the same. ... but because the Father and the Son are so much alike, that he who knows one, knows both.* Aug. *Tract. in Joh. lxx.*

Ipse autem Jesus non credebat semetipsum eis, eo quod ipse nosset omnes. *But Jesus himself did not trust himself to them, because he knew all men.* Jn. 2:24.

N.B. These clauses should be carefully distinguished from the noun clauses introduced by *quia, quoniam* and *quod* dealt with in sections 112 sq.

156a. Clauses of cause introduced by *cum* have the verb in the Subjunctive both in Classical and Ecclesiastical Latin

De omnibus quibus accusor a Judaeis, rex Agrippa, aestimo me beatum apud te cum sim defensurus me hodie. *I think that I am fortunate, king Agrippa, because I am going to defend myself before thee about all the things whereof I am accused by the Jews.* Acts 26:2.

Hi homines conturbant civitatem nostram, cum sint Judaei. *These men disturb our state, because they are Jews.* Acts 16:20.

Rarely an Indicative is found in these clauses:

Ut, cum circa servos talis est Dominus, exemplo suo doceret, qualis circa compares et aequales debeat esse conservus. *That he might teach by his example what a fellow-servant ought to be with respect to his companions and equals, since he himself is such a Lord to his servants.* Cypr. *De bono patientiae.*

Clauses of cause may also be expressed by a Participle or by the Ablative Absolute. See sections 51, 183.

157. (4) **Clauses of Purpose** denote the purpose of the action of the verb in the clause on which they depend.

Clauses of purpose are generally introduced by
ut when affirmative = *that, in order that,*
ne when negative (*ut non* in Ecclesiastical Latin),
quo when comparative.
Mood: Subjunctive always.
These clauses may also be expressed by.
1. A relative clause with the verb in the Subjunctive.
2. The Gerund or Gerundive Participle with *ad* or *causa.*
3. A Future Participle. (In Ecclesiastical Latin a Present Participle may be used in this sense.)
4. A Supine. (This is rare.)

157a. In Ecclesiastical Latin an Infinitive is often used to express purpose as in English and Greek.

This construction is found in the Latin poets, but **not** in Classical prose. It seems to have been a vernacular idiom which came into literary use at a late period.

158.. Purpose expressed by *ut,* etc.

Paenitemini igitur et convertimini, ut deleantur vestra peccata. *Repent therefore and be converted that your sins may be blotted out.* Acts 3:19.

Hic venit in testimonium, ut testimonium perhiberet de lumine. *He came for a testimony in order that he might bear witness about the light.* Jn. 1:7.

Et in manibus tollent te, ne forte offendas ad lapidem. *And they shall bear thee in their hands, that thou dash not thy foot against a stone.* Mt. 4:6.

Nolite judicare ut non judicemini. *Judge not that ye be not judged.* Mt. 7:1.

159. Purpose expressed by a relative clause.

Considerate ergo, fratres, viros ex vobis boni testimonii septem,...quos constituamus super hoc opus. *Look out therefore from among yourselves, brethren, seven men of good report that we may set them over this work.* Acts 6:3.

Tunc summiserunt viros, qui dicerent se audisse eum dicentem verba blasphemiae in Mosen et Deum. *Then they suborned men to say that they had heard him speaking blasphemous words against Moses and God.* Acts 6:11.

160. Purpose expressed by the Gerundive Participle with *ad*.

Propterea et ego amplius non sustinens, misi ad cognoscendam fidem vestram. *Wherefore I also, since I could no longer forbear, sent to know your faith.* 1 Thess. 3:5.

See also Rom. 15:8.

161. Purpose expressed by the Future or the Present Participle.

Post annos autem plures eleemosynas facturus in gentem meam veni. *But after many years I came to give alms to my nation.* Acts 24:17.

Vobis primum Deus suscitans Filium suum, misit eum benedicentem vobis. *For you first God, having raised up his Son, sent Him to bless you.* Acts 3:26.

See also Jn. 6:6.

162. Purpose expressed by the Infinitive.

Venisti huc ante tempus torquere nos? *Hast thou come here before the time to torment us?* Mt. 8:29.

Et circumspiciebat videre eam quae hoc fecerat. *And he looked about to see her that had done this.* Mk. 5:32.

Non enim misit me Christus baptizare, sed evangelizare. *For Christ sent me not to baptize, but to preach the gospel.* 1 Cor. 1:17.

163. (5) **Clauses of Consequence** denote the consequence or result of the action of the verb in the clause on which they depend.

They are introduced by *ut* or *ita ut, so that,* when affirmative and are negatived by *non.*

Mood: Subjunctive always.

Sic enim dilexit Deus mundum, ut Filium suum unigenitum daret. *For God so loved the world, that he gave his only begotten Son.* Jn. 3:16.

Et convenerunt multi, ita ut non caperet neque ad januam. *And many came together, so that there was no room for them even at the door.* Mk. 2:2.

Numquid aquam quis prohibere potest, ut non baptizentur hi qui Spiritum Sanctum acceperunt sicut et nos? *Can any forbid water, that these should be baptized who have received the Holy Ghost as well as we?* Acts 10:47.

Si confiteamur peccata nostra fidelis est et justus ut remittat nobis peccata nostra. *If we confess our sins, he is faithful and just to forgive us our sins.* 1 Jn. 1:9.

These clauses should be observed with special care as the construction of them is so very unlike English.

164. The Infinitive may be used (in the Vulgate) to denote consequence in imitation of the Greek.

O insensati Galatae quis vos fascinavit non obedire veritati? *O foolish Galatians, who has bewitched you that you should not[10] obey the truth?* Gal. 3:1.

Et quomodo conversi estis ad Deum a simulacris, servire Deo vivo et vero. *And how ye were turned to God from idols, to serve the living and true God.* 1 Thess. 1:9.

Anania, cur temtavit Satanas cor tuum, mentiri te Spiritui Sancto? *Ananias, why hath Satan tempted thine heart that thou shouldest lie to the Holy Spirit?* Acts 5:3.

In Rom. 1:10 a Greek Infinitive denoting consequence is trans. by the Genitive of the Gerund.

165. Very rarely clauses of consequence are introduced by *quia,* and once, in a quotation from the Old Testament, by *quod* and *quoniam.*

Quo hic iturus est, quia non inveniemus eum? *Where does he intend to go that we shall not find him?* Jn. 7:35.

See also Mt. 8:27; Mk. 4:40.

Quid est homo quod memor es ejus, aut filius hominis quoniam visitas eum? *What is man that thou art mindful of him, or the son of man that thou visitest him?* Heb. 2:6, cited from Ps. 8:5.

166. (6) **Clauses of Concession** denote some fact which is regarded as likely to prevent or to have prevented the occurrence of the action of the verb in the clause on which they depend.

They are introduced by *cum, quamvis, etsi, licet* = *although.* In the Vulgate the principal clause may be introduced by *sed* or *sed tamen:* see examples below.

In clauses introduced by *cum* in this sense, the verb is always in the Subjunctive. In Classical Latin *quamquam* is followed by a verb in the Indicative and *quamvis* is followed by a verb in the Subjunctive. In Ecclesiastical Latin the Subjunctive is found after both these words. Clauses introduced by *etsi* are similar in construction to clauses of condition. Clauses introduced by *licet* have the verb in the Subjunctive (Indicative in Vulgate).

The tense is the same as that which is used in the English. Negative *non.*

Ecce et naves, cum magnae sint, et a ventis validis minentur, circumferuntur a modico gubernaculo. *Behold also the ships, although they are so big and although they are threatened by strong winds, are turned about by a small helm.* Jas. 3:4.

See also Mt. 26:60.

---

10 This is reading of SC text.

Unum scio, quia caecus cum essem, modo video. *One thing I know, that, although I was blind, now I see.* Jn. 9:25.

Nam cum liber essem ex omnibus, omnium me servum feci. *For although I was free from all men, I made myself a slave of all.* 1 Cor. 9:19.

Quamvis non longe sit ab unoquoque nostrum. *Although he is not far from each one of us.* Acts 17:27.

Quamquam Jesus non baptizaret, sed discipuli ejus. *Although Jesus did not baptize, but his disciples.* Jn. 4:2.

See also Phil. 3:4; Heb. 7:5.

Cum possemus vobis oneri esse...sed facti sumus parvuli in medio vestrum. *Although we might have been burdensome to you...we made ourselves like little children in the midst of you.* I Thess. 2:7.

Etsi omnes scandalizati fuerint: sed non ego. *Although all shall be offended in thee: yet will I never be offended.*

See also Col. 2:5. Mk. 14:29.

Sed licet nos, aut angelus de caelo evangelizet vobis praeterquam quod evangelizavimus vobis, anathema sit. *But although we, or an angel from heaven preach to you any other gospel than that which we have preached to you, let him be accursed.* Gal. 1:8.

Sed licet is qui foris est noster homo corrumpitur.... *But although our outward man decays....* 2 Cor. 4:16.

A clause of concession may also be expressed by a participle or by the Ablative Absolute. See sections 51, 183.

167. (7) **Clauses of Condition** state the condition on which the action of the verb in the clause on which they depend would take place.

A clause of condition and the clause on which it depends make up a sentence which is called a **Conditional Sentence**. In such a sentence the clause of condition states a supposition, and the principal clause states the result of the fulfilment of the supposition.

The clause of condition is called the **Protasis** and the principal clause is called the **Apodosis** of the conditional sentence.

Clauses of condition are introduced by *si*, **if**, *nisi*, unless. Negative *non*.

In Classical Latin if the verb in the principal clause is in the Indicative mood, the verb in the clause of condition is also in the Indicative mood. If the verb in the principal clause is in the Subjunctive mood, the verb in the clause of condition is also in the Subjunctive mood. There are exceptions to this rule; but they are rare and and generally due to a desire to produce a rhetorical effect. In Ecclesiastical Latin the rule given above is not strictly observed.

The construction of conditional sentences varies according as the time of the supposition is **Past, Present**, or **Future**, and according as the condition is regarded as **fulfilled**, or **unfulfilled**.

It is obvious that a condition is never regarded as fulfilled at the time contemplated by the clause on which it depends. It may however be stated in such a way as to imply that it has not been fulfilled.

Consider the sentences

If you are ill I shall send for the doctor.

If you were ill I should send for the doctor.

If you had been ill I should have sent for the doctor.

In the first of these sentences it is left an open question whether the condition has been fulfilled, or not. In the other two sentences it is implied that the condition has not been fulfilled. The first of the two relates to illness extending up to the present time: the second of the two refers to illness in the past.

The two latter sentences illustrate what is meant by an **unfulfilled conditional sentence**.

168. Present or past suppositions implying nothing as to the fulfilment of the condition.

A Present or Past tense of the Indicative is used in the clause of condition. Almost any part of the verb may be used in the principal clause.

> Si judico ego, judicium meum verum est. *If I judge, my judgment is true.* Jn. 8:16.

> Si Filius Dei es, dic ut lapides isti panes fiant. *If thou art the Son of God, command these stones to become loaves...* Mt. 4:3.

> Si Abraham ex operibus justificatus est, habet gloriam. *If Abraham was justified by works, he has whereof to glory.* Rom. 4:2.

> Si vero ex Deo est, non poteritis dissolvere eos. *If it is really of God, you will not be able to break them up.* Acts 5:39.

169. Present or Past suppositions implying that the condition has not been fulfilled.

The Imperfect or Pluperfect Subjunctive is used both in the clause of condition and in the principal clause. The Imperfect Subjunctive denotes continued action in past time, or action extending up to the present moment. The Pluperfect Subjunctive denotes action in past time.

> Si adhuc hominibus placerem, Christi servus non essem.
> *If I were still pleasing men, I should not be the slave of Christ.* Gal. 1:10.

> Si diligeretis me, gauderetis utique. *If ye loved me, ye would certainly rejoice.* Jn. 14:28.

> Non haberes potestatem adversum me ullam, nisi tibi datum esset de super. *Thou wouldst have no power at all against me unless it had been given thee from above.* Jn. 19:11.

> Si non esset hic malefactor, non tibi tradidissemus eum. *If this man were not a malefactor, we would not have given him up to thee.* Jn. 18:30.

> Si opera non fecissem in eis, quae nemo alius fecit, peccatum non haberent. *If I had not done among them the works that no man else did, they would not have sin.* Jn. 15:24.

> Domine, si fuisses hic, frater meus non fuisset mortuus. *Lord, if thou hadst been here, my brother would not have died.* Jn. 11:21.

170. If one of the **Modal verbs** such as *possum, debeo, oportet* or a **Periphrastic** tense made up of the Future Participle or the Gerund or Gerundive with part of *esse* stands in the principal clause of a conditional sentence in which there is a Subjunctive in the clause of condition, the **Indicative** mood of such verbs is used instead of the Subjunctive.

> Nisi esset hic a Deo, non poterat facere quicquam. *If this man were not of God, he could do nothing.* Jn. 9:33.

> Dimitti poterat homo hic, si non appellasset Caesarem. *This man might be let go, if he had not appealed to Caesar.* Acts 26:32.

171. The following are examples of sentences in which the rule that, if there is an Indicative in the principal clause, there should be an Indicative in the clause of condition is not observed.

Bonum erat ei, si natus non fuisset homo ille. *It was good for that man, if he had not been born.* Mt. 26:24.

Nam concupiscentiam nesciebam, nisi lex diceret: Non concupisces. *For I did not know covetousness, if the law had not said: Thou shalt not covet.* Rom. 7:7.

172. Future Suppositions. There are two forms of future suppositions.
　　1. The more vivid form.
　　2. The less vivid form.

The Future or Future Perfect Indicative is used in the more vivid form. The Present Subjunctive is used in the less vivid form.

In English the Present Indicative is often used in the Protasis of these conditional sentences. This use is really incorrect: the Latin is much more accurate in its use of tenses: consider the force of the Latin Future and Future Perfect tenses in the examples given below.

If the action expressed in the Protasis of the conditional sentence is represented as taking place *before* the action denoted by the verb in the principal clause, the Future Perfect is properly used, because the action denoted by the principal clause is itself still future. Strictly speaking the Future should only be used in the Protasis when the time denoted by the Protasis and Apodosis is identical. For example:

Dum hic ero, te amabo. *As long as I am here, I shall love you.*

It will be noticed however that this principle is not strictly observed.

Si quis autem templum Dei violaverit, disperdet eum Deus. *But if any man defile the temple of God, him will God destroy.*　　1 Cor. 3:17.

Si omnes scandalizati fuerint in te, ego numquam scandalizabor. *If all men shall be offended in thee, yet will I never be offended.* Mt. 26:33.

Haec tibi omnia dabo, si cadens adoraveris me. *All these things will I give thee, if thou wilt fall down and worship me.*　　Mt. 4:9.

Fidelis sermo: nam si commortui sumus, et convivemus: si sustinebimus, et conregnabimus: si negabimus, et ille negabit nos. *Faithful is the saying: for if we have died with him, we shall also live with him: if we endure, we shall also reign with him: if we deny him, he also will deny us.*　　2 Tim. 2:11.

173. The use of the less vivid form is rare.

Quid enim proficit homo, si lucretur universum mundum, se autem ipsum perdat, et detrimentum sui faciat? *For what does it profit a man if he should gain the whole world, but lose himself, and work his own destruction?* Lk. 9:25.

Sic est regnum Dei, quemadmodum si homo jaciat sementem in terram.... *So is the kingdom of God as if a man should cast a seed into the earth...* Mk. 4:26.

See also 1 Cor. 7:8.

174. In accordance with Hebrew usage, sentences similar in meaning to Conditional Sentences are found in the Vulgate where the conditional clause is expressed by (*a*) an inversion, (*b*) an Imperative.

(*a*) Tristatur aliquis vestrum? oret aequo animo et psallat. Infirmatur quis in vobis? inducat presbyteros Ecclesiae. *Is any sad among you? let him pray with a calm mind and let him sing psalms. Is any sick among you? let him send for the elders of the Church.* Jas. 5:13.

(*b*) Petite, et dabitur vobis: quaerite, et invenietis: pulsate, et aperietur vobis. *Ask, and it shall be given to you: seek, and ye shall find: knock, and it shall be opened to you.* Mt. 7:7.

175. (8) **Clauses of Comparison** compare the action or state denoted by the verb in the clause on which they depend to the action or state denoted in the clause of comparison.

They are introduced by *ut, sicut, prout, quomodo, tanquam, quasi,* etc., *as, as if.* Negative *non.*

The verb in clauses of comparison is in the **Indicative**, if it is implied that the comparison is **real**.

If it is implied that the comparison is **not real**, the verb may be in the **Subjunctive**

Sometimes only a Participle is used and sometimes the verb is omitted altogether in the clause of comparison.

Ita et viri debent diligere uxores ut corpora sua. *So men ought to love their wives as their own bodies.* Eph. 5:28.

Non ergo oportuit et te misereri conservi tui, sicut et ego tui misertus sum? *Oughtest thou not therefore to have had pity on thy fellow slave, even as I had pity on thee?* Mt. 18:33.

Ut quomodo Christus surrexit a mortuis...ita et nos in novitate vitae ambulemus. *That as Christ rose from the dead...so we also may walk in newness of life.* Rom. 6:4.

Consilium autem do tanquam misericordiam consecutus a Domino. *But I give my advice as one that has received mercy from the Lord.* 1 Cor. 7:25.

Ostendens se tanquam sit Deus. *Showing himself as if he were God.* II Thess. 2:4.

Diliges proximum tuum tanquam te ipsum. *Thou shalt love thy neighbour as thyself.* Mk. 12:31.

His qui sub lege sunt, quasi sub lege essem, cum ipse non essem sub lege, ut eos, qui sub lege erant, lucri facerem. *To those that are under the law as if I were under the law, although I was not under the law, that I might gain them that were under the law.* 1 Cor. 9:20.

Carissimi, nolite peregrinari in fervore qui ad temptationem vobis fit, quasi novi aliquid vobis contingat. *Beloved, do not be disturbed at the fiery trial which has come upon you to test you, as if some new thing were happening to you.* 1 Pet. 4:12.

Optulistis mihi hunc hominem, quasi avertentem populum. *Ye have brought to me this man as one that is turning away the people....* Lk. 23:14.

Sic curro, non quasi in incertum: sic pugno, non quasi aerem verberans. *So run I not as uncertainly: so fight I not as one that beateth the air.* 1 Cor. 9:7.

Sometimes a clause of consequence is expressed by *sicut* or *sic* followed by *et.*

Fiat voluntas tua sicut in caelo et in terra. *Thy will be done in earth as it is in heaven.* Mt. 6:10.

PARTICIPLES

176. A Participle is a **verbal adjective** sharing the characteristics of both verbs and adjectives.

As a verb it has a subject, and, if it is the Participle of a transitive verb, it has an object. It governs the same case as the verb from which it is derived. It has also tense and voice.

As an adjective it agrees with the noun which it qualifies in number, gender and case.

The Latin language is very short of Participles: it only has:

A Present Participle Active.

A future Participle Active.

A Past Participle Passive.

In the case of **deponent verbs** the Past Participle is used in an active sense, as well as a passive.

The time denoted by the tense of a Participle is relative to the time of the main verb, and not to the time of speaking, or writing.

177. Properly speaking the **Present Participle** denotes action going on at the **same time** as the action of the main verb, but in Ecclesiastical Latin the Present Participle is continually used to represent the Aorist Participle in Greek and to denote action which took place before the action of the main verb. See examples.

The **Future Participle** denotes action which is expected to take place.

The **Past Participle** is also a **Perfect Participle** and so denotes past action complete and so continuing to have its effect at the time of the action of the main verb as well as simple past action.

178. Examples of the use of the tenses of the Participle:

Present Participle in the sense of action contemporaneous with that of the main verb.

Igitur qui dispersi erant pertransibant evangelizantes verbum. *Those therefore that were scattered went everywhere preaching the word.* Acts 8:4.

Viri autem illi qui comitabantur cum eo, stabant stupefacti, audientes quidem vocem, neminem autem videntes. *But the men who were travelling with him stood amazed, hearing the voice, but seeing no man.* Acts 9:7.

Notice the use of the Past Participle *stupefacti* in a Perfect sense.

Present Participle in the sense of action previous to that of the main verb.

Ascendens autem, frangensque panem et gustans, satisque allocutus usque ad lucem, sic profectus est. *But having gone up and having broken bread and eaten, and having addressed them a long time even until dawn, so he departed.* Acts 20:11.

Notice that the Present Participle and the Past Participle are used in exactly the same sense in this passage.

See also Mk. 3:13; Eph. 2:14, 15.

179. Future Participle in the sense of expected action.

Genimina viperarum, quis ostendit vobis fugere a ventura ira? *O generation of vipers, who hath warned you to flee from the wrath to come?* Lk. 3:7.

180. Past Participle in sense of past or perfect action.

Demoratus autem inter eos dies non amplius quam octo aut decem, descendit Caesaream. *And having remained among them not more than eight or ten days he descended to Caesarea.* Acts 25:6.

181. A Participle may be used either **adjectivally** or **adverbially.**

When it is used adjectivally it limits the meaning of the noun which it qualifies just like an adjective. A participle may also be used by itself in this sense, the noun with which it agrees being understood. Adjectival Participles are generally best translated by an adjectival clause, an adjective or a noun.

When it is used adverbially it is equivalent to an adverbial clause modifying some verb in the sentence. Adverbial Participles are generally best translated by a suitable adverbial clause.

The context must decide which kind of adverbial clause the Participle in question is equivalent to. The Participle itself does not denote time, purpose, cause, concession, or condition, but the context implies one of these ideas, and the Participle admits it.

Participles are used much more frequently in Latin than in English, and this is the reason why it is so often advisable to translate a Participle by a clause.

182. Adjectival Participles. These are generally best translated by a relative clause, or by a noun.

> Nolumus autem vos ignorare, fratres, de dormientibus. *But we do not wish you to be ignorant, brethren, concerning those that are asleep.* I Thess. 4:13.

> Quam pius es petentibus, sed quid invenientibus? *How good thou art to those that seek, but what to those that find?* St Bernard.

> Qua cessabunt persequentes, et regnabunt patientes. *Where the persecutors shall cease, and the patient shall reign.* Hym. Lat.

The use of participles as nouns is characteristic of Late Latin.

> Credentes = *believers.* Diffidentes = *unbelievers.*

> Discentes = *disciples.*

183. Adverbial Participles.

Equivalent to a clause of Time.

> Orantes autem, nolite multum loqui. *But when ye pray, do not say much.* Mt. 6:7.

> Oportuit ergo te mittere pecuniam meam nummulariis, et veniens ego recepissem utique quod meum est cum usura. *You ought to have put out my money to the bankers, and then, when I came, I should have received my own with usury.* Mt. 25:27.

Equivalent to a clause of **Cause.**

> Peccavi tradens sanguinem justum. *I have sinned, because I have betrayed righteous blood.* Mt. 27:4.

> See also Acts 4:21, 12:3; 2 Pet. 1:19.

Equivalent to a clause of **Concession.**

> Et nullam causam mortis invenientes in eum, petierunt a Pilato ut interficerent eum. *And although they found no cause of death in him, yet they asked Pilate that they might slay him.* Acts 13:28.

> See also 2 Pet. 1:12; Jude, 5.

Equivalent to a clause of **Purpose.**

The future participle is generally used in this sense; but in Ecclesiastical Latin a present participle may be so used.

Post autem annos plures eleemosynas facturus in gentem meam veni. *But after many years I came to make offerings to my nation.* Acts 24:17.

Sine videamus an veniat Helias liberans eum. *Let us see if Elias will come to save him.* Mt. 27:49.

Vobis primum Deus suscitans Filium suum, misit eum benedicentem vobis. *To you first God, having raised up his Son, sent him to bless you.* Acts 3:26.

Equivalent to a clause of **Condition.**

Tempore enim suo metemus, non deficientes. *For in his own time we shall reap, if we faint not.* Gal. 6:9.

A quibus custodientes vos, bene agetis. *If ye keep yourselves from these, ye shall do well.* Acts 15:29.

See also Rom. 2:27, 12:20.

184. After verbs denoting ceasing, continuing, making an end or failing a participle is used to complete the sense, as in Greek.

Et factum est cum consummasset Jesus praecipiens duodecim discipulis suis.... *And it came to pass when Jesus had made an end of giving commands to his twelve disciples....* Mt. 11:1.

Vos autem, fratres, nolite deficere bene facientes.... *But you, brethren, do not cease to do well....* II Thess. 3:13.

Petrus autem perseveravit pulsans. *But Peter continued knocking.* Acts 12:16.

See also Acts 5:42; Eph. 1:16; Col. 1:9.

185. A peculiar use of the Present Participle which is an attempt to reproduce the Hebrew Infinitive Absolute is found in the Vulgate

The Pres. Part. is used with a mood of the same verb to make a strong or positive statement.

Conterens non conteram domum Jacob. *I will not utterly destroy the house of Jacob.* Amos 9:8.

Videns vidi afflictionem populi mei. *I have surely seen the affliction of my people.* Acts 7:34.

See also Heb. 6:14; Mt. 13:14.

The same sense may also be expressed by an Ablative of the Gerund or by the Ablative of a noun of kindred meaning to the verb.

Praecipiendo praecipimus vobis ne doceretis in nomine isto. *We have strictly charged you that ye should not teach in this name.* Acts 5:28.

Qui maledixerit patri vel matri, morte moriatur. *Whosoever curses father or mother, let him surely die.* Mt. 15:4.

Desiderio desideravi hoc pascha manducare vobiscum antequam patiar. *I have greatly desired to eat this Passover with you before I suffer.* Lk. 22:15.

A Pres. Part. may also be used in the sense of the Ablative of the gerund.

Quis autem vestrum cogitans potest adjicere ad staturam suam cubitum unum? *Which of you by thinking can add one cubit to his stature?* Mt. 6:27.

THE GERUND, GERUNDIVE PARTICIPLE AND SUPINE

186. These parts of the Latin verb have no exact equivalents in English, although the English verbal noun ending in *ing* is equivalent to some uses of the Gerund.

The Gerund and Supine are verbal nouns and the Gerundive is a verbal adjective.

The Nom. case of the verbal noun is expressed in Latin by the Infinitive and so is the Accusative case, except in uses where the verbal noun stands after a preposition.

The Genitive, Dative and Ablative cases of the verbal noun and the Accusative case, when standing after a preposition, are expressed by the Gerund.

The Gerund is not used very often in the Vulgate

For the sake of clearness some simple examples of each case of the verbal noun are given first and then some examples from the Vulgate etc.

Nominative. Edere jucundum est. *To eat (or eating) is pleasant. Accusative.* Dicit edere jucundum esse. *He says that eating is pleasant.*

Accusative (with a prep.). Omnia ad edendum parata sunt. *All things are prepared for eating.*

Genitive. Amor edendi magnum malum est. *The love of eating is a great evil.*

Dative. Dat operam edendo. *He gives attention to eating.*

Ablative. Vivimus edendo. *We live by eating.*

187. Examples of the use of the Gerund in the Vulgate:

Et dedit illis potestatem curandi infirmitates. *And he gave them the power of curing diseases.*Mk. 3:15; Mt. 11:15.

Deus autem spei repleat vos omni gaudio et pace in credendo. *But may the God of hope fill you with all joy and peace in believing.* Rom. 15:13.

Quae quaestum magnum praestabat dominis suis divinando. *Who brought much gain to her masters by soothsaying.*Acts 16:16.

See also Acts 10:33; 1 Cor. 12:24; 1 Tim. 5:21.

188. A peculiar use of the Ablative of the Gerund which is employed to translate a Present or Aorist Participle in the Greek is found in the Vulgate This is generally best translated by a present participle in English.

Qui pertransivit bene faciendo et sanando omnes oppressos a diabolo. *Who went about doing good and healing all that were oppressed by the devil.* Acts 10:38.

Hodie, in David dicendo, post tantum temporis....*Saying in David: "To-day, after so long a time...."* Heb. 4:7.

In casulis habitando cum Isaac.... *Dwelling in tents with Isaac....* Heb. 11:9.

In quo et laboro, certando secundum operationem ejus, quam operatur in me in virtute. *In which I also labour, working according to his operation which he works in me with power.* Col. 1:29.

A similar use is found in the "Stabat Mater."

Vidit suum dulcem Natum
Moriendo desolatum.

And in Augustine:

Nec jam ingemiscebam orando ut subvenires mihi. *Confess.* 6:3.

189. In the Vulgate translation of the Psalms (which is not Jerome's direct translation from the Hebrew, but a revised form of the Old Latin) the Ablative of the Gerund with *in* is found in a sense which is best translated into English by a clause of time.

This is also found in Augustine.

Example:

> In convertendo inimicum meum retrorsum.... *When mine enemy is turned back....* Ps. 9:4.

> In deficiendo ex me spiritum meum, et tu cognovisti semitas meas. *When my spirit failed within me, thou knewest my paths.* Ps. 141:4.

> See also 101:23, 125:1.

190. In Classical Latin if the verb is transitive and the object expressed the **Gerundive Participle** is generally used instead of the Gerund.

The Gerundive is not a noun, but an adjective, and, as such, agrees with its noun in number, gender and case.

As the Gerundive is in the passive voice in Latin and the verbal noun is in the active voice in English, the noun with which it agrees will be that which is the object of the verbal noun in English.

Thus where we write in English.:

> They sent ambassadors for the sake of seeking peace,

the Latin has something equivalent to:

> They sent ambassadors for the sake of peace to be sought.

By a construction known as the Gerundive Attraction the word that would be the object if the Gerund were used is drawn into the **case** of the Gerundive, if this is in any other case than the Accusative, and the Gerundive still agrees with it in number and gender.

Thus instead of the Gerund construction

> Miserunt legatos ad petendum pacem,

we write

> Miserunt legatos ad petendam pacem.

Instead of

Causa opprimendi legionem. *For the sake of destroying the legion,* we write Causa opprimendae legionis.

Instead of Opprimendo legiones. *By destroying the legions,* we write Opprimendis legionibus.

This Gerundive construction is nearly always used in the Accusative and Dative and generally in the Genitive and Ablative The Genitive Plural is avoided.

Examples of the Gerundive construction from the Vulgate:

> Ad dandam scientiam salutis plebi ejus.... *To give the knowledge of salvation to his people....* Lk. 1:77.

> Dico enim Christum Jesum ministrum fuisse circumcisionis, propter veritatem Dei, ad confirmandas promissiones patrum. *For I say that Christ Jesus was a minister of the circumcision, on account of the truth of God, to confirm the promises of the fathers.* Rom. 15:8.

> See also Mt. 26:12; 1 Thess. 3:5.

191. In Ecclesiastical Latin the Gerund is found governing a direct object.

> Hoc autem ipse de se, non profecto jactando virtutem, sed deflendo potius defectum, quem sibi per curam pastoralem incucurrisse videbatur, referre consueverat. *This he used to say about himself, not certainly by way of boasting of his virtue, but rather by way of lamenting his shortcomings, which he seemed to have incurred through the pastoral office.* Bede, *Hist. Ecclesiastical*

> Ego autem dico vobis: quoniam omnis, qui viderit mulierem ad concupiscendum eam, jam moechatus est eam in corde suo. *But I say to you that*

every one who looketh on a woman to lust after her hath already committed adultery with her in his heart. Mt. 5:28.

See also Mk. 3:15, quoted above, and Rom. 1:5.

192. In the Nom. case and the Accusative case (when used as the subject of an infinitive) the Gerund and the Gerundive have a meaning which is quite distinct from that which has been described above. They have a sense of obligation or duty.

The Gerund is used when the verb is Intransitive, or when the verb is Transitive and the object is not expressed.

As stated above, the Gerund is in the Active voice and the Gerundive is in the Passive voice and agrees with its subject in number, gender and case.

The name of the person on whom the duty lies is put in the Dative case. If the verb governs a Dative, the Ablative with *a* is used to express the person on whom the duty lies, to avoid ambiguity.

Examples:

Gerund.

Currendum est mihi. *I must run.*

Parentibus nostris a nobis parendum est. *We must obey our parents.*

Gerundive.

Mater tua amanda est. *Your mother is to be loved,* or *You must love your mother.*

Hostes nobis vincendi sunt. *The enemy are to be conquered by us,* or *We must conquer the enemy.*

Examples from the Vulgate:

Gerund.

Horrendum est incidere in manus Dei viventis. *It is a thing to be feared to fall into the hands of a living God.* Heb. 10:31.

Qui praedicas non furandum, furaris? *Thou who preachest that a man should not steal, dost thou steal?* Rom. 2:21.

Gerundive.

Filius hominis tradendus est in manus hominum. *The Son of man must be given up into the hands of men.* Mt. 17:22.

By a very exceptional construction the Gerundive is used in the sense of and parallel with the Future Participle.

At illi existimabant eum in tumorem convertendum et subito casurum et mori. *But they thought that he would swell up and suddenly fall down and die.* Acts 28:6.

THE SUPINE

193. The Supine ending in *um* expresses purpose. It is rare in Latin.

> Et quicumque potum dederit uni ex minimis istis calicem aquae frigidae tantum...non perdet mercedem suam. *And whosoever shall give only a cup of cold water to one of the least of these to drink...he shall not lose his reward.* Mt. 10:42.

The Supine ending in *u* is only used in certain expressions in the sense of the Ablative case of a verbal noun.

> Auditu audietis et non intelligetis.... *In hearing ye shall hear and shall not understand....* Mt. 13:14, from Isa. 6:9.

> Qui ergo tribuit vobis Spiritum et operatur virtutes in vobis: ex operibus legis, an ex auditu fidei? *He therefore that giveth to you the Spirit and worketh mighty works among you: doth he it by the works of the law, or by the hearing of faith?* Gal. 3:5.

> See also Isa. 2:16.

METHODS OF ASKING QUESTIONS

194. In Classical Latin direct questions which may be answered by either *yes* or *no* are expressed by adding the particle *ne* to an emphatic word at the beginning of the sentence.

In the Vulgate there is often nothing but the context to show if a sentence is a question or not.

> Pilatus vocavit Jesum et dixit ei: Tu es rex Judaeorum? *Pilate called Jesus and said to him: Art thou the king of the Jews?* Jn. 18:33.

195. If an affirmative answer is expected to the question it is introduced by *nonne* and in the Vulgate by *an.*

> Domine, Domine, nonne in nomine tuo prophetavimus? *Lord, Lord, did we not prophecy in thy name?* Mt. 7:22.

> An nescitis quoniam sancti de mundo judicabunt? *Do ye not know that the saints shall judge concerning the world?* 1 Cor. 6:2.

> See also Mt. 26:53; Rom. 3:29,6:3. *Numquid non* is also found in the Vulgate in this sense: Rom. 10:18.

196. If a negative answer is expected to the question it is introduced by *num* in Classical Latin and by *numquid* in the Vulgate

> Respondit Pilatus: Numquid ego Judaeus sum? *Pilate answered: Am I a Jew?* Jn. 18:35.

Num is apparently not found in the Vulgate New Testament It is found in the Old Testament

> Num custos fratris mei ego sum? *Am I my brother's keeper?* Gen. 4:9.

Both methods of asking a question are seen in this example:

> Alii dicebant: Hic est Christus. Quidam autem dicebant: Numquid a Galilaea venit Christus? Nonne scriptura dicit: Quia ex semine David...venit Christus? *Others said: This is Christ. But certain said: Does Christ come out of Galilee? Does not the scripture say that Christ comes of the seed of David?* Jn. 7:41.

> See also Mk. 4:21.

197. In the Vulgate *si* is often used in imitation of Greek to introduce both direct and indirect questions.

Dixitque ad eos: Si Spiritum Sanctum accepistis credentes? At illi dixerunt ad eum: Sed neque si Spiritus Sanctus est, audivimus.   Acts 14:2.
See also Acts 10:18, 21:37   Acts 19:2

198. Questions may be introduced by the interrogative pronoun *quis* or by expressions compounded with it such as *quomodo* or *ut quid*, which is an imitation of the Greek ἵνα τί or εἰς τί.

See Mt. 9:4, 26:8; Acts 7:26; 1 Cor 10:29.

Quid is used in the sense of *cur*=why in Mt. 20:6.

Alternative or double questions are expressed by *utrum...an*, see Jn. 7:17, or by *an* alone in the second member of the question. The latter is the usual method in the Vulgate

Tu es qui venturus es, an alium expectamus? *Art thou he that should come, or are we to look for another?* Mt. 11:3.

Quem vultis dimittam vobis: Barabbam, an Jesum qui dicitur Christus? *Which do you wish that I should release for you: Barabbas, or Jesus who is called Christ?* Mt. 27:17.

Notice the use of the interrogative pronoun *quem* here where *utrum* would have been used in Classical Latin

See also Jn. 18:34.

ADJECTIVES

199. An adjective whether used as an attribute of a noun or to complete a predicate agrees with the noun which it qualifies in number, gender and case.

Sometimes, however, if the noun is a collective noun, the adjective agrees rather with the idea that is signified by the noun than with the grammatical number and gender of the noun (*constructio ad sensum*).

Sed turba haec, quae non novit legem, maledicti sunt. *But this crowd which knows not the law are cursed.*   Jn. 7:49.

See also Jas. 3:8; Rev. 7:9.

Multitudo militiae caelestis laudantium Deum et dicentium....
A multitude of the heavenly host (of angels) praising God and saying....
Lk. 2:13.

200. Adjectives are often used as equivalent to nouns, the masculine denoting men, or people in general of the kind described by the adjective, the feminine women, the neuter things.

Resurrectio justorum et iniquorum. *A resurrection of the just and the unjust.* Acts 24:15.

Invisibilia enim ipsius...per ea quae facta sunt intellecta conspiciuntur. *For the invisible things of him...being understood by the things that are made, are perceived.*   Rom. 1:20.

The neuter of the adjective may be used in the sense of an abstract noun. *Salutare*=salvation, Lk 2:30.

201. The adjective *unus* is used in the Vulgate in the sense of the indefinite article. This use became general in the Romance languages.

Et accessit ad eum una ancilla dicens: Et tu cum Jesu Galilaeo eras. *And there came to him a maid and said: Thou also wert with Jesus the Galilaean.* Mt. 26:69.

See also Mt. 21:19.

202. The adjective *omnis* is used with a negative to express a strong negative statement or command in imitation of Hebrew

Et nisi breviati fuissent dies illi, non fieret salva omnis caro.... *And unless those days had been shortened, no living thing would be saved.* Mt. 24:22.

Omnis sermo malus ex ore vestro non procedat. *Let no corrupt speech proceed out of your mouth.* Eph. 4:29.

See also Rom. 3:20; 1 Cor. 1:29; Rev. 18:22.

COMPARISON OF ADJECTIVES

203. The positive degree of an adjective may be used in the Vulgate in the sense of a comparative.

Bonum est tibi ... in vitam intrare ... quam mitti in gehennam. *It is better for thee to enter into life than to be cast into Gehenna.* Mt. 18:9.

The positive may be used in the sense of a superlative.

Quod est magnum mandatum in lege? *Which is the greatest commandment in the law?* Mt. 22:36.

The comparative may be used in the sense of a superlative.

Major autem horum est charitas. *But the greatest of these is love.* 1 Cor. 13:13.

The superlative may be used in the sense of the comparative.

Quod minimum quidem est omnibus seminibus. *Which indeed is less than all seeds.* Mt. 13:32; Heb. 11:4.

204. The ordinary const. after an adj. in the comparative degree in Classical Latin to express the object with which the comparison is made is to put the word which denotes this object in the Ablative case, or to use *quam*.

Amen dico vobis, non surrexit inter natos mulierum major Johanne Baptista. *Verily I say to you, there has not arisen any one greater than John the Baptist among those born of women.* Mt. 11:11.

Qui amat patrem aut matrem plus quam me, non est me dignus. *He who loves father or mother more than me is not worthy of me.* Mt. 10:37.

In the Vulgate in imitation of Hebrew the preps. *a, ex, prae, super* may be used after an adjective in the comparative degree, or even a Genitive case, in imitation of Greek.

See Lk. 13:2, 18:14; 2 Cor. 12:2; Heb. 2:7, 3:3; Ps. 18:11, 138:6, and section 32 of this book.

Page intentionally left blank

VOCABULARY

a : see ab

ab, *prep.* : + *abl.* : by (agent), from

ablativus, -a, -um, *adj.* : that which pertains to taking away something

abnormitas, -atis, *f.* : abnormality, strangeness

abominabilis, -is, -e, *adj.* : detestable, hateful, worthy of destruction

absoluo, -ere, -solui, -solutum : free (bonds), release; acquit; pay off

absolute, *adv.* : absolutely

absolutus, absoluta, absolutum, *adj.* : absolute

absque, *prep* + *abl.* : without, apart from, away from; but for; except for; were it not for

abstractio, abstractionis, *f.* : abstraction

abstraho, -ere, -traxi, -tractum : abstract, separate, remove; split

absum, esse, afui : be away, be absent; be lacking

abutor, -eris, -i, abusus sum : waste, squander; abuse; misuse; use up; spend; exhaust; misapply (word); curse

ac, *conj.* : and, and also, and besides

accedit, *impersonal* : it is added

accedo, -ere, -cessi, -cessum : come near, approach; agree with; be added to

accidens, -entis, *n.* : accident

accidentaliter, *adv.* : accidentally, opposite of essentialiter

accido, -ere, -cidi : happen, turns out, befall, come to pass, occur

accipio, -ere, -cepi, -ceptum : to take, grasp, receive, accept, undertake; admit, let in, hear, learn; obey

accipio, -ere, -cepi, -ceptum : to take, grasp, receive, accept; hear, learn; obey

accommodo, -are : adapt, adjust to, fit, suit; apply to, fasten on; apply/devote oneself to

accuso, -are : accuse, blame

actio, -onis, *f.* : act, action, activity, deed; incident

activus, -a, -um, *adj.* : active, practical

actualis, -is, -e, *adj.* : actual, practical, active

actualitas, -tatis, *f.* : reality, existence

actuo, actuare : to implement, actuate, perfect, make actual

actus, -us, *m.* : deed, act, work

ad, *prep.* + *acc.* : to, up to, towards; near, at; until; according to

adaequatio, adaequationis, *f.* : a making equal, equalization, equation

adaequo, -are : equalize, make equal in height; compare (to); be equal

additio, additionis, *f.* : addition, the act of adding

addo, -ere, -didi, -ditum : add, insert, attach to, say in addition

adeo, *adv.* : to such an extent

adhibeo, -ere, -ui, -itum : summon, invite, bring in; consult; put, add; use, employ

adhuc, *adv.* : thus far, till now, to this point; hitherto; yet, as yet; still; besides

adiaceo, -ere, -cui, - : lie near to, lie beside; be adjacent to

adipiscor, -i, adeptus sum : gain, secure, win, obtain; arrive at, come up to/into; inherit; overtake

adjectivus, adjectiva, adjectivum, *adj.* : that is added (to the noun: grammatical sense); adjective

admirativus, -a, -um, *adj.* : arousing admiration, admirable

admitto, -ere, -misi, -missum : let in, admit, receive; grant, permit

admoveo, -ere, -movi, -motum : move up, bring near; draw near, approach

adnecto, -ere, -nexui, -nexum : tie to, bind to; fasten on; attach, connect, join, annex

adnoto, -are : note, notice, become aware; state; designate

adsum, esse, adfui : be near, be present

adverto, (advorto) -ere, -verti, -versum : turn/face to/towards; direct/draw one's attention to

adultus, -a, -um : grown up, full grown, mature, ripe, adult; at its peak/height/full strength

aedificatio, aedificationis, *f.* : house, building

aedificator, aedificatoris, *m.* : builder, contractor, maker, creator

aedificium, -ii, *n.* : building; edifice, structure

aedifico, -are : build, erect, construct

aeger, -gra, -grum : sick, ill

aequalis, -e, *adj.* : equal, comrade; person of one's age/rank/ability, contemporary; equivalent

aequalitas, -atis, *f.* : evenness; equality (of age/status/merit/distribution), uniformity, symmetry

aeque, *inv.* : equally, justly, fairly; in same/like manner/degree, just as; likewise, also

aequivaleo, aequivalere : to have equal power; to be equivalent

aequivocus, aequivoca, aequivocum, *adj.* : equivocal, ambiguous

aequo, -are : level, make even

aer, aeris, *m.* : air (one of 4 elements); atmosphere, sky; cloud, mist, weather; breeze; odor

aestimativus, -a, -um, *adj.* : estimating, valuating, pertaining to the sentient faculty of valuation or judgment

aetas, -atis, *f.* : lifetime, age; period; time, era

Aethiops, Aethiopis, *m.* : an Ethiopian; a black person

affectibilis, -is, -e, *adj.* : able to be moved to emotion or desire

affectio, -onis, *f* : mental condition, mood, feeling, disposition; affection, love; purpose

affectivus, affectiva, affectivum, *adj.* : affective; of willing/desiring

affectus, -us, *m.* : disposition, state (of body/mind), mood, emotion; affection, passion, love

affero, afferre, attuli, allatum : bring to, bring forth, allege, produce

afficio, -ere, -feci, -fectum : affect, make impression; move, influence

affingo, affingere, affinxi, affictum : to add to, attach

affirmatio, affirmationis, *f.* : an affirmation, assertion

affirmo, -are : affirm, assert (dogmatically/positively); confirm; emphasize

ago, -ere, egi, actum : act, drive, urge, conduct; spend (time with cum); thank (with gratias); deliver (speech)

aio, (ait) *defective verb*: say, assert; say yes/so, affirm, assent; prescribe/lay down (*leg.*)

Albertus, -i, *m.* : Albert, (Albertus Magnus, St. Albert the Great)

albitudo, albitudinis, *f.* : whiteness

albus, -a, -um : white, pale, fair, hoary, gray; bright, clear; favorable, auspicious, fortunate

alibi, *adv.* : elsewhere, in another place; in other respects , otherwise; in another matter

alioquin, *adv.* : otherwise, in other/some respects; besides, else; in any case; in general

aliquam, *adv.* : abbreviating the phrase in aliquam partem => in some degree; ~ multum => largely, to a large extent; ~ multi/multum => fair number/amount

aliquando, *adv.* : sometime (or other), at any time, ever; finally; before too late; at length

aliqui, aliqua, aliquod, *indef. adj.* : some, any

aliquis, aliquid : 1. *pron.* anyone/anybody/anything; someone 2. *adj.* some, such

aliter, *adv.* : otherwise, differently; in any other way (aliter ac => otherwise than)

alius, -a, -ud : the one ... the other (alius ... alius)

allicio, allicere, allexi, allectum : draw gently to, entice, lure, induce

alter, altera, alterum, *indef. pron.* : the one ... the other (alter ... alter); otherwise

alteratio, alterationis, *f.* : alteratio, alterationis

altus, -a, -um, *adj.* : high, tall; deep

amans, -antis : lover, sweetheart; mistress; one who is fond/affectionate

amarus, -a, -um : bitter, brackish, pungent; harsh, shrill; sad, calamitous; ill-natured, caustic

amitto, -ere, -misi, -missum : lose; send away, disperse, pardon

amo, -are : love, be fond of

amor, -oris, *m.* : love, affection

amotio, -onis, *f.* : removal, removing

analogia, analogiae, *f.* : a ratio, proportion; an analogy

analogus, analoga, analogum, *adj.* : proportional; analogous

angelicus, angelica, angelicum, *adj.* : angelic; of an angel; belonging to angels

angustus, -a, -um : narrow, steep, close, confined; scanty, poor; low, mean; narrow-minded, petty

anima, -ae, *f.* : soul, spirit, vital principle; life; mind; wind

animal, -alis, *n.* : animal, living thing, creature, beast

animalis, -e, *adj.* : animal, pertaining to animals

animalitas, animalitatis, *f.* : animal nature, animal form; animality, the abstract concept of being an animal

animo, -are : animate, give life; revive, refresh

animus, -i, *m.* : mind; intellect; soul; feelings; heart; spirit, courage, character, pride; air

annulus, -i, *m.* : one year old

ante, *prep.* +*acc.* : in front/presence of, in view; before (space/time/degree); over against, facing

antea, *adv.* : before, before this; formerly, previously, in the past

antecedo, -ere, -cessi, -cessum : precede, go before, surpass

antepraedicamenta, -orum, *neuter plural* : the Antepraedicaments (the preliminary notions necessary for knowledge of the categories); the title of the first three chapters of Aristotle's Categories

antichristus, -i, *m.* : the Antichrist, by extension any figure opposed to Christ or Christian doctrine

antiquus, -a, -um : the men (*pl.*) of old, the ancients, the early authorities/writers; ancestors

appareo, -ere, -ui, -itum : appear; be evident

appello, -are : call; address; accuse; name

appendicium, -ii, *n.* : appendage; payment for the right to construct; in the *plural* only, dependents (of a house, church, or monastery)

appendix, appendicis, *f.* : an appendix, supplement, annex

appetibilis, appetibilis, appetibile, *adj.* : desirable, sought after

appetitus, appetitus, *m.* : appetite, desire; esp. natural/instinctive desire

appeto, -ere, -i(*v*)i, -itum : seek, grasp after, desire; assail; strive eagerly for; approach, near

applicatio, -onis, *f.* : application, inclination; joining, attaching; attachment of client to patron

applico, -are : connect, place near; apply

appono, -ere, -posui, -positum : place near, put/apply/add to; appoint, assign

apprehendo, -ere, -prendi, -prensum : seize (upon), grasp, cling to, lay hold of; apprehend

apprehensibilis, -is, *adj.* : intelligible, understandable, that can be understood

apprehensio, apprehensionis, *f.* : seizing upon, laying hold of; (philosophical) apprehension, understanding

approbo, -are : approve, commend; prove; confirm; justify; allow

approprio, appropriare, appropriavi, appropriatum : appropriate, make one's own

apto, -are : adapt, fit, apply, adjust; prepare, furnish

apud, *prep*+*acc* : at, by, near, among; at the house of; before, in the presence/writings/view of

aqua, -ae, *f.* : water; sea, lake; river, stream; rain, rainfall (*pl.*), rainwater; spa; urine

arbor, -oris, *f.* : tree; tree trunk; mast; oar; ship; gallows; spearshaft; beam

architectus, -i, *m.* : architect, master-builder; inventor, designer, maker, author, deviser

Aristoteles (Ἀριστοτέλης), -is, *m.* : Aristotle

arma, -orum, *n. plural*: arms, weapons

armo, -are : equip, fit with armor; arm

ars, artis, *f.* : skill, craft, art; trick, wile; science, knowledge; method, way; character (*pl.*)

artefactus, -a, -um : from arte + factus = make by art, man made

artifex, -icis, *m.* : artist, actor; craftsman; master of an art; author, maker; mastermind, schemer

artificiosus, artificiosa, -um, *adj.* : skillfully done; technical, by the rules, prescribed by art; artificial

assecutio, -onis, *f.* : perception, comprehension, knowledge

assequor, -i, -secutus sum : follow on, pursue, go after; overtake; gain, achieve; equal, rival; understand

assero, -ere, -serui, -sertum : assert, remark, claim

assertio, -onis, *f.* : assertion

assigno, -are : assign, distribute, allot

assimilo, assimilare, assimilavi, assimilatum : compare, make like to, imitate, simulate

assimilor, assimilari, assimilatus sum, *deponent* : to be compared, become like

assumo, -ere, -sumpsi, -sumptum : assume, receive, take, raise

at, *conj.* : but, but on the other hand; on the contrary; while, whereas; but yet; at least

atque, *conj.* : and, as well as

atqui, *inv.*, et pourtant, eh bien: but, yet, notwithstanding, however, rather, well/but now; and yet, still

attamen, *adv.* : nevertheless, nonetheless

attendo, -ere, -tendi, -tentum : turn/stretch towards; apply; attend/pay (close) attention to, listen carefully

attingo, -ere, -tigi, -tactum : wipe/smear on

attribuo, -ere, -tribui, -tributum : assign, attribute; grant, pay; appoint

attributio, attributionis, *f.* : attribution, assignment of a quality

aufero, fers, ferre, abstuli, ablatum : bear/carry/take/fetch/sweep/snatch away/off, remove, withdraw; steal, obtain

Augustinus, Augustini, *m.* : St. Augustine (Bishop of Hippo, 354-430, author of *Confessions, City of God*)

aurum, -i, *n.* : gold (metal/color), gold money, riches

aut, *conj.* : or, or rather/else; either...or (aut...aut) (emphasizing one)

autem, *conj.* : but (*postpositive*), on the other hand/contrary; while, however; moreover, also

auxilium, -ii, *n.* : help, assistance, aid; supporting resource/force; auxiliaries (*pl.*)

avello, -ere, -vulsi, -vulsum : tear/pluck/wrench away/out/off; separate by force, part; take away, wrest

avis, -is, *m.* : bird; sign, omen, portent

barbarus, -a, -um : barbarian, uncivilized person; foreigner (not Greek/Roman)

bellua, -ae, *f.* : beast, wild animal; monster, brute

bene, *adv.* : well, very, quite, rightly

Bernardus, -i, *m.* : Bernard, especially St. Bernard of Clairvaux

Boetius, -i, *m.* : Boetius was responsible for Latin translations of portions of Greek philosophy, providing a bridge for these ideas to cross over into the Middle Ages

Bonaventura, -ae : St. Bonaventure (1221-1274), Italian medieval scholastic theologian and seventh General of the Order of Friars Minor.

bonitas, -atis, *f.* : goodness, integrity, moral excellence; kindness, benevolence, tenderness

bonus, -a, -um : good, moral, honest, brave; man of honor, gentleman

brutum, bruti, *n.* : beast, animal

caecitas, -atis, *f.* : blindness; mental/moral blindness, lack of discernment

caecus, -a, -um : blind; unseeing

caecus, -a, -um : blind; unseeing; dark, gloomy, hidden, secret; aimless, confused, random; rash

Caesar, Caesaris, *m.* : a Roman family name, especially of Julius Caesar; by extension, a title applied to the Roman emperors, and after Diocletian's establishment of the tetrarchy, to additional offices of command (initially the second in authority after the Augustus of the East and of the West)

calor, -oris, *m.* : heat; warmth, glow; warm/hot/summer heat/weather; fever; passion, zeal; love

canon, -onis: *m.*; canon, norm, rule

canto, -are : sing; recite; praise

cantus, -us, *m.* : song, chant; singing

capacitas, capacitatis, *f.* : capacity, largeness, ability, power of comprehension

capillus, -i, *m.* : hair; hair of head; single hair

capio, -ere, cepi, captum : take, seize

caput, -itis, *n.* : head; leader; top

careo, -ere, -ui, -iturum : be without, free from; lack, lose

caritas (charitas), caritatis, *f.* : charity; love

Cartesianus, -a, -um, *adj.* : Cartesian, pertaining to the philosophy or mathematical system of Rene Descartes

Cartesius, -ii, *m.* : Rene Descartes (French philosopher)

categoria, categoriae, *f.* : category, class of predicables (logic)

catholicus, catholica, catholicum, *adj.* : catholic, universal; Roman Catholic

causa, -ae, *f.* : cause; case; for the sake/purpose of (preceded by *gen.*), on account of, with a view to

causo, causare, causavi, causatum : to cause

causor, -ari : allege an excuse/reason, object; excuse oneself; plead a cause, bring action

censeo, -ere, censui, censum : think/suppose, judge; recommend; decree, vote, determine; count/reckon; assess

cera, -ae, *f.* : wax, beeswax; honeycomb; wax-covered writing tablet, letter; wax image/seal

cerebrum, -i, *n.* : brain; top of the head, skull; bud; seat of senses/intelligence; anger/wrath

certitudo, certitudinis, *f.* : certainty, certitude; assurance

certus, -a, -um : fixed, settled, firm; certain; trusty/reliable; sure; resolved, determined

ceterus, -a, -um, *adj.*: other, rest, remaining

Christus, Christi, *m.* : Christ

Cicero, Ciceronis, *m.* : Marcus Tullius Cicero, Roman orator and statesman

circa, *prep + acc.* : around, on the bounds of; about/near (space/time/numeral); concerning; with

circulus, -i, *m.* : circle; orbit, zone; ring, hoop; belt, collar; company; cycle; circumference

civitas, -atis, *f.* : community, city, town, state; citizens; citizen rights, citizenship; naturalization

civis, -is, *m.* : citizen, free person

clarus, -a, -um : clear, bright, gleaming; loud, distinct; evident, plain; illustrious, famous

clemens, -entis, *adj.* : merciful, lenient; mild, gentle, quiet, peaceful, easy, moderate; compliant

cogitabilis, cogitabilis, cogitabile, *adj.* : conceivable, thinkable, imaginable, cogitable

cogitatio, -onis, *f.* : thinking, meditation, reflection; thought; intention; plan; opinion, reasoning

cogito, -are : think; consider

cognitio, -ionis, *f.* : acquaintance (with a person or thing) ; idea, notion; knowledge

cognitivus, -a, -um, *adj.* : related to knowing; cognitive

cognitrix, cognitricis, *adj.* : capable of understanding, that which knows (e.g alma cognitrix)

cognoscibilis, -e, *adj.* : recognizable, discernible

cognoscitivus, cognoscitiva, cognoscitivum, *adj.* : knowing, having power of knowing, intellectually aware

cognosco, -ere, -novi, cognitum : become acquainted with/aware of; recognize; learn, find to be; inquire, examine

collatio, -ionis, *f.* : meeting, gathering, assembly, conference; collection; discussion

collectio, -onis, *f.* : collection, accumulation; gathering, abscess; recapitulation, summary; inference

colligo, -ere, -legi, -lectum : bind, tie together, collect; obtain; recover; sum up; deduce, infer; compute, add up

color, -oris, *m.* : color; pigment; shade, tinge

coloratus, colorata, -um, *adj.* : colored

columna, -ae, *f.* : pillar, column

comedo, comedere, comedi, comesus : eat up; finish eating; consume, devour; waste, squander

comito, -are : accompany, go along with

commodus, -a, -um : desirable, agreeable; good (health/news)

communicabilitas, communicabilitatis, *f.* : communicability

communico, -are : communicate, discuss, impart; consult

communis, -e, *adj.* : common; neutral, impartial

compar, comparis (*gen.*), *adj.* : equal, equal to; like, similar

comparatio, -ionis, *f.* : comparison, weighing of merits; preparation, making ready; provision; arrangement

comparativus, comparativa, comparativum, *adj.* : involving consideration of *relative* merits; *comparative*

comperio, -ire, -peri, -pertum : learn/discover/ find (by investigation); verify/know for certain; find guilty

competo, -ere, -petivi (ii), -petitum : be sound/capable/adequate/competent/admissible

compleo, -ere, -plevi, -pletum : finish, complete, perfect

complexio, complexionis, *f.* : encircling; combination, association, connection; summary

compono, componere, composui, compositum : construct, build; arrange, compile, compose; organize

compositio, compositionis, *f.* : composition, arrangement, combination

computo, -are : reckon, compute, work out

conatus, -us, *m.* : attempt, effort; exertion, struggle; impulse, tendency; endeavor, design

conceptio, -ionis, *f.* : conception, action of conceiving, pregnancy; idea, notion, formula, system

conceptus, -us, *m.* : concept, thought, purpose

concilium, -ii, *n.* : public gathering, meeting; popular assembly, council; hearing; debate

concipio, -ere, -cepi, -ceptum : form, devise; understand, imagine; conceive

conclusio, conclusionis, *f.* : logical conclusion; deduction; conclusion, finish

concomitor, concomitari, concomitatus sum : to attend, accompany

concretus, concreta, -um, *adj.* : composed, formed; composite; concrete; solid

concurro, -ere, -curri, -cursum : charge, fight, engage in battle; come running up/in large numbers; rally

conditio, conditionis, *f.* : quality, condition; term; situation, position, arrangement

confero, -ferre, -tuli, -latum : discuss/debate/confer; oppose; pit/match against another; blame; bestowith assign

conficio, -ere, -feci, -fectum : finish off; kill, dispatch; defeat finally, subdue/reduce/pacify; chop/cut up

confido, -ere, confisus sum : have confidence in, rely on; believe, be confident

conformabilis, -e, *adj.* : conformable

conformo, conformare, conformavi, conformatum : shape, mold skillfully; outline, describe; train, educate

congrego, -are : collect, bring together, assemble; concentrate

congruens, -entis : congruent, corresponding to, similar, matching; appropriate, fitting; proper

congruo, -ere, -ui : agree, coincide, correspond, unite, combine

coniunctio, -ionis, *f.* : conjunction (word); combination; association, affinity

coniungo, -ere, -iunxi, -iunctum : connect, join together; marry; connect, compound; add; associate

conor, aris, ari : attempt/try/endeavor, make an effort; exert oneself; try to go/rise/speak

conscientia, -ae, *f.* : (joint) knowledge, complicity (of crime); conscience; sense of guilt, remorse

consentaneus, -a, -um : agreeable; consistent, appropriate, fitting; in harmony with

consequenter, *adv.* : consequently, as a result

consequor, -i, -cutus sum : seek after, aim at; achieve, reach; obtain; acquire, gain; grasp, comprehend

conservatio, -ionis, *f.* : preservation, conservation, keeping (intact); observance, maintenance (duty)

conservo, -are : keep safe, save (from danger); preserve, maintain

considero, -are : consider, investigate

considero, -are : examine, look at, inspect; consider closely, reflect on/contemplate; investigate

consimilis, -e, *adj.* : like, very similar; similar in all respects

consisto, -ere, -stiti : stand together/fast; consist of/be reckoned in; rest/depend upon; be unaltered

consortium, -i, *n.* : possession in common, sharing property; community life

conspiro, -are : plot/conspire

constituo, -ere, -tui, -tutum : establish/create/institute; draw up, arrange/set in order; make up, form; fix

constitutio, -ionis, *f.* : ordinance, decree, decision; position, ordering; destiny; definition of a term

construo, -ere, -struxi, -structum : make, build, construct

consuesco, -ere, -suevi, suetum : to form a habit; be in the habit of

consultatio, -ionis, *f.* : meeting/opportunity for debate; subject for consideration, problem, question

contemno, -ere, -tempsi, -temptum : treat with/hold in contempt, scorn, disdain; despise; keep away from, avoid

contineo, -ere, -tinui, -tentum : keep/hold/ hang together; surround, enclose, contain, limit; concentrate

contingenter, *adv.* : contingently; conditionally

contingo, -ere, -tigi, -tactum : to touch, affect emotionally; happen, befall, turn out, come to pass

contra, *adv* : conversely; on the contrary; to-wards/up to, in direction of

contractio, contractionis, *f.* : contraction; abridgement

contradico, contradicere, contradixi, contra-dictum : contradict; speak against, oppose

contradictorius, contradictoria, contradictori-um, *adj.* : containing a contradiction

contrarietas, contrarietatis, *f.* : contrast, oppo-site; opposition, contrariety; misfortune

contrarius, -a, -um : opponent, adversary; antagonist

convenio, -ire, -veni, -ventum : to convene, come together; be agreed upon/arranged (*passive*)

converto, -ere, -verti, -versum : turn upside down; invert, transpose; convert

copulo, -are : connect, join physically, couple; bind/tie together, associate, unite, ally

cor, cordis, *n.* : heart; mind, soul, spirit; in-tellect/judgment; sweetheart; souls (*pl.*), persons

corono, -are : wreathe, crown; surround

corporeus, corporea, corporeum, *adj.* : corpo-real, material, physical

corpus, -oris, *n.* : material object, body

corruptibilis, corruptibile, *adj.* : corruptible, liable to decay, perishable

credo, -ere, -didi, -ditum : lend (money) to, give credit; believe, think, accept as true

creo, -are : produce, create; elect, appoint

crispus, crispa, crispum, *adj.* : curled, curly

cuiusmodi, *adv.* : of whatsoever kind or sort

culpa, -ae, *f.* : offense; error; (sense of) guilt; fault/defect (moral/other); sickness/injury

culpabilis, culpabile, *adj.* : reprehensible, de-serving of blame; guilty

cum, *inv.* : 1. *Preposition + abl.* = with 2. *con-junction* = when, since, although

cunctus, -a, -um : all (usually *pl.*); all together, the whole, entire

cur, *adv.* : why, wherefore; for what reason/pur-pose?; on account of which? because

currus, -us, *m.* : chariot, light horse vehicle; triumphal chariot; triumph; wheels on plow; cart

Damascenus, Damascena, Damascenum, *adj.* : of/from Damascus; St. John Damascene

damnatus, damnata, -um, *adj.* : condemned; found guilty; damned

damno, -are, -avi, -atum : to condemn, discred-it, damn

de, *prep. + abl.* : from; about, concerning; ac-cording to; with regard to

debeo, -ere, -ui, -itum : owe; be indebted; ought, must, should

debilito, -are : weaken, disable, impair

decem, *adj.* num. : ten; (ten men)

decerno, -ere, -creui, -cretum : decide, deter-mine, resolve; decree; judge

declino, -are : decline; deflect, divert

decursus, -us, *m.* : descent; downward course/ slope; a race, course

defectus, defectus, *m.* : failure, absence

deficio, -ere, -feci, -fectum : fail, disappoint, let down; pass away; become extinct, die

definio, -ire, -ivi, -itum : define, bound, limit; restrict; determine; specify, sum up; assert

definitio, -onis, *f.* : classification; pronounce-ment; definition; argument based on definition of term

definitivus, definitiva, definitivum, *adj.* : defini-tive, explanatory; involving definition

deliberatio, -onis, *f.* : deliberation/consultation (with others), consideration; deliberative style speech

delibero, -are : weigh, consider, deliberate

demonstratio, -ionis, *f.* : demonstration, indi-cation; identification

demonstrativus, demonstrativa, demon-strativum, *adj.* : *demonstrative*; by logical demonstration

denique, *adv.* : finally, in the end; and then; at worst; in short, to sum up; in fact, indeed

denominativus, denominativa, denominativum, *adj.* : naming, designating, derived, pertaining to derivation

denomino, -are : denominate, designate; give a name to

denoto, -are : observe; indicate/point out; imply

dens, dentis, *m.* : tooth; tusk; ivory; tooth-like thing, spike; distructive power, envy, ill will

dependenter, *adv.* : dependently

dependeo, -ere : hang down from; depend, depend on; be derived from

derivo, -are : draw off, deduce, derive

desidero, -are : want, desire; miss, lack, need

despero, -are : despair (of); give up hope

destituo, -ere, destitui, destitutum : desert, leave, abandon, give up; disappoint

destruo, -ere, -struxi, -structum : pull down; destroy, ruin

desum, -esse, defui : be wanting (with *dat.*), fail; abandon, desert

determino, determinare, determinavi, determinatum : delimit, set bounds to; define; designate, mark out

detestabilis, -e, *adj.* : abominable, detestable

detestor, detestari, detestatus sum : to call down solemn curse on, execrate; detest, loathe

detraho, -ere, -traxi, -tractum : drag down, pull away; take away; remove; detract

deuotio, -ionis, *f.* : devotion/consecrating; fealty/allegiance; piety; prayer; zeal; consideration

deus, -i, *m.* : god; God (Christian text); divine essence/being, supreme being; statue of god

dico, -are : dedicate, consecrate, set apart; devote; offer

dico, -ere, -dixi, -dictum : say, talk; tell, call; name, designate

dictio, -ionis, *f.* : saying; prediction; jurisdiction; pleading, defense; delivery, speech

dicto, -are : say repeatedly; dictate (for writing); compose

dictum, -i, *n.* : saying, word; maxim; bon mot, witticism; order

differentia, -ae, *f.* : difference/diversity/distinction; distinguishing characteristic; different kind

differo, -ferre, distuli, dilatum : put off; delay; differ; scatter, disperse

diffundo, -ere, -fudi, -fusum : pour out, spread out, diffuse

digitus, -i, *m.* : le doigt (de pied), l'orteil (ad digitum : finger; toe; a finger's breath

dignitas, -atis, *f.* : worth; dignity, position, rank; authority, office; self-respect, grace

dignus, -a, -um, *adj.* : worthy, worthy of, deserving, deserved; fit, proper

diligo, diligere, dilexi, dilectum : love, hold dear; value, esteem, favor

directivus, directiva, directivum, *adj.* : directive; helpful, positive; directing

dirigo, -ere, direxi, directum : direct, steer, guide, align; strighten

discerno, -ere, -crevi, -cretum : see, discern; distinguish, separate

disciplina, -ae, *f.* : teaching, instruction, education; training; discipline, method, science

discipulus, -i, *m.* : student, pupil, trainee; follower, disciple

discursivus, -a, -um, *adj.* : inferring, concluding, pertaining to the power of connected thinking

disgrego, disgregare, disgregavi, disgregatum : separate; divide; disperse, scatter, divide

disparitas, disparitatis, *f.* : difference; discrepancy; inequality

dispositio, -ionis, *f.* : layout; orderly arrangement/disposition of arguments/words/time/activities

dissimilitudo, -tudinis, *f.* : unlikeness, difference

distinctio, distinctionis, *f.* : distinction, difference

distinguo, -ere, -stinxi, -stinctum : distinguish, separate, divide, part; adorn, decorate

districte, *adv.* : strictly, severely

diversus, -a, -um : opposite; separate, apart; diverse, unlike, different; hostile

divido,-ere, -visi, -visum : divide, separate, break up; distribute; distinguish

divinitas, -atis, *f.* : divinity, quality/nature of God; divine excellence/power/being; divining

divinus, -a, -um : divine

divisio, -ionis, *f.* : division; distribution

divello, -ere, -velli, -vulsum : tear away, tear to pieces; break up; estrange

do, dare, dedi, datum : give; surrender, give over; send to die; ascribe, attribute

doceo, docere, docui, doctum : teach, show, point out

doctor, -oris, *m.* : teacher; instructor; trainer

doctrina, -ae, *f.* : education; learning; science; teaching; instruction; principle; doctrine

doctus, -a, -um : learned, wise; skilled, experienced, expert; trained; clever, cunning, shrewd

dogmatizo, dogmatizare, dogmatizavi, dogmatizatum : propound a dogma; dogmatize

dominium, -ii, *n.* : rule, dominion; ownership; banquet, feast

dominor, -ari : be master/despot/in control, rule over, exercise sovereignity; rule/dominate

domus, -us, *f.* : house, building; home, household; (domu => at home)

dormio, -ire, -iui, -itum : sleep

dubitatio, -ionis, *f.* : doubt, irresolution, uncertainty; wavering, hesitation; questioning

dubium, -ii, *n.* : doubt; question

duco, -ere, duxi, ductum : lead, command; think, consider, regard; prolong

dulce, *adv.* : a sweet drink, sweets (*pl*)

dulcedo, inis, *f.* : sweetness, agreeableness; charm

dum, *conj.* : while, as long as, until; provided that

dummodo, *inv.* : provided (that) (+ subj)

dumtaxat, *conj.* : to this extent, no more than; as long as; only, precisely; merely; at any rate

duo, -ae, -o : two

duplex, -icis : twofold, double; divided; two-faced

dupliciter, *adv.* : in two ways, doubly

e : see ex

e.g. (exempli gratia) : for example

edo, edere, edidi, editum : eat; consume, devour; spend money on food; destroy

educo, -ere : lead out; draw up; bring up

effatum, effati, *n.* : axiom, proposition, a saying

effectus, -us, *m.* : execution, performance; effect

efficaciter, *adv.* : efficaciously, effectively, efficiently

efficio, -ere, effeci, effectum : bring about; effect, execute, cause; accomplish; make, produce; prove

effodio, -ere, -fodi, -fossum : dig out, excavate; gouge out

effor, -ari, -atus sum : utter; declare; speak

efformo, efformare, efformavi, efformatum : to form, shape, fashion

effundo, -ere, -fudi, -fusum : stretch/spread out, extend; spread (sail); loosen/slacken/fling, give rein

egeo, -ere, egui : need (with *gen./abl.*), lack, want; require, be without

elaboratus, -a, -um, *adj.* : acquired, produced by labor

electio, -ionis, *f.* : choice, selection

eleemosyna, eleemosynae, *f.* : alms; gift to a church

elicio, -ere, -cui, -citum : draw forth, entice, elicit, coax

eligo, -ere, -legi, -lectum : pick out, choose

eminens, -entis : lofty; prominent; eminent

enim, *conj.* : namely (*postpositive*); indeed; in fact; for; I mean, for instance, that is to say

ens, entis : being, a being; present active participle of esse

entitas, entitatis, *f.* : character of being

entitativus, entitativa, entitativum, *adj.* : of the nature of a being

enuntiatio, -onis, *f.* : declaration, proposition, enunciation

enuntio, -are : reveal; say; disclose; report

enuntio, enuntiare, enuntiavi, enuntiatum : to say, express, declare

eo, *adv.* : there, to that place; on this account, therefore; to that degree, so far

eo, ire, ivi (ii), itum : go, walk; march, advance

equidem, *inv.* : truly, indeed; for my part

equus, -i, *m.* : horse

erga, *prep.*+ *acc.* : towards, opposite (friendly)

ergo, *conj.* : therefore; well, then, now

erro, -are : wander; err

error, -oris, *m.* : wandering; error; deception

erumpo, -ere, -rupi, -ruptum : break out, burst/ sally forth; erupt

esse : see sum

essendi : gerund of esse; actus essendi = act of being; existence

essentia, essentiae, *f.* : essence, substance, being, actuality

essentialis, essentialis, essentiale, *adj.* : essential, pertaining to the essence

essentialiter, *adv.* : essentially, by essence

et, *conj.* : and, and even; also, even; (et ... et = both ... and)

etenim, *inv.* : and indeed, because, since, as a matter of fact (independent reason, emphasis)

ethicus, ethica, ethicum, *adj.* : pertaining to ethics, ethical

etiam, *adv.* : now too, as yet, still, even now; and also, besides, furthermore; actually

etsi, *conj.* : although, though, even if; albeit

etymologia (ethymologia), etymologiae, *f.* : etymology

eucharístia, -ae, *f.* : thanksgiving, the Holy Eucharist

europaeus, -a, -um, *adj.* : European, of or belonging to Europe

evenio, -ire, -veni, -ventum : come out/about/ forth; happen; turn out

evoluo, -ere, -volui, -volutum : roll out, unroll; disclose, unfold; extricate; pursue; explain

ex, *prep.* : + *abl.* : out of, from; by reason of; according to; because of, as a result of

excedo, -ere, -cessi, -cessum : pass, withdraw, exceed

excellens, -entis : distinguished, excellent

excellentia, excellentiae, *f.* : excellence, superiority; merit;

excessus, -us, *m.* : departure; death; digression

excipio, excipere, excepi, exceptum : to except, make an exception of, exclude; to receive; to support, sustain

excito, -are : wake up, stir up; excite, arouse

excludo, -ere, -clusi, -clusum : shut out, shut off; remove; exclude

excogito, -are : think out; devise, invent, contrive

exemplar, aris, *n.* : model, pattern, example, original, ideal; copy

exemplaris, exemplaris, exemplare, *adj.* : exemplary, serving as example or pattern

exemplum, -i, *n.* : sample, specimen, representative; precedent, case; pattern, model; warning

exeo, -ire, -ii, -itum : leave, go out; issue, emerge; sprout

exequor, -i, -cutus sum : pursue; pursue with vengeance; accomplish

exerceo, -ere, -cui, -citum : exercise, train, drill, practice

exhibeo, -ere, -ui, -itum : present; furnish; exhibit; produce

exigo, -ere, -egi, -actum : demand

exinde, *adv.* : thence, from that

existentia, -ae, *f.* : existence

existentia, existentiae, *f.* : existence; that by which essence becomes actual

existimatio, -ionis, *f.* : opinion; reputation; judgement; credit

existimo, -are : value; think, suppose; estimate; judge

existo (exsisto), -ere, exstiti, exstitum : exist, be visible, emerge, appear

experientia, -ae, *f.* : trial, experiment; experience

expeto, -ere, -ii, -itum : ask for; desire; aspire to

explicatio, -onis, *f.* : explanation

explico, -are, -vi, -atum : unfold, extend; set forth, explain

explico, explicare, explicavi, explicatum : to explain; to unfold, extend; set forth, display

expono, -ere, -posui, -positum : set forth; abandon, expose; publish; explain

expostulo, -are : ask, demand vehemently, require, dispute

exprimo, -ere, -pressi, -pressum : squeeze, press out; imitate, copy; portray; pronounce, express

extendo, -ere, -tendi, -tensum (-tum) : stretch out; extend; enlarge; continue, prolong

extensio, extensionis, *f.* : extension, the act or process of extending

externus, -a, -um : outward, external; foreign, strange

exterus, -a, -um : outer/external; outward; on outside, far; of another country, foreign; strange

extra, *prep.* + *acc.* : outside of, beyond, without, beside; except

extraneus, -a, -um : external, extraneous, foreign; not belonging to one's family or household

extremitas, extremitatis, *f.* : end, extremity, border, perimeter, an extreme case

extremus, -a, -um : the rear (*pl.*)

extrinsecus, extrinseca, extrinsecum, *adj.* : outside, external; extrinsic; unessential; extraneous

exurgo, -ere, -surrexi, -surrectum : rise (to one's feet); stand, get up; come to being

facies, ei, *f.* : shape, face, look; presence, appearance; beauty; achievement

facio, -ere, feci, factum : do, make; create; cause, fashion; compose; accomplish

factor, factoris, *m.* : the producer, maker; perpetrator

factum, -i, *n.* : fact, deed, act; achievement

facultas, -atis, *f.* : means; ability, skill; opportunity, chance; resources (*pl.*), supplies

fallacia, -ae, *f.* : deceit, trick, stratagem; deceptive behavior or an instance of this

fallo, -ere, fefelli, falsum : deceive; be mistaken; beguile, cheat

falsitas, falsitatis, *f.* : falsehood, untruth

falsus, -a, -um, *adj.* : wrong, lying, fictitious, false

familia, -ae, *f.* : household; household of slaves; family; clan

feles, felis, *f.* : a cat

felix, -icis, *adj.* : favorable; lucky; happy, successful, fruitful; blessed

fere, *adv.* : almost; about, nearly; generally, in general; (with negatives) hardly ever

fero, ferre, tuli, latum : bring, bear; tell speak of; consider; carry off, win, receive, produce; get

ferramentum, ferramenti, *n.* : iron tool

ferrum, -i, *n.* : iron; any tool of iron;weapon, sword

fides, ei, *f.* : 1. faith, loyalty; honesty; credit; confidence, trust, belief; good faith

figura, -ae, *f.* : shape, form, figure, image; beauty; style; figure of speech

filius, -ii, *m.* : son

finalis, finalis, finale, *adj.* : of or pertaining to the end; concluding, final; of or relating to purpose, purposeful

fingo, -ere, finxi, -fictum : make up (story/excuse); pretend, pose; forge, counterfeit; act insincerely

finio, -ire, -ivi, -itum : limit, end; finish; determine, define; mark out the boundaries

finis, -is, *f.* : boundary, end, limit, goal; (*pl.*) country, territory, land

fio, fieri, factus sum : be made, become; happen, take place

fluo, -ere, fluxi, fluxum : flow, stream; emanate, proceed from; fall gradually

fons, fontis, *m.* : spring, fountain; source; principal cause

fore, future infinitive of esse

foris, *inv.* : outside, out of doors, abroad

forma, -ae, *f.* : form, figure, appearance; beauty; mould, pattern

formalis, formalis, formale, *adj.* : formal; theoretical

formaliter, *adv.* : formally; positively

fortitudo, inis, *f.* : strength, courage, valor; firmness

fortuitus, -a, -um : casual, accidental, fortuitous, happening by chance

frigus, -oris, *n.* : cold; cold weather, winter; frost

fugio, -ere, fugi : flee, fly, run away; avoid, shun; go into exile

fulcio, -ire, fulsi, fultum : prop up, support

fulgor, -oris, *m.* : lightening, flash; brightness, glittering; glory

fundamentum, -i, *n.* : foundation; beginning; basis

fundo, -are : found, establish, set in place, secure

fundo, -are : pour, cast (metals); scatter

fundo, -ere, fusi, fusum : pour, cast (metals); scatter, shed, rout

furor, -ari, *deponent* : madness, rage, fury, frenzy

futurus, -a, -um, part. fut. de sum : about to be; future

gallus, -i, *m.* : cock, rooster

gaudeo, -ere, gavisus sum : be glad, rejoice

gemino, -are : double; pair (with)

generalis, -e, *adj.* : general, generic; shared by/ common to a class/kind; of the nature of a thing

generaliter, *adv.* : generally, in general

generatim, *adv.* : generally, in general; by kinds

generatio, generationis, *f.* : the act of generation, the process of procreating

generatio, -onis, *f.* : generation, action/process of procreating, begetting; generation of men/family

genero, -are : beget, father, produce

gens, gentis, *f.* : tribe, clan; nation, people; Gentiles

genus, -eris, *n.* : kind, class, rank; mode, method; race, family

gero, -ere, gessi, gestum : bear, carry, wear; carry on; manage, govern; (se gerere = to conduct oneself)

gladius, -i, *m.* : sword

gloria, -ae, *f.* : glory, fame; ambition; renown; vainglory, boasting

gradus, -us, *m.* : step; position

graecus, graeca, graecum, *adj.* : Greek; from Greece

gratia, -ae, *f.* : favor, grace; gratitude, thanks (*pl.*)

gratis, *adv.* : without payment, for nothing

gratus, -a, -um : pleasing, acceptable, agreeable, welcome; dear, beloved; grateful, thankful

gutta, guttae, *f.* : drop, spot, speck

habeo, -ere, habui, habitum : have, hold, consider, think, reason; manage, keep; spend or pass (time)

habitatio, habitationis, *f.* : lodging, residence

habitudo, habitudinis, *f.* : condition

habitus, -us, *m.* : habit, condition, disposition; clothing, religious garb

haeresis, haeresis, *f.* : heresy

haud, *inv.* : not, not at all, by no means; not (as a particle)

hereticus, heretica, hereticum, *adj.* : heretical

hic, *adv.* : here, in this place; in the present circumstances

hic, haec, hoc : here, in this place; in the present circumstances

hinc, *adv.* : from here, from this source/cause; hence, henceforth

hinnibilis, -is, -e, *adj.* : able to neigh (e.g. a horse)

hisce, = his (hic, haec, hoc)

homo, -minis, *m.* : man, human being, person, fellow; (novus homo => nouveau riche)

hora, -ae, *f.* : hour; time; season; (Horae => the Seasons)

huiusmodi, *adv.* : of this sort

humanitas, -atis, *f.* : human nature/character/ feeling; kindness/courtesy; culture/civilization

humanus, -a, -um : human; kind; humane, civilized, refined

humor, humoris, *m.* : fluid, liquid

hydrogeneus, -a, -um, *adj.* : of hydrogen

hypostasis, hypostasis (hypostasim, *accusative*), *f.* : basis, foundation; single substance (a concrete individualized nature); a rational single substance

iam, *adv.* : now, already, by/even now; besides; (non ~ => no longer; ~ pridem => long ago)

ibi, *adv.* : there, in that place; thereupon

ictus, -us, *m.* : blow, stroke; musical/metrical beat

idcirco, *adv.* : on that account; therefore

idea, ideae, *f.* : idea

idem, eadem, idem, *pronoun* and *adj.* : same, the same, the very same, also

identicus, identica, identicum, *adj.* : identical

identifico, identificare, identificavi, identificatum : to identify

ideo, *inv.* : therefore, for the reason that, for that reason

idest (id est) : that is

igitur, *conj.* : therefore (*postpositive*), consequently

ignavia, -ae, *f.* : idleness, laziness; faintheartedness

ignis, -is, *m.* : fire, brightness; passion, glow of passion

ille, illa, illud : that; those (*pl.*); also *demonstrative*; that person/thing; the well known; the former

illumino, -are : illuminate, give light to

illustro, -are : illuminate; make clear, elucidate; enlighten

imaginarius, -a, -um : imaginary

imaginativus, imaginativa, imaginativum, *adj.* : imaginative

imaginor, -ari, -atus sum : to imagine, conceive, picture to oneself

imbuo, imbuere, imbui, imbutum : wet, soak, dip; give initial instruction (in)

imitatio, -onis, *f.* : imitation, copy, mimicking

immediate, *adv.* : directly, immediately

immediatus, immediata, -um, *adj.* : non-mediated, underived, direct; immediate

immo, *inv.* : no indeed (contradiction); on the contrary, more correctly; indeed, nay more

immobilis, -e, *adj.* : immovable; immobile; unmoved; steadfast; slow to act

immoderatus, -a, -um : unlimited, immoderate, disorderly

immortalis, -e, *adj.* : immortal; eternal

immutabilis, -e, *adj.* : unchangeable/unalterable; (rarely) liable to be changed

immuto, -are : change, alter, transform

impedio, impedire, impedivi, impeditum : to hinder, obstruct

importo, -are : bring in, convey; import; bring about, cause

impossibilis, impossibilis, impossibile, *adj.* : impossible

impressio, impressionis, *f.* : impression, impressed mark

imprimo, -ere, -pressi, -pressum : impress, imprint; press upon; stamp

in, *prep.* : +*acc.* into; +*abl.* in, about, in the midst of; according to, among

inadaequo, inadaequare, inadaequavi, inadaequatum : to make unequal, to be unequal

inanis, -e, *adj.* : void, empty, hollow; vain; inane, foolish

inanitas, inanitatis, *f.* : emptiness, vanity

incarnatio, incarnationis, *f.* : incarnation, embodiment

inchoatio, inchoationis, *f.* : beginning, germ; first element, principle, cause

incommunicabilis, incommunicabilis, incommunicabile, *adj.* : unable to be communicated, incommunicable

incomplete, *adv.* : incompletely

incompletus, -a, -um, *adj.* : incomplete

inde, *adv.* : thence, thenceforth; from that place/time/cause; thereupon

indico, -are : point out, show, indicate

indifferens, -entis, *adj.* : indifferent

indigeo, -ere, -ui : to want, need, lack, require (with *gen.* or *abl.*)

indistinctus, indistincta, indistinctum, *adj.* : not separated; indistinct, obscure

indiuiduus, -a, -um : indivisible, inseparable

individualiter, *adv.* : individually

individuo, -are, -avi, -atum : to form an individual, individuate

indivisibilis, indivisibilis, indivisibile, *adj.* :

indivisible, inseparable

indivisus, indivisa, indivisum, *adj.* : undivided, indivisible

induco, inducere, induxi, inductum : induce, influence; introduce

indumentum, -i, *n.* : garment, robe; something put on; (mask, sauce)

induo, -ere, indui, indutum : put on, clothe, cover; dress oneself in

inelaboratus, -a, -um, *adj.* : not elaborate, unworked

infans, -antis, *m.* : infant; child

inferior, -oris : *comparative* of inferus (low, below)

infero, inferre, intuli, illatum : to infer

infidelis, infidelis, infidele, *adj.* : infidel, unbelieving, treacherous, disloyal

infinitus, -a, -um : boundless, unlimited, endless; infinite

infirmo, -are : weaken; diminish

inflexio, inflexionis, *f.* : modification, adaption; bending

influentia, influentiae, *f.* : influence

influo, influere, influxi, influxum : to flow into; to flow; to influence

informo, -are : shape, form; fashion; form an idea of

infra, *prep.* : + *acc.* : below, lower than; later than

infundo, -ere, -fudi, -fusum : pour in, pour on, pour out

ingenium, -ii, *n.* : trick, clever device

ingredior, -i, -gressus sum : advance, walk; enter, step/go into; undertake, begin

inhaerentia, -ae, *f.* : inherent quality

inhaereo, -ere, -haesi, -haesum : to adhere to, inhere

inhibeo, -ere, -bui, -bitum : restrain, curb; prevent

inimicus, -i, *m.* : enemy, foe

initialis, -e, *adj.* : initial, first

innitor, -i, nixus sum : lean/rest on (with *dat.*), be supported by (with *abl.*)

innotesco, -ere, innotui : become known, be made conspicuous

innuo, -ere : nod or beckon (to)

inquit (*defective verb*) : he replied

insculpo, insculpere, insculpsi, insculptum : carve (in or on), engrave; engrave on the mind

inspicio, -ere, -spexi, -spectum : examine, inspect; consider, observe

instar (*indeclinable*) : image, likeness, resemblance

instinctus, -us, *m.* : inspiration; instigation

instituo, instituere, institui, institutum : set up, establish, found, institute; build

instrumentalis, instrumentalis, instrumentale, *adj.* : instrumental

instrumentaliter, *adv.* : instrumentally

instrumentarius, -a, -um, *adj.* : instrumental

instrumentum, -i, *n.* : tool, tools; equipment, apparatus; instrument; means; document (*leg.*), deed

insum, -esse : exist in, be in; belong to; be involved in

insuper, *inv.* : above, on top; in addition (to); over

integer, -gra, -grum, *adj.* : untouched, entire, whole, complete

integraliter, *adv.* : entirely

integritas, -atis, *f.* : soundness; chastity; integrity

integritas, integritatis, *f.* : soundness; chastity; integrity

intellectio, -ionis, *f.* : comprehension

intellectivus, -a, -um, *adj.* : intellectual; knowing intellectually (as distinct from discursively); the opposite of rationalis

intellectualis, intellectualis, intellectuale, *adj.* : intellectual, of the mind or understanding

intellectus, -us, *m.* : comprehension/understanding; recognition/discerning; intelect; meaning/sense

intellegíbilis, -is, -e, *adj.* : intelligible, intellectual

intellego (or intelligo), intellegere, intellexi, intellectum : understand; realize

intelligo : see intellego

intendo, -ere, -tendi, -tentum : hold out; stretch, strain, exert

intensio, intensionis, *f.* : stretch, extension; spasm; concentration, aim

intentio, -onis, *f.* : thought; purpose, intention

intentionalis, intentionalis, intentionale, *adj.* : intentional

intentionaliter, *adv.* : intentionally

inter, *prep.* + *acc.* : between, among; during; (inter se = to each other, mutually)

intercedo, -ere, -cessi, -cessum : intervene; intercede; exist/come between

interim, *adv.* : meanwhile, in the meantime; at the same time; however, nevertheless

internus, -a, -um, *adj.* : inward, internal; domestic

intra, *prep* + *acc* : inside ; *adv* : within, inside; during; under

intranscendens, -entis, *adj.* : non-transcendant ; a property which pertains to one species or group but not to others (opposite of transcedentalis)

intrinsecus, intrinseca, intrinsecum, *adj.* : inward, internal

introductio, introductionis, *f.* : innovation; introduction, preface

inveho, -ere, -vexi, -vectum : carry/bring in, import; ride (*pass.*), drive, sail, attack

invenio, -ire, -veni, -ventum : come upon; discover, find; invent

investigo, -are : investigate; search for

invicem, *adv.* : in turn; by turns; reciprocally, mutually (ab invicem => from one another)

involuo, -ere, -volui, -volutum : wrap (in), cover, envelop; roll along

Ioannes, Ioannis, *m.* : John

ipse, ipsa, ipsum : himself/herself/itself; the very/real/actual one; in person; themselves (*pl.*)

is, ea, id *pronoun* : he, she, it, they; also *demonstrative*, that

iste, -a, -ud *demonstrative pronoun*: that, that of yours, that which you refer to; such

ita, *adv.* : thus, so; therefore

italus, itala, italum, *adj.* : Italian

itaque, *conj.* : and so, therefore

item, *inv.* : likewise; besides, also, similarly

iterum, *inv.* : again; a second time; for the second time

iudicium, -ii, *n.* : trial; opinion; judgement/sentence/verdict; court, judicial investigation

iudico, -are : judge, give judgement; sentence; decide

iungo, -ere, iunxi, iunctum : join, unite

ius, iuris, *n.* : law (*pl.* only *nom.* and *acc.*), right; duty; justice; that which is binding; oath

iustitia, -ae, *f.* : justice; equality; righteousness

iuvenis, -is, *m.* : youth, young man/woman

labefacio, labefacere, labefeci, labefactum : to loosen, shake, subvert

laedo, -ere, -si, -sum : strike; hurt, injure, wound; offend, annoy

lapido, -are : throw stones at; stone

lapis, idis, *m.* : stone; milestone; jewel

lateo, -ere, latui : lie hidden, lurk; live a retired life, escape notice

later, lateris, *m.* : brick, brickwork

latitudo, inis, *f.* : width, breadth, extent

laudo, -are : recommend; praise, approve, extol; call upon, name; deliver eulogy on

laxus, -a, -um : wide, loose, roomy, slack, open, lax

leo, -onis, *m.* : lion

lex, legis, *f.* : motion, bill, law, statute; principle; condition

liber, -bri, *m.* : book, volume; inner bark of a tree

liber, era, erum : book, volume; inner bark of a tree

liber, -era, -erum : free; (liberi, *pl.*) children

libertas, -atis, *f.* : freedom, liberty; frankness of speech, outspokenness

libet, libere, libuit, libitus est : it pleases, it is agreeable; ad libitum = at will

licet, *conj.* : although, granted that

licet, -ere, licuit, licitum est : *impersonal verb*; it is allowed, lawful, or permitted, one may

lignum, -i, *n.* : wood; firewood; timber; gallows/cross; tree of the cross; staves (*pl.*)

ligo, ligare, ligavi, ligatum : bind, tie, fasten; unite

linea, -ae, *f.* : string, line (plumb/fishing); (alba ~ => white line at end of race course)

liquefacio, liquefacere, liquefeci, liquefactum : to melt, liquefy

littera, -ae, *f.* : letter (alphabet); (*pl.*) letter, epistle; literature, books, records, account

localis, localis, locale, *adj.* : local; pertaining to place

Lockius, Lockii, *m.* : John Locke (1632-1704), English philosopher

loco, locare, locavi, locatum : place, put, station; arrange

locus, -i, *m.* : place, seat, rank, position; passage in book

logice, *adv.* : logically; by use of logic

logicus, logica, logicum, *adj.* : logical, pertaining to logic

longus, -a, -um : long; tall; tedious, taking long time; boundless; far; of specific length/time

loquor, -i, locutus sum : speak, tell; talk; mention; say, utter; phrase

lucrum, -i, *n.* : gain, profit; avarice

lumen, inis, *n.* : light; lamp, torch; eye (of a person); life; day, daylight

lupus, -i, *m.* : wolf; grappling iron

lux, lucis, *f.* : light, daylight, light of day; (prima luce => at daybreak); life; world; day

magis, *adv.* : to a greater extent, more nearly; rather, instead; more

magnitudo, -dinis, *f.* : size, magnitude, bulk; greatness. importance, intensity

maior, -oris : ancestors (*pl.*)

maius, *adv.* : more

male, *adv.* : badly, ill, wrongly, wickedly, unfortunately; extremely

malum, -i, *n.* : evil, mischief; disaster, misfortune, calamity, plague; punishment; harm/hurt

maneo, -ere, mansi, mansum : remain, stay, abide; wait for; continue, endure

manifestatio, manifestationis, *f.* : manifestation; manifesting; demonstration, revelation

manifeste, *adv.* : clearly

manifesto, manifestare, manifestavi, manifestatum : make visible/clearer/evident/plain; reveal, make known; disclose

manus, -us, *f.* : hand, fist; gang, band of soldiers; handwriting

marmor, -oris, *n.* : marble, block of marble, marble monument/statue; surface of the sea

materia, -ae, *f.* : matter; means, occasion

materialis, -is, -e, *adj.* : material

materialiter, *adv.* : materially

mathematicus, -i, *m.* : mathematician; astrologer

mechanicus, mechanica, mechanicum, *adj.* : mechanical

mediate, *adv.* : indirectly, by steps

mediatus, -a, -um, *adj.* : intermediate, mediated

medicina, -ae, *f.* : art/practice of medicine, medicine; clinic; treatment, dosing; remedy, cure

medicinalis, -is, -e, *adj.* : healing, salutary, medicinal

medicus, -i, *m.* : doctor, physician

medio, mediare, mediavi, mediatum : to mediate, to divide, to be in the middle

medium, -ii, *n.* : middle, center; medium, mean; midst, community, public; publicity

melius, *adv.* : better

membrum, -i, *n.* : member, limb, organ

memoria, -ae, *f.* : memory, recollection; history; time within memory (~ tenere => to remember)

mendacium, -ii, *n.* : lie, lying, falsehood, untruth; counterfeit, fraud

mens, -entis, *f.* : mind; reason, intellect, judgement; plan, intention, frame of mind; courage

mensura, mensurae, *f.* : measure, length

mentior, iris, iri, titus sum : lie, deceive, invent; imitate; feign; pretend; speak falsely about

mereo, -ere, -rui, -ritum (mereri, eor, itus sum) : earn; deserve, merit

merus, -a, -um : unmixed (wine), pure, only; bare, mere, sheer

metaphysica, -ae, *f.* : metaphysics

metaphysice, *adv.* : metaphysically

metaphysicus, metaphysica, metaphysicum, *adj.* : metaphysical

miles, itis, *m.* : soldier; foot soldier; soldiery; knight (medieval)

minime, *adv.* : hardly, by no means

minimus, -a, -um, *adj.* : smallest, littlest, least important

minor, -or, -us, *comparative adj.* : smaller, lesser, less important

minor, -oris : those inferior in rank/grade/age, subordinate; descendants (*pl.*)

minus, *adv.* : less; not so well; not quite

mirabilis, -e, *adj.* : wonderful, marvelous, astonishing, extraordinary

miraculum, -i, *n.* : wonder, marvel; miracle, amazing event

mirus, -a, -um : wonderful, strange, remarkable, amazing, surprising, extraordinary

misceo, -ere, -ui, mixtum : mix, mingle; embroil; confound; stir up

miser, -a, -um : the wretched (*pl.*)

miseria, -ae, *f.* : misery, distress, woe, wretchedness

misericordia, -ae, *f.* : pity, sympathy; compassion, mercy; pathos

modalis, -is, -e, *adj.* : modal

modo, *adv.* : but, if only; but only

modulus, moduli, *m.* : a measure (e.g. like a measuring cup)

modus, -i, *m.* : manner, mode, way, method; rule, rhythm, beat, measure, size; bound, limit

moneo, -ere, -ui, -itum : remind, advise, warn; teach; admonish; foretell, presage

moralis, moralis, morale, *adj.* : moral, concerning ethics

morbus, -i, *m.* : sickness, illness, weakness; disease; distress; vice

morior, -i, mortuus sum : die, expire, pass/die/ wither away/out; fail; decay

mortalis, -e, *adj.* : mortal, transient; human, of human origin

motivus, motiva, motivum, *adj.* : that which sets something in motion; causa motiva = efficient cause; ratio motiva = motive

motus, -us, *m.* : movement, motion; riot, commotion, disturbance; gesture; emotion

moveo, -ere, movi, motum : move, stir, agitate, affect, provoke, disturb

mox, *adv.* : soon, next (time/position)

multa, -ae, *f.* : fine; penalty

multiplicabilis, multiplicabilis, multiplicabile, *adj.* : that which can be multiplied; multiple, manifold

multiplico, -are : multiply, increase

multitudo, dinis, *f.* : multitude, great number; crowd; rabble, mob

multo, *adv.* : much, by much, a great deal, very; most; by far

mundus, -i, *m.* : universe, heavens; world, mankind

munus, -eris, *n.* : service; duty, office, function; gift; tribute, offering; bribes (*pl.*)

musicus, -a, -um : belonging to poetry or music, musical

mutatio, -onis, *f* : change, alteration; interchange, exchange

muto, mutare, mutavi, mutatum : move, change, shift, alter

mutuus, -a, -um, *adj.* : borrowed, lent; mutual, in return

mysterium, mysterii, *n.* : mystery, a secret

nam, *conj.* : for, on the other hand; for instance

nascor, -i, natus sum : be produced spontaneously, come into existance/being; spring forth, grow; live

natura, -ae, *f.* : nature; birth; character

naturalis, -e, *adj.* : physical/natural scientist; physicist; natural philosopher

naturaliter, *adv.* : naturally, normally

navis, -is, *f.* : ship

nec, *adv.* : nor, and...not; not...either, not even

necessario, *adv.* : unavoidably, without option; necessarily, of necessity; inevitably/unavoidably

necessarius, -a, -um, *adj.* : inevitable, fateful; urgent/critical; unavoidable/compulsory; natural (death)

necesse, *adj. inv.* : necessary, essential; unavoidable, compulsory, inevitable; a natural law; true

necessitas, -atis, *f.* : need/necessity; inevitability; difficult straits; poverty; obligation; bond

negatio, -onis, *f.* : denial, negation

negativus, -a, -um, *adj.* : negative

nego, -are : deny, refuse; say ... not

negotior, -ari : do business, trade

nemo, neminis : no one, nobody

nempe, *adv.* : truly, certainly, of course

neque, *adv.* : nor (neque...neque=neither... nor); neque solum...sed etiam=not only... but also

nequeo, nequire, nequivi(ii), nequitum : be unable, cannot

niger, -gra, -grum, *adj.* : black, dark; unlucky

nihil, *invariable*, *n.* : nothing

nihilum, nihili, *n.* : alternate form of nihil; nothing, nonesense

nimio, *adv.* : by a very great degree, far

nimirum, *adv.* : without doubt, evidently, forsooth

nimis, *adv.* : very much; too much; exceedingly

nimium, *adv.* : too, too much; very, very much, beyond measure, excessive, too great

nisi, *conj.* : if not; except, unless

no, nare, navi, natatum : swim, float

nobilis, -e, *adj.* : nobles (*pl.*)

nobilitas, -atis, *f.* : nobility/noble class; (noble) birth/descent; fame/excellence; the nobles; rank

noceo, -ere, nocui, nocitum : harm, hurt; injure (with *dat.*)

nocivus, nociva, -um, *adj.* : harmful, injurious; noxious

nomen, inis, *n.* : name, family name; noun; account, entry in debt ledger; sake; title, heading

nomino, -are : name, call

non, *neg.* : not, by no means, no; (non modo ... sed etiam (*conj.*) => not only ... but also

nondum, *adv.* : not yet

nonnullus, -a, -um : some (*pl.*), several, a few

nos, *pronoun*: we

nosco, -ere, novi, notum : get to know; learn, find out; recognize; examine, study

noster, -tra, -trum, *possessive adj. and pron.* : our, ours, our own; our men (*pl.*)

notio, -onis, *f.* : notion, idea, conception

notior, ioris : *comparative* of notus, -a, -um : known, familiar, notable

notus, -a, -um, *adj.* : known

novus, nova, -um, *adj.* : new, fresh, young

nugatorius, -a, -um, *adj.* : frivolous, trifling

nullus, -a, -um : no one

num, *inv.* : if, whether; now, surely not, really, then (asking question expecting neg)

numero, -are : count; consider; relate; number, enumerate

numerus, -i, *m.* : number, sum, total, rank; numerical strength; category; rhythm, cadence

numquam, *inv.* : never

nunc, *adv.* : now, today, at present

nuncupo, -are : call, name; express

ob, *prep. + acc* : on account of, for the sake of, for; instead of; right before

obeo, -ire, -ii, -itum : go to meet; die; fulfill, perform

obicio, -ere, -ieci, -iectum : throw before, cast; object, oppose

objectivus, objectiva, objectivum, *adj.* : objective

objectum, -i, *n.* : object, thing

obliquitas, obliquitatis, *f.* : a sidelong or slanting direction

obliquus, -a, -um : slanting; oblique

obsto, -are, -stiti, -staturum : oppose, hinder; (with *dat.*)

obtineo, -ere, -tinui, -tentum : get hold of; maintain; obtain

occasio, -onis, *f.* : opportunity; chance; pretext, occasion

occasionalis, -e, *adj.* : occasional

occasionaliter, *adv.* : occasionally

occido, -ere, occidi, occisum (ob + caedo) : kill, murder, slaughter

occisio, occisionis, *f.* : murder, killing; slaughter

occulto, -are : hide; conceal

occurro, -ere, -curri, -cursum : run to meet; oppose, resist; come to mind, occur (with *dat.*)

oceanus, oceani, *m.* : ocean

oculus, -i, *m.* : eye

odi, odisse: *defective verb*, perf. with pres. meaning; hate, detest

omitto, -ere, -misi, -missum : lay aside; omit; let go; disregard

omnino, *adv.* : entirely, altogether; after negatives => at all; with numerals=> in all

omnipotens, omnipotentis, *adj.* : all-powerful, omnipotent

omnis, -e, *adj.* : all men (*pl.*), all persons

opera, -ae, *f.* : work, care; aid; service, effort, trouble; (dare operam => to pay attention to

opera, -ae, *f.* : work, care; aid; service, effort, trouble; (dare operam => to pay attention to)

operatio, -onis, *f.* : operation, work, toil, trade, business, virtue, action

operor, -ari, -atus sum : labor, toil, work; perform (religious service), attend, serve; devote oneself

oportet, oportere, oportuit (*defective verb*) : it is right/proper/necessary

oppono, -ere, -posui, -positum : place opposite, oppose

oppositio, -onis, *f.* : opposition

ops, opis, *f.* : power, might; help; influence; (*pl.*) => resources, wealth

opus, operis, *n.* : need; work

opus, operis, *n.* : need; work; (opus est => is useful, beneficial); fortifications (*pl.*), works

orator, -oris, *m.* : speaker, orator

ordino, -are : order, arrange, set in order; adjust, regulate; compose

ordo, -inis, *m.* : row, order; succession; series

organum, organi, *n.* : musical instrument, organ, organ of the body

origo, -ginis, *f.* : origin, source; birth, family; race

orior, -iris, -iri, ortus sum : rise, arise; spring from, appear; be descended; begin, proceed, originate

ornatus, -us, *m.* : decoration, ornamentation

os, oris, *n.* : mouth, speech, expression; face; pronunciation

ostendo, -ere, -tendi, -tentum : show; reveal; make clear, point out, display, exhibit

ovis, -is, *f.* : sheep

oxygeneus, -a, -um, *adj.* : having oxygen, oxygenized (e.g. aer oxygeneus = oxygen-rich air)

pantheismus, pantheismi, *m.* : pantheism

Papa, Papae, *m.* : Pope

paries, -etis, *m.* : wall, house wall

pars, partis, *f.* : part, region; share; direction; role; portion, piece; party, faction, side

participatio, participationis, *f.* : participation, sharing (in)

particula, particulae, *f.* : small part, a little bit, a particle

particularis, particularis, particulare, *adj.* : particular; partial, of/concerning a (small) part

passim, *adv.* : here and there; everywhere

passio, passionis, *f.* : passion, suffering, a change which is undergone, receptivity, passivity

passivus, passiva, passivum, *adj.* : random, indiscriminate; *passive*, being acted on

pateo, -ere, patui : stand open, be open; be well known

pater, patris, *m.* : father (pater familias, patris familias, *m.* => head of family, household)

patiens, -entis : patient, enduring

patior, -i, passus sum : suffer; allow; undergo, endure; permit

patria, -ae, *f.* : native land; home, native city; one's country

paucus, -ae, -a, *adj.* : only a small/an indefinite number of people (*pl.*), few; a few; a select few

paulatim, *adv.* : little by little; gradually

paulo, *adv.* : by a little; by only a small amount; a little; somewhat

Paulus, Pauli, *m.* : Paul

pauper, eris : a poor man

pecco, -are : sin, do wrong

pecunia, -ae, *f.* : money; property

pendeo, -ere, pependi, - : hang, hang down; depend

penes, *prep. acc.* : in the power of, in the hands of (person); belonging to

penicillus, penicilli, *m.* : painter's brush or pencil; style

penna, -ae, *f.* : feather, wing

per, *prep.* : + *acc.* : through (space); during (time); by, by means of

percipio, percipere, percepi, perceptum : secure, gain; perceive, learn, feel

perfectio, perfectionis, *f.* : perfection, completion; bringing to completion

perfectivus, -a, -um, *adj.* : perfective, that which perfects something; that which leads or directs something toward perfection

perfectus, -a, -um : perfect, complete; excellent

perficio, -ere, -feci, -fectum : complete, finish; execute; bring about, accomplish; perfect

perimo, -ere, -emi, -emptum : kill, destroy; remove completely

Peripateticus, Peripatetica, Peripateticum, *adj.* : of/belonging to the Peripatetic (Aristotelian) school of philosophy

perluciditas, perluciditatis, *f.* : the quality of being transparent

permaneo, -ere, -mansi, -mansum : last, continue; remain; endure

pernicies, iei, *f.* : ruin; disaster; pest, bane; curse; destruction, calamity; mischief

perpendo, -ere, perpendi, perpensum : weigh carefully; assess carefully

perseitas, perseitatis, *f.* : the condition of existing in and of oneself (a per se attribute of God)

persevero, -are : persist, persevere; continue

persona, -ae, *f.* : mask; character; personality

personalitas, -atis, *f.* : personality, character

perspicio, -ere, -spexi, -spectum : see through; examine; observe

perspicuitas, -atis, *f.* : clearness

perspicuus, -a, -um : transparent, clear; evident

pertineo, -ere, -tinui : reach; extend; relate to; concerns, pertain to

pertingo, pertingere : to reach, to get as far as

perversitas, perversitatis, *f.* : perversity

pes, pedis, *m.* : foot; (pedem referre => to retreat)

pessimus, -a, -um, *adj.* : worst (*superlative* of malus)

peto, -ere, -ivi, -itum : beg, entreat, ask (for); reach towards, make for

Petrus, Petri, *m.* : Peter

phantasia, phantasiae, *f.* : fancy, imagined situation; mental image, imagination

phantasma, phantasmatis, *n.* : a sensible image

philosophia, -ae, *f.* : philosophy, love of wisdom

philosophus, -i, *m.* : philosopher

physicus, -a, -um, *adj.* : physical, of physics, of nature, natural

physicus, -i, *m.* : physicist, natural philosopher; natural scientist

pictura, -ae, *f.* : painting, picture

pictus, picta, pictum, *adj.* : painted

pietas, -atis, *f.* : responsibility, sense of duty; loyalty; tenderness, goodness; pity; piety

placeo, -ere, -cui, -citum : please, satisfy

planta, -ae, *f.* : sole (of foot); (esp. as placed on ground in standing/treading); foot

Plato, Platonos/is, *m.* : Plato; (Greek philosopher 429-347 BC, disciple of Socrates)

plerique, aeque, aque : the majority, most

plerumque, *adv.* : generally, commonly; mostly, for the most part; often, frequently

plurimum, *adv.* : most/great number of things; greatest amount; very much; the most possible

plurimus, -a, -um : very many, many a one; the most people, very many/great number of people

plus, *adv.* : more, too much, more than enough; more than (with number); higher price/value (*gen.*)

plus, pluris, *comparative adj.* : more, several, many

poenalis, -is, -e, *adj.* : penal, punishing, culpable, sinful, worthy of punishment

Polycletus (Πολύκλητος), -i, *m.* : a Greek sculptor in bronze of the fifth and the early 4th century BC

Pompeius, Pompei, *m.* : a Roman family name, especially Gnaeus Pompeius Magnus (Pompey the Great) triumvir with Julius Caesar

pono, -ere, posui, positum : put, place, set; station

porrigo, -ere, -rexi, -rectum : stretch out, extend

porro, *adv* : at a distance, further on, far off, onward; of old, formerly, hereafter; again

positio, positionis, *f.* : position, arrangement, place

possibilis, possibilis, possibile, *adj.* : possible

possibilitas, -atis, *f.* : possibility, power

possideo, -ere, -sedi, -sessum : seize, hold, be master of; possess, occupy; inherit

possum, posse, potui : be able, can; multum posse => to have much (more, most) influence or power

post, *adv.* : + *acc.* : behind (space), after (time); subordinate to (rank)

postpraedicamenum, -i, *n.* : postpredicament; any of the five relations considered by Aristotle at the end of his work on the ten predicaments or categories: viz. opposites (ἀντικείμενα), of four kinds; and the conceptions before or priority (πρότερον), of five kinds; at once or simultaneity (ἅμα), of two kinds; motion (κίνησις), of six kinds; and having (ἔχειν), of eight kinds

postremus, -a, -um : last; worst; lowest

postulo, -are : demand, claim; require; ask/pray for

potens, -entis : powerful, strong; capable; mighty

potentia, -ae, *f.* : force, power, political power

potestas, -atis, *f.* : power, rule, force; strength, ability; chance, opportunity

potissimus, -a, -um : chief, principal, most prominent/powerful; strongest; foremost

practice, *adv.* : in act, really, in effect

practicus, practica, practicum, *adj.* : practical, active

prae, *adv* : before, in front; in view of, because of

praecedo, -ere, -cessi, -cessum : go before, precede; surpass, excel

praeceptor, -oris, *m.* : instructor, master, teacher

praecipue, *adv.* : especially; chiefly

praecipuus, -a, -um : particular, especial

praecisivus, -a, -um, *adj.* : That cuts off, separates, or defines one (person or thing)

186

from another or others, as in precisive abstraction; characterized by precision or exactitude

praedecessor, praedecessoris, *m.* : predecessor

praedicabilis, -is, -e, *adj.* : able to be said of an object; subst. *pl. n.*, praedicabilia, the predicable (the universal attributes common to things, namely, genus, species, difference, property, and accident); praiseworthy

praedicamentum, -i, *n.* : that which is predicted or predicated

praedicatio, -ionis, *f.* : predication (logic); publication, public proclamation; prediction; preaching

praedico, -are : proclaim, declare, make known; preach; predicate (logic)

praeparatorius, -a, -um, *adj.* : preparatory

praesens, -entis : present; at hand; existing; prompt, in person; propitious

praesentia, -ae, *f.* : present time; presence

praestans, praestantis, *adj.* : excellent, outstanding

praesto, -are : excel, surpass; furnish, supply, fulfill

praesumo, -ere, -sumpsi, -sumptum : presume, take for granted, take before, anticipate

praesuppositio, praesuppositionis, *f.* : assumption; presupposition

praeter, *adv.* : beyond,before

praeteritus, -a, -um : past

presentia : see praesentia

primarius, primaria, primarium, *adj.* : in the first rank, distinguished

primitas, primitatis, *f.* : priority, preeminence, of the first rank

primo, *adv.* : at first; in the first place; at the beginning

primoris, -e, *adj.* : nobles (*pl.*), men of the first rank

primum, *adv.* : at first; in the first place

primus, -a, -um *adj.* : first, chief; nobles (*pl.*)

princeps, -ipis, *m.* : leader, first man; *adj.* first, primary

principalis, principalis, principale, *adj.* : chief, principal

principaliter, *adv.* : primarily/principally/in first place; directly/without intermediary; imperially

principium, -ii, *n.* : beginning, source, origin

principor, principari, principatus sum : to rule, to rule over (+ *gen.* or *dat.*)

prior, -oris : superior/elder monk; (later) second in dignity to abbot/head of priory, prior

prioritas, prioritatis, *f.* : priority

prius, *inv.* : earlier, before, previously, first

privatio, -onis, *f.* : a privation, deprivation, taking away

privo, -are : deprive, rob, free

pro, *prep.* : + *abl.* : on behalf of; for; as, like

procedo, -ere, -cessi, -cessum : proceed; advance; appear

produco, -ere, -duxi, -ductum : lead forward, bring out; reveal; induce; promote

productio, productionis, *f.* : production, bringing forth; lengthening (e.g. of time or of a syllable)

profluo, -ere, -fluxi, -fluxum : flow forth or along; emanate (from)

progredior, -i, gressus sum : go, come forth, go forward, march forward; advance. proceed. make progress

prohibeo, -ere, -bui, -bitum : hinder, restrain; forbid, prevent

proinde, *adv.* : hence, so then

prophetia, prophetiae, *f.* : prophecy; prediction; body of prophets

propinquus, -a, -um : *relative*

propius, *adv.* : more nearly (*comparative* of popre)

propono, -ere, posui, positum : display; propose; relate; put or place forward

proportio, -onis, *f.* : proportion, relation between parts

proportionatus, -a, -um, *adj.* : proportionate

proportiono, proportionavi, proportionare, proportionatum : to proportion

propositio, -onis, *f.* : proposition, text, proposal, statement; the offerings carried by the people during the offertory

proprietas, -atis, *f.* : quality; special character; ownership

proprius, -a, -um : own, very own; individual; special, particular, characteristic

propter, *prep* + *acc.* : near; on account of; by means of; because of

propterea, *adv.* : therefore, for this reason; (propterea quod => because)

prorsus, *adv.* : forwards, right onward; absolutely, entirely, utterly, by all means; in short

prosequor, -i, secutus sum : escort; pursue; describe in detail

prout, *conj.* : as, just as; exactly as

proximus, -a, -um : proche ; primus... proximum : neighbor; nearest one

proximus, proxima, proximum, *adj.* : nearest, closest, next; most recent

prudens, -entis : aware, skilled; sensible, prudent; farseeing; experienced

pulsus, pulsus, *m.* : stroke; beat; pulse; impulse

pungo, -ere, pupugi, punctum : prick, puncture; sting (insect); jab/poke; mark with points/pricks; vex/trouble

punio, -ire, -ivi, -itum : punish, inflict punishment; avenge, extract retribution

pure, *adv.* : purely, clearly

purus, -a, -um, *adj.* : clear, limpid, pure

puto, -are : think, believe, suppose

qua, *conj.* et *adv.* : where; by which route

quaelibet (from quilibet). *indefinite pronoun* : *indefinite pronoun* : whoever, whichever, whatsoever

quaero, -ere, -sivi, -situm : search for, seek, strive for; obtain; ask, inquire, demand

quaestio, -ionis, *f.* : questioning, inquiry; investigation

qualis, -e, *adj.* : what kind/sort/condition (of); what is (he/it) like

qualitas, -atis, *f.* : character/nature, essential/distinguishing quality/characteristic; mood (grammar)

quam *adv.* how, how much; than (with *comparative*); as (with *superlative*)

quamlibet, *adv.* : however, however much

quamquam, quanquam + ind. : though, although; yet; nevertheless

quamvis, *conj.* : however much; although

quandam (quamdam) : see quidam

quando, *conj.* : when; after si, nisi, ne, num = aliquando = sometimes; *conj.* : when, since, because; (si quando => if ever)

quantitas, -atis, *f.* : magnitude/multitude, quantity, degree, size; (specified) amount/quanity/sum

quanto, *adv.* :(by) how much

quantum, *inv.* : so much as; how much; how far

quare, *inv.* : in what way? how? by which means, whereby; why; wherefore, therefore, hence

quasi, *conj.* : comme si; *adv.* : as if, just as if, as though; as it were; about

quatenus, *adv* : how far, to what point, how long?; (*rel.*) as far as, in so far as, since, till

quemadmodum, *inv.* : in what way, how; as, just as; to the extent that

queo, -ire, -ii or, -ivi, -itum : be able

qui, quae, quod: *rel. pron.*; who, which, what, that; interr. *adj.*: which, what, what kind of; *indef. adj.*: any; *indef. pron.*: anyone, anything

quia, *conj.* : because

quibuscum : quibus (*ablative* of qui) + cum

quicumque, quaecumque, quodcumque, *indefinite pronoun* : whosoever, whatsoever

quid: *interrogative pron.* : what?, why?

quidam, quaedam, quoddam/quiddam: a certain, a certain one, somebody, something

quidditas, quidditatis, *f.* : quiddity, what a thing is, essence of a thing; (answers question quid est res)

quidem, *adv.* : indeed (*postpositive*), certainly, even, at least; ne...quidem -- not...even

quiduis : whatever it be, whatsoever you please

quies, etis, *f.* : quiet, calm, rest, peace; sleep

quiesco, -ere, quievi, quietum : rest, keep quiet; be inactive; sleep

quilibet, quaelibet, quodlibet, *indefinite pronoun* : whoever, whichever, whatsoever

quin, *inv.* : so that not, without; that not; but that; that; (quin etiam => moreover)

quinimmo, *adv.* : indeed, in fact; but truly, furthermore

quinque, *adj. inv.* : five

quintus, -a, -um, *adj.* : fifth

quippe, *inv.* : of course; as you see; obviously; naturally; by all means

quisque, quaeque, quodque, *indef. pron.* & *adj.* : whoever, whatever, each, every

quisquis, quidquid or quicquid : whatever, whatsoever; everything which; each one; each; everything; anything

quivis, quaevis, quodvis, *indef. adj.* : any, any you please, any at all

quoad, *conj.* : + subj. : as long as, until

quocirca, *conj.*; on that account, therefore

quocumque, *inv.* : wherever, to/in any place/ quarter to which/whatever, whithersoever; anywhere

quodammodo, *adv.* : in a certain way, in a certain measure

quodlibet (from quilibet), *indefinite pronoun* : whichever, whatsoever

quomodo, *adv.* : how, in what way; just as

quoniam, *conj.* : because, since, seeing that

quoque, *adv.* : likewise/besides/also/too; not only; even/actually; (after word emphasized)

quot, *inv.* : how many; of what number; as many

rabio, rabere (also, rabo, rabare) : to be furious, to rage, to rave

radícitus, *adv.* : by the roots, radically, completely, utterly

ratio, -onis, *f.* : account, reckoning; plan; prudence; method; reasoning; rule; regard

ratiocinatio, ratiocinationis, *f.* : reasoning; esp. a form of argument, syllogism

ratiocinor, -ari, ratiocinatus sum, *deponent* : reckon, compute, calculate, infer, conclude

rationalis, -e, *adj.* : theoretician; accountant

rationalitas, -atis, *f.* : reasonableness, rationality

realis, realis, reale, *adj.* : real

realitas, realitatis, *f.* : reality

realiter, *adv.* : really

recens, -entis : fresh, recent; rested

receptio, receptionis, *f.* : recovery; receiving/ reception; retention

recipio, recipere, recepi, receptum : recover, receive, take back

recordatio, -ionis, *f.* : recollection

recta, *adv.* : directly, straight

recte, *adv.* : vertically; rightly, correctly, properly, well

rectus, -a, -um : right, proper; straight; honest

reddo, reddere, reddidi, redditum : return; restore; pay back; translate

redigo, -ere, -egi, -actum : drive back; reduce; render

reduco, -ere, -duxi, -ductum : lead back, bring back; restore; reduce

reduplicativus, -a, -um, *adj.* : having a double explanation; enuntiatio reduplicativa (e.g. Christ suffered inasmuch as he was man, but not inasmuch as he was God)

refero, ferre, tuli, latum : give back; renew; report; return, pay back (referre gratiam => return thanks); refert, *impersonal* : it concerns, it befits

reflexio, -onis, *f.* : a bending back, reflection

refuto, refutare, refutavi, refutatum : to refute

regnum, -i, *n.* : royal power; power; control; kingdom

regula, regulae, *f.* : ruler, straight edge (drawing); basic principle, rule, standard

regulatio, regulationis, *f.* : a regulation, the act of regulation or the state of being regulated

regulo, regulare, regulavi, regulatum : to direct, regulate

reiicio, reiicere, reieci, reiectum : to throw back, repulse, refuse, reject

reipsa : from re (res) + ipsa

relatio, -ionis, *f.* : reference to standard, relation; repayment

relinquo, -ere, reliqui, relictum : leave behind, abandon; (*pass.*) be left, remain

reliquus, -a, -um : the rest of/remaining/available/left; surviving; future/further; yet to be/owed

remaneo, -ere, -mansi, -mansum : stay behind; continue, remain

remedium, -i, *n.* : remedy, cure; medicine

remitto, -ere, -misi, -missum : send back, remit

remotus, -a, -um : remote

removeo, -ere, -moui, -motum : move back; put away; withdraw; remove

reperio, -ire, repperi, repertum : discover, learn; find out; invent

repraesentativus, repraesentativa, repraesentativum, *adj.* : representative, representing something else (as a statue represents a man)

repraesento, -are : represent, depict; show; manifest

reprehendo, reprehendere, reprehendi, reprehensum : hold back, seize, catch; blame

reprobo, reprobare, reprobavi, reprobatum : condemn, reject

repugnantia, repugnantiae, *f.* : resistance, opposition; contradiction; repugnance

repugno, -are : fight back, oppose; be incompatible with; disagree with

requiro, -ere, -quisiui, -quisitum : require, seek, ask for; need; miss, pine for

res, rei, *f.* : thing; event, affair, business; fact; cause

respectus, -us, *m.* : looking back (at); refuge, regard, consideration (for)

respicio, -ere, -spexi, -spectum : look back at; gaze at; consider

respondeo, respondere, respondi, responsum : answer

respuo, -ere, -ui, - : reject, spit out; turn away, repel; spurn, refuse

retineo, -ere, -ui, -tentum : hold back, restrain; retain, preserve

REUBAU, acronym : the scholastic mnemonic for remembering the transcendental terms, namely res, ens, verum, bonum, aliquid, unum

revera, *adv.* : in fact; in reality, actually

revoco, -are : call back, recall; revive; regain

risibilis, risibilis, risibile, *adj.* : that can laugh; risible

risibilitas, risibilitatis, *f.* : the power to laugh

ruber, rubra, rubrum : red, ruddy, painted red

rudis, -e : undeveloped, rough, wild; coarse

rursus, *inv.* : turned back, backward; on the contrary/other hand, in return, in turn, again

sacer, cra, crum : sacred; consecrated; accursed

sacramentum, -i, *n.* : sum deposited in a civil process, guaranty; oath of allegiance; sacrament

sacrificium, -ii, *n.* : sacrifice, offering to a deity

saltem, *inv.* : at least, anyhow, in all events; (on to more practical idea); even, so much as

salus, utis, *f.* : health; prosperity; good wish; greeting; salvation, safety

sancio, -ire, sanxi, sanctum : confirm, ratify; sanction; dedicate

sanctimonialis, sanctimonialis (*gen. plural* = sanctimonialium), *f.* : a nun, a religious

sanctus, -a, -um : holy; a saint

sane, *adv.* : reasonably, sensibly; certainly, truly; however; yes, of course

sanitas, -atis, *f.* : sanity, reason; health

sano, -are : cure, heal; correct

sanus, -a, -um : sound; healthy; sensible; sober; sane

satisfactoria, -ae, *f.* : satisfaction, purgation, justification

schola, -ae, *f.* : school; followers of a system/ teacher/subject; thesis/subject; area with benches

scholasticus, -i, *m.* : student/teacher, one who attends school; one who studies, scholar

scholion (σχόλιον), -ii, *n.* : a short writing, disputation, or significant interpretation

scientia, -ae, *f.* : knowledge, science; skill

scilicet, *adv.* : one may know, certainly; of course

scio, -ire, sciui, scitum : know, understand

Scotus, -i, *m.* : a person from Scotland; the philosopher Duns Scotus

sculptor, sculptoris, *m.* : a sculptor

se (*acc.,* *abl.*), sui (*gen.*), sibi (*dat.*) *reflexive pron.* : himself, herself, itself, themselves

seclusus, seclusa, seclusum, *adj.* : remote, secluded

secreto, *adv.* : separately; secretly, in private

sectio, -ionis, *f.* : section, division

secum, = cum + se

secundarius, -a, -um, *adj.* : secondary

secundarius, -a, -um, *adj.* : secondary, inferior

secundum, + *acc* : according to; along, next to, following/immediately after, close behind

secundus, -a, -um : following, next; second; favorable

secus, *adv.* : otherwise; *prep.* : along, beside

sed, *conj.* : but, but also; yet; however, but in fact/truth; not to mention; yes but

seipse, -ipsa, -ipsum, *reflexive pronoun* : he himself, she herself, it itself

semino, seminare, seminavi, seminatum : to plant, sow, scatter

semper, *adv.* : always

senex, senis, *m.* : old man

sensatio, -onis, *f.* : knowledge through the senses, perception, observation

sensibilis, sensibilis, sensibile, *adj.* : perceptible, sensible; detectable by the senses

sensorius, sensoria, sensorium, *adj.* : sensory

sensus, -us, *m.* : feeling, sense

sententia, -ae, *f.* : opinion, feeling; sentence, thought; vote

separatim, *adv.* : apart, separately

separatio, separationis, *f.* : separation; division; severing

separo, -are : divide, distinguish; separate

sepulcrum, -i, *n.* : grave, tomb

sequor, -i, -secutus sum : follow; escort; support; obey, observe; pursue, chase

seraphicus, seraphica, seraphicum, *adj.* : Seraphic, like an angel; a common epithet of St. Francis, St. Bonaventure, St. Thomas Aquinas, and others

serra, serrae, *f.* : a saw

servo, -are : watch over; protect, keep, guard, preserve, save

sese, *pron.* : variant form of se

seu, *conj.* : or

sex, *numeral* : six

si, *conj.* : if, if only; whether; (quod si => but if) (si quis, quid => if anyone, thing)

sic, *adv.* : thus, so; as follows; in another way; in such a way

sicut, *inv.* : as, just as; like; in the same way; as if; as it certainly is; as it were

sicuti, *inv.* : as, just as; like; in the same way; as if; as it certainly is; as it were

significabilis, -e, *adj.* : that which has meaning, significative, meaningful

significatio, -ionis, *f.* : signal, outward sign; indication, applause; meaning; suggestion, hint

significo, -are : signify, indicate, show

signo, -are : mark, stamp, designate, sign; seal

signum, -i, *n.* : indication; seal; sign, proof; signal, standard; image, statue

similis, -e, *adj.* : like, similar, resembling

similiter, *inv.* : similarly

similitudo, inis, *f.* : likeness, imitation; similarity, resemblance; by-word; parable

simplex, -icis : single; simple, unaffected

simplex, simplicis, *adj.* : single, simple,

simpliciter, simplicius, simplicissime *adv.* : simply/just; without complexity; candidly/openly/frankly

simul, *adv.* : at the same time; likewise; also; simultaneously; at once

simultas, -atis, *f.* : enmity, rivalry; hatred

sin, *conj.* : but if; if on the contrary

sine, *prep.* + *abl.* : without

singularis, -e, *adj.* : alone, unique; single, one by one; singular, remarkable

singulariter, *adv.* : separately, singly, one by one

singulus, singula, singulum, *adj.*: every, individual, separate; (*pl.*) a piece

sino, -ere, sivi, situm : allow, permit

siquidem, *conj.* : accordingly; if indeed/in fact/it is possible, even supposing; since/in that

situs, -us, *m.* : situation, position, site

sive, (seu) *inv.* : or if; or; sive ... sive => whether ... or

sol, solis, *m.* : the sun

soleo, -ere, solitus sum : be in the habit of; become accustomed to

soliloquium, -ii, *n.* : soliloquy, talking to one's self

solus, -a, -um : only, single; lonely; alone, having no companion/friend/protector; unique

sors, sortis, *f.* : lot, fate; oracular response

sortior, iris, iri, itus sum : cast or draw lots; obtain by lot; appoint by lot; choose

species, ei, *f* : sight, appearance, show; splendor, beauty; kind, type

specto, -are : observe, watch, look at, see

speculum, -i, *n.* : mirror, looking glass, reflector; copy, imitation

spero, -are : hope for; trust; look forward to; hope

spes, ei, *f.* : hope, anticipation; expectation

spiritualis, -is, -e, *adj.* : belonging to the spirit, spiritual

spiritualiter, *adv.* : in a spiritual sense, spiritually

statua, -ae, *f.* : statue; image

sto, stare, steti, statum : stand, stand still, stand firm; remain, rest

stricte, *adv.* : exactly, strictly

stuppa (also stipa, stupa) -ae, *f.* : coarse part of flax (used for starting fires), tow, cotton

sub, *prep.* : + *abl.* : under

subdo, -ere, -didi, -ditum : place under, apply; supply

subiicio, -ere, -ieci, -iectum : throw under, place under; make subject

subintellego, subintellegere, subintellexi, subintellectus (= ἐπινοῶ) : assume that which is not expressed, understand, supply in thought, understand a little

subjectivus, -a, -um, *adj.* : subordinate, subjective

subjectum, -i, *n.* : subject

sublatus, -a, -um: see tollo, tollere

subsidium, -ii, *n.* : help, relief; reinforcement

subsistentia, -ae, *f.* : substance, reality, source or means of subsisting

subsisto, -ere, -stiti, - : exist, be; halt, stand; cause to stop

substantia, substantiae, *f.* : nature; substance

substantialis, substantialis, substantiale, *adj.* : essential; substantial; substantive; of/belonging to essence/substance

substantivus, substantiva, substantivum, *adj.* : self-existent; substantive

substo, substare : to hold firm, stand under

successio, successionis, *f.* : succession

sufficienter, *adv.* : sufficiently, adequately

sufficio, -ere, -feci, -fectum : be sufficient, suffice

sum, esse, fui, futurum : to be, to exist

summus, -a, -um : highest, the top of; greatest; last; the end of

sumo, -ere, sumpsi, sumptum : take up; begin; suppose, assume; select; purchase

sumo, sumere, sumpsi, sumptus (also, sumtus) : to take, grasp, understand

sumptus, -us, *m.* : cost, charge, expense

super, *prep.* : + *abl.* , upon/on; over, above

superabundo, superabundare, superabundavi, superabundatum : to be very abundant

superadditio, -tionis, *f.* : a further addition

superaddo, superaddere, superaddidi, superadditum : to add to, to add over and above

superior, -oris : *comparative adjective* => superus, supera, -um, above, high; higher, upper

supernaturaliter, *adv.* : supernaturally

superpono, -ere, -posui, -positum : lay or put or set over

supertranscendentalis, -is, -e, *adj* : supertranscendantal; that which applies not only to real beings but also to imaginary ones

suppono, -ere, -posui, -positum : place under; substitute; suppose

suppositio, -onis, *f*: meaning, hypothesis, supposition

supra, *adv.* or *prep.* : above, beyond; over

suscipio, -ere, -cepi, -ceptum : undertake; support; accept, receive, take up

sustentaculum, -i, *n.* : nourishment, sustenance, support

sustento, -are : endure, hold out

sustineo, -ere, -tinui, -tentum : support; put up with; sustain

suus, -a, -um : *adj.* : his, hers, its, their

synderesis (συναίρεσις), synderesis, *f.* : synderesis or synteresis; A name for that function or department of conscience which serves as a guide for conduct; conscience as directive of one's actions as distinguished from syneidesis (That function or department of conscience which is concerned with passing judgement on acts already performed).

systema, -atis, *n.* : system

talis, -e, *adj.* : such; so great; so excellent; of such kind

taliter, *adv.* : in such a manner, so

tamen, *adv.* : yet, nevertheless, still

tamquam, *adv.* : as, just as; as it were, so to speak; as much as

tanquam, *adv.* : see tamquam

tanto, *adv.* : by so much, so much the; *adj.* see tantus

tantum, *adv.* : so much, so far; hardly, only

tantumdem (tantundem), *adv.*: as much, just as much

tantus, tanta, tantum, *adj.* : of such size; so great, so much

tempus, -oris, *n.* : time, condition, right time; season, occasion; necessity

termino, terminare, terminavi, terminatum : mark the boundaries of, form the boundaries of; restrict; conclude

terminus, -i, *m.* : boundary, limit, end; terminus

terrestris, -e, *adj.* : by or on land, terrestrial

tertius, -a, -um : third

testificor, testificari, testificatus sum, *deponent* : to assert solemnly, testify (to a fact); demonstrate

theatrum, -i, *n.* : theater

theologia, theologiae, *f.* : theology

theologicus, theologica, theologicum, *adj.* : theological

theologus, theologi, *m.* : a theologian

theorema, -atis, *n.* : theorem, proposition, formula

thesaurus, (thens-), -i, *m* : treasure chamber/ vault/repository; treasure; hoard; collected precious objects

Thomas, *indeclinable*, or Thoma, -ae, *m.* : Thomas

thomista, -ae, *m.* : a follower of the teaching of Thomas Aquinas; a Thomist

timiditas, -atis, *f.* : timidity

tollo, tollere, sustuli, sublatum : lift, raise; destroy; remove, steal; take/lift up/away

tot, *adv.* : so many, such a number of; as many, so many; such a great number of

totalis, totalis, totale, *adj.* : total; entire

totaliter, *adv.* : completely, wholly

totus, -a, -um : the whole, all, entire, total, complete; every part; all together/at once

tracto, -are : draw, haul, pull, drag about; handle, manage, treat, discuss

tractus, -us, *m.* : dragging or pulling along; drawing out; extent; tract, region; lengthening

trado, -ere, -didi, -ditum : hand over, surrender; deliver; bequeath; relate

tragoedus (also, tragaedus), -i, *m.* : a tragic actor

traho, -ere, traxi, tractum : draw, drag, haul; derive, get

transcendentalis, -is, -e, *adj.* : transcendental

transcendo, -ere, -scendi, -scensum : transcend; to be common to all (phil.)

transeo, -ire, -ii, -itum : go over, cross

transformo, -are : change in shape, transform

transmutatio, -onis, *f.* : change

tres, tres, tria: three

tribus, -us, *m.* : third part of the people; tribe, hereditary division (Ramnes, Tities, Luceres)

Tullius, -i, *m.* : the name of a Roman gens, especially Marcus Tullius Cicero

tum, *adv.* : then, next; besides; at that time; (cum...tum => not only...but also)

tunc, *adv.* : then, thereupon, at that time

turbatio, -ionis, *f.* : disturbance

turpis, -e, *adj.* : ugly; nasty; disgraceful; indecent; base, shameful, disgusting, repulsive

tyro (also, tiro) -onis, *m.* or *f.* : beginner, recruit, novice

ubi, *interogative* or *relative adv.* : where, whereby

ullus, -a, -um : any

ulterior, -oris, *comparative adj.* : farther

ultimus, -a, -um, *superlative adj.* : last, farthest, most recent

ultra, *adv.* : farther ; *prep. + acc.* : beyond, on the other side, on that side; more than, besides

una, *adv.* : together, together with; at the same time; along with

unde, *interogative* or *relative adv.* : from where, whence, from what or which place; from which; from whom

unicus, -a, -um : only, sole, single, singular, unique; uncommon, unparalleled; one of a kind

unio, -onis, *f.* : union

unio, unire, univi, unitum : unite, combine into one

unitas, -atis, *f.* : unity

universalis, -is, -e, *adj.* : universal, of all

univocus, univoca, univocum, *adj.* : univocal, single-meaning

unus, -a, -um : alone, a single/sole; some, some one; only (*pl.*); one set of (denoting enity)

unusquisque & unumquodque, each one, every

uro, -ere, ussi, ustum : burn

usurpo, -are : seize upon, usurp; use

usus, -us, *m.* : use, enjoyment; experience, skill, advantage; custom

ut (uti) : with indicative : as, when; with subjunctive : that, in order that

uterque, utraque, utrumque: both, each of two

uti, = ut: in order that; that, so that; as, when; (ut primum => as soon as)

utilis, -e, *adj.* : useful, profitable, practical, helpful, advantageous

utor, -i, usus sum : use, make use of, enjoy; enjoy the friendship of (with *abl.*)

utpote, *adv.* : as, in as much as

utrinque, *adv.* : on both sides; from both sides; at both ends

v.g., abbreviation of verbi gratia : for example

vagor, -ari : wander, roam

vagus, vaga, vagum, *adj.* : roving, wandering

valeo, -ere, -ui, -itum : be strong, powerful; (vale => goodbye/farewell); prevail

variatio, variationis, *f.* : variation, difference, change

varietas, -atis, *f.* : variety, difference; mottled appearance

vario, -are : change, alter, vary

varius, -a, -um : different; various, diverse; changing; colored; party colored, variegated

varius, -a, -um : different; various, diverse; variegated

vas, vasis, *n.* : vessel, dish; vase

vehemens, vehementis, *adj.* : violent, severe, vehement

vel, *adv.* : or (vel... vel... : either ... or)

velut, *inv.* : just as, as if

venator, -oris, *m.* : hunter

venenum, -i, *n.* : poison; drug

ver, -eris, *n.* : spring; spring-time of life, youth

verbum, -i, *n.*: word; proverb; verba dare alicui => to cheat, to deceive someone

veritas, -atis, *f.* : truth, honesty

vero, *inv.* : but; yes; in truth; certainly; truly, to be sure; however

verso, -are : change, turn, treat, deliberate

versor, -ari, -atus sum : move about; live, dwell; occupy one's self with

verto, -ere, verti, versum : turn, turn around; change, alter; overthrow, destroy

verum, *conj.* : yes; in truth; certainly; truly, to be sure; however; (rare form, usu. vero)

verus, -a, -um : true, real, genuine, actual; properly named; well founded; right, fair, proper

vid., abbreviation of vide : see; used to refer a reader to a passage or source located elsewhere

volo, velle, volui : to wish, want

Page intentionally left blank

Page intentionally left blank

BIBLIOGRAPHY

BLAISE, A., *Lexicon latinitatis medii aevi : praesertim ad res ecclesiasticas investigandas pertinens = Dictionnaire latin-français des auteurs du Moyen-age*, Brepols, Turnhout (Belgium) 1994.

———, *Manuel du latin chrétien*, Brepols, Turnhout (Belgium) 1986.

BUSA, S.J., R. - ALARCÓN, E., «Index Thomisticus & Corpus Thomisticum», 2000, in http://www.corpusthomisticum.org/.

DEFERRARI, R. J., *A Latin-English dictionary of St. Thomas Aquinas : based on the Summa theologica and selected passages of his other works*, St. Paul Editions, Boston, MA 1986.

DEFERRARI, R. J. - BARRY, M. I. - McGUINESS, I., *A lexicon of Saint Thomas Aquinas : based on the Summa theologica and selected passages of his other works*, Loreto Publications, Fitzwilliam, NH 2004.

DONAT, S. J., J., *Ontologia*, Felicianus Rauch, Oeniponte 1914.

FORCELLINI, E. - FACCIOLATI, J. - FURLANETTO, G., *Totius latinitatis lexicon consilio et cura Jacobi Facciolati, opera et studio Ægidii Forcellini,*, Typis Seminarii, Patavii 1827.

LEWIS, C. T. - SHORT, C., *A Latin dictionary*, Oxford University Press, Oxford 1984.

NUNN, H. P. V., *An introduction to ecclesiastical Latin*, University Press 1922.

REEB, G. - CORNOLDI, G. M., *Thesaurus philosophorum seu distinctiones et axiomata philosophica*, P. Lethielleux 1891.

SCANLON, C. C. - SCANLON, C. L., *Second Latin*, Tan Books and Publishers, Rockford, IL 1976.

SCANLON, C. C. - SCANLON, C. L. - THOMPSON, N. W., *Latin grammar : grammar, vocabularies, and exercises in preparation for the reading of the missal and breviary*, Tan Books, Rockford, IL 1976.

SIGNORIELLO, N., *Lexicon peripateticum philosophico-theologicum in quo scholasticorum distinctiones et effata praecipua explicantur*, Pignatelli 1872.

Smith, W. - Hall, T. D., *A copious and critical English-Latin dictionary*, New York : Harper & brothers 1871, in http://archive.org/details/copiouscritica-le00smit [1-8-2012].

Springhetti, A., *Latinitas fontium philosophiae scholasticae*, Pontificium institutum altioris latinatis, Romae 1967.

Stelten, L. F., *Dictionary of ecclesiastical Latin*, Hendrickson, Peabody, MA 2003.

4520714R10116

Made in the USA
San Bernardino, CA
23 September 2013